CUT THE FAT, NOT THE MUSCLE

COST-IMPROVEMENT STRATEGIES FOR LONG-TERM PROFITABILITY

NORMAN KOBERT

PRENTICE HALL
Englewood Cliffs, New Jersey 07632

Prentice-Hall International (UK) Limited, *London*
Prentice-Hall of Australia Pty. Limited, *Sydney*
Prentice-Hall Canada, Inc., *Toronto*
Prentice-Hall Hispanoamericana, S.A., *Mexico*
Prentice-Hall of India Private Limited, *New Delhi*
Prentice-Hall of Japan, Inc., *Tokyo*
Simon & Schuster Asia Pte. Ltd., *Singapore*
Editora Prentice-Hall do Brasil, Ltda., *Rio de Janeiro*

10   9   8   7   6   5   4   3   2   1

Library of Congress Cataloging-in Publication Data

Kobert, Norman.
  Cut the fat, not the muscle : cost-improvement strategies for
long-term profitability / Norman Kobert.
    p.   cm.
  Includes index.
  ISBN 0-13-292443-9
  1. Cost control. I. Title.
HD47.3.K62 1994
658.15'52—dc20   94–30049
                                             CIP

ISBN 0-13-292443-9

PRENTICE HALL
Career & Personal Development
Englewood Cliffs, NJ 07632

Simon & Schuster, A Paramount Communications Company

Printed in the United States of America

This book is dedicated to the support group that surrounds me with love, social, educational and economic contributions, challenging questions, individual pride and consistent loyalty—my family!

Also by the Author

Managing Inventory for Cost Reduction

Inventory Strategies

The Aggressive Management Style

Managing Time

CONTENTS

Chapter 3: GAINING CONSENSUS FOR COST REDUCTION STRATEGIES TO IMPROVE ASSET MANAGEMENT   31

Chapter 4: HOW TO USE GROUP CONSENSUS TO SELECT AREAS OF COST REDUCTION/PROFIT IMPROVEMENT OPPORTUNITIES   51

CHAPTER 9: MANAGING YOUR TIME MORE EFFICIENTLY CAN SNOWBALL INTO A COMPANY-WIDE EFFORT   159

CHAPTER 10: CONTINUOUS IMPROVEMENT (KAIZEN) THROUGH CONTINUOUS ANALYSES   183

Chapter 11: INCREASE PRODUCTIVITY BY POOLING THE HUMAN RESOURCE'S TALENTS   217

PREFACE

The words change, but the cost-reduction song remains the same. The key management terms for today's cost-cutting approaches include downsizing, rightsizing, restructuring, benchmarking, outsourcing and partnering, re-engineering, retrenchment, and function driven analyses. These have replaced the older terms such as management-by-objectives, cost/benefit analysis, make-or-buy studies, procedural/manpower overview, profit/volume and asset utilization analyses, group technology, and similar terms for cost-cutting programs.

No matter what they're called, all of these cost-cutting tools reflect the misconceptions and mistakes of past managements and their ingrained practices of operation. By failing to admit past mistakes, current management is condemned to repeat them by continuing present practices in seeking or maintaining profitability. At the same time, sporadic efforts are made at applying across-the-board cost-cutting sweeps without analyzing their effects on future profitable performance.

Although some old cost-cutting strategies have fallen by the wayside over the years, reducing the work force is still the most popular because it produces immediately discernible results.

In the heat of battle within any industry and against growing new local and foreign competition—and in some cases to merely maintain their own job security—top management demands immediate action. Future profits are relegated to a concern for the next generation of managers. In this environment, good soldiers move quickly to reduce the personnel roster as their first, and sometimes only, cost-reduction effort.

Staff reductions should be only one of the approaches to cutting costs, not the sole concerted effort to overcome the deficiencies of past managerial practices. This book presents a wide variety of bold techniques which can not only cut costs, but also provide a profitability dominated approach to future actions and expenditures.

No one will question cutting the fat, but future profitability is at stake when you cut into the muscle, bone, and nerves of the corporate entity. For this reason, the conventional approach to cost reduction needs to be reconsidered. This approach decrees:

1. Do the same things as before, but at a reduced cost.
2. Accomplish this by cutting operating expenses and capital budgets across-the-board by a mandated fixed percentage.
3. Then, as a possible next step, rethink how the entity can and should be doing business.

The contention of this book is that step #3 should be performed prior to, or at the very least during, the actions taken in stages #1 and #2. There is a major difference between, "Cut costs now!" and "Improve profits now and in the foreseeable future." The latter relies on the accepted techniques of problem-solving and decision-making, which begin with establishing realistic and agreed upon objectives, as well as the criteria for success.

Consider that almost any cost reduction strategy will bring some desired results at some point in time. However, analyzing how your company should be doing business not only enables you to improve profits in the short run, but also to establish a program for long-term profitability.

This book offers numerous techniques for cost reduction with an eye toward the future. You will see how to gain a consensus for cost-reduction strategies, then use that consensus to zero in on specific areas of cost-cutting. You will learn how to leverage cost reductions to increase long-term profitability, how to ensure continuous improvements through continued analysis, and how to use true costing techniques to locate and cut the fat in your company. When personnel cutbacks are necessary, this book shows you how to conduct organizational realignments and increase productivity through talent pooling and cross training.

After reading over this broad range of available cost-cutting techniques, you can select a strategy for gaining long-term profitability that includes short-term selective cost reductions that fit into an overall cost reduction strategy. This is the cut-the-fat, not-the-muscle theory in actual practice.

Norman Kobert

IMPROVING FUTURE PROFITABILITY TAKES MORE THAN JUST SLASHING COSTS

No one doubts that excessive costs should be reduced, if not eliminated, whenever and wherever they are found to exist. Likewise, the severity of a company's economic health will determine both the depth and imminence of specific cost-cutting mandates. This is accepted cost reduction dogma.

However, there is a point where such simple cost-cutting should be incorporated into the philosophy and strategies of longer-term, planned profit improvement. This is where the company's management launches an investment in profitability planning, which obviously includes cost reductions, but adds cost investment in the overall mix of strategies.

The distinction between applying simple cost-cutting techniques and that of adopting a plan for investment for future profits is the theme of this book. An effective program weds short-term actions of cutting out the fat with "avoidance of damage to muscle, nerve, and bone" of the corporate entity. The whole corporate body must be analyzed in the longer view, in order to maximize return on investment through increased and ongoing profitability. In this way, cost-cutting is but one of a myriad of profit planning strategies, not the sole or primary management technique that is employed.

WATCH OUT FOR ACROSS-THE-BOARD COST-CUTTING

The usual steps taken by those managements that face losses or sharp shrinkages in profitability include the following:

- mandated, across-the-board cuts in all expenditures and capital spending
- closing "unprofitable and non-essential" operations
- implementing staged or immediate termination of "non-essential" employees

The above steps, by themselves, imply the following:

- All expenditures can be cut by the same percentage, since they **equally** contribute to unnecessary costs that can no longer be tolerated.
- An analysis of unprofitable products, locations, and services has resulted in a decision that their potential profitability does not match what can be anticipated from the remaining product lines, services, and sites.
- Personnel will be terminated who have been involved in producing products and services no longer required for future profitability.

It is expected that the above actions will permit continued production of the remaining products and/or services that will now contribute to a much improved profit projection. This is predicted to occur even as the remaining personnel and other assets continue to provide goods and services with the same efficiencies and motivated actions as in the past.

Obviously, many of these assumptions do not work out as planned. The statement made in hindsight usually is, "Well, we saved the company! Through cost reductions we bought the time to be able to, now, plan future profitability schemes." Thus, the initial cost-cutting becomes the survival plan; not part of a longer-range approach to profit planning. The danger may be that vigorous across-the-board cost-cutting may indiscriminantly cut nerves, muscle, and bone, as well as the fat.

AVOID CUTTING TOO MUCH, TOO FAST

Three examples of cost-cutting that may cut muscle as well as fat are:

1. **Manufacturing Capacity.** A management directive may eliminate or drastically reduce over-capacity to match current

demand forecasts, resulting in employee redundancies. But, an equal percentage reduction in the budget for new product development, or for installing a better forecasting procedure, may dramatically damage next year's profit picture. Assuming that all cost reductions are **equal** can lead to poorly chosen applications of corporate axe-wielding. It is the very inequality of costs contributing to the profit equation that represents an opportunity for well-directed management cost improvements. In Chapter Four, you will read more about inequalities of inputs vs. outputs and learn how to develop more effective cost improvement strategies.

2. **Maintenance and Repair Personnel.** It is not unusual to clamor for a reduction in maintenance and repair budgets as production demand is reduced. After all, both the preventive maintenance schedule and the use of spare parts is related to equipment use, not merely to elapsed calendar time. However, maintenance personnel are generally not just a lump of average skills and experience; rather, they possess single purpose skills (simple electrical or mechanical experiences) as well as complex and flexible skills (electronic problem detection and repair, as well as across-the-board welding skills). An investment in cross-training may be a more logical approach to reducing future personnel costs. Thus, immediate, but selective personnel reductions, if required, would be far more effective than a bold swipe of the cost-cutting blade. Likewise, maintenance inventories are established to meet preventive as well as demand schedules, such that inventory cost is subservient to the critical needs of specific parts. You can procure a simple electrical switch at the local hardware store if you stockout of this non-critical item; but, the whole plant could be closed for days if you are forced to await delivery of a critical, low-cost item from a foreign supplier.

3. **Support Staff.** Reduction in the size of support staff is a first goal of most cost reduction efforts in service companies. A professional services' firm will seek immediate savings from a reduction in office administration and para-professional services. The equivalent increase in non-professional time, which may now have to be expended by the professional staff, is barely considered, if at all. In a legal or accounting professional association, administrative expense staff cuts could result in an immediate reduction of out-of-pocket indirect costs, which may then be matched by an attendant loss of billable time by professional staff. An investment in a study of minimum required

administrative support, as well as alternate means of processing and accounting, may well be a more logical approach to cutting costs than that which simply assumes cutting the fat impairs no other functions.

As you can see from these examples, it is a far better practice to analyze, and then squeeze costs out of assets, than to seek immediate cost savings which may reduce essential services. In addition, since all cost reductions do not equally contribute to positive (and negative) effects that drop to the bottom line, a well-planned cost reduction program must use this knowledge of cost effectiveness differentials when selecting management strategies. In Chapter Three you will learn how to analyze such inequalities for use in defining management cost improvement actions.

BE TOUGH ON ALL DISCRETIONARY SPENDING

In over 35 years of consultancy and training experiences, I continue to be amazed at the number of companies that act decisively to cut costs, but waffle in expending the effort, time and money to determine the proper allocation and expected profit-making results from authorized expenditures.

We can see this dichotomy of management resolve in the following two examples:

Maintaining bad habits: All internal company expenses may be drastically cut, while the credit and purchasing departments continue to practice as before. Poor credit checks, salesperson domination of collection practices, improper extensions of payment terms for receivables, overriding of acceptable incoming quality levels for production expediency sake, and the granting of permission for exaggerated claims allowances . . . all of these actions will result in losses which are both unprofitable and frequently unexpected. These types of loose practices may very well continue after simple expense-cutting decrees have been applied to all the company departmental budgets. Thus, travel and advertising expenses, office equipment upgrades, and training will be reduced on a mandatory basis, while other discretionary, cost-additive practices will continue because they have not been investigated.

Training suppliers: One of the major features of Just-In-Time (JIT) applications by the purchasing function is to reduce the number of suppliers while increasing the quality of products received coupled with improved delivery performance. Many other savings come from training the selected few suppliers about your products, your customers and unique manufacturing processes. In today's market situation, presenting your suppliers with a long list of statistical specifications is a practice that should be reinforced with face-to-face training of their personnel. This is a far better practice than to assume that the chosen few certified suppliers will perform well in the future because of their past performance. Vendor training will probably prove to be an increased and ongoing cost as an integral part of a Just-In-Time cost reduction application.

Cost analysis is not a discretionary expense. When drastically cutting costs, one of the costs that may have to be increased is cost analysis, especially when investigating the fertile area of discretionary spending. The name of the game is cost analysis through cost knowledge, not just "what is it?" but "what does it do?" Thus, an effective cost improvement program may add costs to improve profitability, subsequent to a determination of the effectiveness of various expenditures.

HOW TO IDENTIFY DISCRETIONARY COSTS

To label a cost discretionary is to assume that management has an option with regard to the amount and timing of that particular expenditure. In the extreme situation, this is probably true.

Isolating discretionary costs will depend on the managerial freedom that is inherent in your particular position, as well as related to the aggressive management philosophy which you choose to assume within the boundaries of your implied authority.

Let's begin with the obvious. Discretionary costs can be reduced at will where you isolate your parameters of stated or implied authority and responsibility. Chapter Seven addresses in depth the issues that confront most managers when applying a cost reduction program that is either directed from above or self-imposed. The key is to isolate the perception and the reality of discretionary costs. It is these costs that will be analyzed for profit improvement through either reduction or enhancement.

A manager may suggest the elimination of certain data that is collected, generated and received. You may cite examples of the costs of this data distribution activity as both unnecessary and unwanted. However, what about other departments that receive this information? Will they support this proposition? Will your request for a cost reduction impinge on the needs (real or imagined) expressed by other groups? If you receive "useless" information that is required by others, what is the cost savings that might accrue from leaving your individual department off the distribution list? Probably, not much.

Where an increase in one area's expenditures will require budget reductions in other areas of operation, such a cost reduction option should be agreed by all, not just mandated for action by all affected parties. This is dogma, since, until you eliminate any area of activity, its personnel must be motivated to continue contributing to the success of the whole enterprise. In other words, many cost reduction approaches will be effective where the concepts are sold, negotiated and compromised for the benefit of all concerned. This makes the cost improvement program "ours" not just "theirs."

Therefore, the first question should be, "Why are we spending this sum at all?" Elimination of a discretionary cost is the highest form of cost improvement, followed, in order of effectiveness, by cost reductions and/or postponement of expenditures.

Following the attempts to eliminate a cost altogether, the next priority in selecting a discretionary cost reduction option should relate to the projected magnitude of the resultant increased profits.

SPENDING MONEY TO MAKE MONEY

Spending money to make money is an age-old business philosophy. Its relevancy to cost reduction should not be overlooked, since many one-shot, cut-the-fat directives do not allow for this option.

Obviously, if the patient is dying, quick action is far more advisable than suggesting, "Let's form a committee to analyze and propose solutions." However, in the normal operations of any enterprise, cost reduction should be an ongoing activity as these proposed actions relate to and result in increased profitability. Thus, spending money to make money should be an easily utilized option available to all managers when examining discretionary expenditures for cost reductions that lead to increased profitability.

As stated in the previous section, cost analysis is a key element in the search for profit-making opportunities from selective cost reductions. If cutting costs in one area provides the opportunity for profit improvement by investment in another area, this is an example of the gains from having cost analysis pinpoint available options. The following case study is an example of a one-sided strategy, resulting from a lack of specific cost knowledge to provide alternatives.

CASE STUDY: MAKING INCREASED MARKET SHARE THE SOLE OBJECTIVE

A major food processing company in the Southwest was totally focused on the primary corporate strategy of increasing market share.

Promotions and dismissals in the sales and marketing group hinged on results reported in the industry trade publication. The annual budget and all expenditure adjustments throughout the year were based on the success or failure in reaching the product line market share goals.

It was a stated company commandment that the road to increased profitability could only be achieved through an aggressive expenditure to increase market share. Requests for capital improvements for production processes had to meet the test of their relevance to the stated overall goal. Will new equipment, revised process flow, recruitment of production management personnel result in meeting this primary goal? If not, new production budget requests were postponed or rejected, even though basic cost reductions were demonstrated in the documented proposals.

A new divisional manager, recruited from outside the food processing industry, was appointed just prior to the week that a capital equipment request for $420,000 was forwarded to design and procure a reservoir and water recovery pumping system. The water bill from the local pumping plant was approximately $47,000 per month, and 95% of this water was used in the processing requirement to quickly cool produced products down to ambient temperatures. An examination showed that this 95% of water consumed never touched the food product, but was only used to cool the outside package. After performing this function, the water was pumped into the sewage system.

At first, the request was reviewed on a simple mathematical basis. The company was being asked to spend $420,000 to save $535,000 (95% × $47,000 × 12) per year. However, the second pass through the capital budget committee revealed that these funds could only be made available by reducing that which would be committed to the new sales support project.

When presented with the above options, the new divisional manager asked the sales and marketing director to provide a five-year analysis of expenditures used to attain new customers. In addition, he requested compilation of the ratio of sales and marketing costs presently required to service existing customers as a percent of total selling price.

To his surprise, these figures were not readily known or available. Instead, he discovered the following:

- After one week of category adjustments and number manipulations, the sales and marketing director developed a cost for servicing present customers. This was the first time such an analysis had been prepared.
- After one month, there was no agreement as to the actual amount of previous and ongoing expenditures that were under-

taken to gain new customers. The only ratio that existed showed that increases in market share did not seem to be remotely related to bottom line profitability, even on a lead/lag basis.

- The production manager's request for a water recovery system was not based on an agreed forecast of capacity use as it related to projected sales; it was derived from the proposer's extrapolation of past capacity usage.

Based on the above determinations, the new divisional manager produced a policy statement that demanded that all approvals for future expenditures for both cost reductions and market share improvements must:

- be presented with back-up data relating to such definitive items as the cost of getting a new customer and the cost of making a sale,
- be provided to the budgetary committee based on agreed projections of future sales to production requirements on existing and future capacity, and
- relate to traceable, future bottom-line profitability.

The new divisional manager proclaimed that improving profitability took preference over increased market share or production cost improvements for any claims on the company treasury. The company management no longer had carte blanche approval of the strategy that increasing market share was the only objective for cost allocation. In the future, all cost improvements would be driven by results that would appear as traceable profits dropping to the bottom line.

COST ANALYSIS MAY MASK COST REDUCTION OPTIONS

It is common practice to review cost figures and accept their basis as reliable. Some examples of errors that may be masked by the use of such information are:

- The carrying cost of inventory is one of the most misconstrued figures routinely bandied about by managers who justify inventory cost reductions. They confuse fixed, mixed and variable costs when they state, "The carrying cost of our inventories is 20%, such that any inventory reduction of $100,000 will drop $20,000 to the bottom line as an increased profit." This statement does not account for the ongoing cost of the warehouse, supervision, materials handlers and utilities which will probably exist even if the inventory is reduced by as much as 50%. Unless you eliminate the fixed costs of warehousing, personnel and power, they will continue to be absorbed by (allocated to) a smaller inventory. Such "savings" may actually result in producing higher unit inventory costs. The variable cost of converting cash to inventory by purchase and manufacture is traceable to improving bottom line profitability, but at a much lower rate than that proscribed by a fictitious inventory carrying cost.

- Systems and procedures analysts frequently quote the cost of purchase orders and correspondence in terms of cost per document originated. Thus, a purchase order is said to cost $72.34 when generated, and a routine letter costs $13.95 to send. Ridiculous! If those cost estimates were true, write 1,000 less purchase orders next year to see if you save $72,340; originate and send 1,000 less letters next year and then seek out the $13,950 savings. Consider: if that bogus theory were acceptable, one could reduce the unit cost of most document preparation by increasing the volume of documents produced!

Cost analysis must include an evaluation of fixed, mixed and variable costs as they are allocated to the unit of output, whether that is a product or a service. Cost per unit averaging can mask both cost reduction and pricing opportunities for increased profitability.

In Chapter Five, you will receive a detailed approach to analyzing costs for cost reduction. The major feature of that discussion will be to demonstrate those cost analysis approaches which could be useful tools for cost improvement, not merely for summarizing history.

ANALYZE COST ALLOCATION CAREFULLY

Allocating costs can be an excruciating exercise for some managers. The task involves detailed and very specific analysis of data as well as the application of good business judgment, which may fly in the face of political forces within the company. This is especially true where overhead and indirect cost allocations are applied by dictum, across-the-board and on an averaging basis.

"This is the way we have always done it!" will be the rationale for continuing the process of straight percentage cost allocations and rejecting studies for accurate analyses. The manager requesting an analysis of indirect and overhead cost allocations may risk being labelled a procrastinator. "We are seeking cost reductions and you are concerned with cost applications. If you just cut your costs, your analysis request would be academic!"

Remember that the personnel who are helping you in the analysis of overhead cost allocations are themselves part of the overhead expense . . . and the people who must approve your capital budget proposals must weigh your priorities against theirs in the overall corporate division of available assets.

Conversely, well-defined and agreed allocations of overhead and indirect costs will provide data for options regarding:

- areas in which to concentrate limited management and cash resources for maximum gain,
- opportunities for applying leveraged actions to reduce costs that increase revenues and will drop profits to the bottom line,
- individual specific pricing modifications to improve market share and overall profitability, and
- application of measurements and/or incentives that are based on cost reductions that lead to profit improvements.

Throughout the following chapters, you will note the heavy emphasis placed on analysis before action, as well as on gaining consensus for those proposals that impinge on other organizational elements. You must also consider that analysis without action may be busywork at best. Likewise, plans without controls are usually doomed by the very inertia of those who feel more comfortable with the status quo. Therefore, in Chapters Nine and Ten techniques will be proposed for both gaining necessary support and controlling the installation of your recommended improvements.

ELIMINATING UNASSIGNABLE COSTS

It certainly sounds logical. Eliminate all costs that cannot be realistically assigned to a profit or cost center. In practice, however, you will find that it is far more acceptable by all parties concerned to reduce an allocation, while elimination may be impossible to consider.

This position is taken because if every cost center decided that a particular cost is logically not absorbable by all the individual groups, then why does that cost continue to exist? Management is not a popularity contest; it is a results contest! Therefore, the justification of an allocation must not be on the basis of "liking the work of George's group" but rather on the perceived and actual contribution made to the absorbing function.

The ground rules for allocation of indirect and overhead costs will therefore establish a modus operandi for reviewing the need for the provided services, as well as the size of the investment that is desired. This occurs, because, as average cost allocations are converted to a percentage-by-need application:

- some presently provided overhead and indirect services may be eliminated,
- some services will be shown to be required by a fewer number of cost centers, thus increasing the allocation to those centers that have a continuing need for these services, and
- the resultant re-application of allocated costs may define the magnitude of the support costs required . . . most likely at a reduced rate, since the costs of these services will now be borne by fewer organizational elements.

The technique for analyzing allocation of costs is called ABC (Activity Based Contribution). This tool has been used to more accurately define the application of overhead and indirect costs to the supported cost center activities. In Chapter Eight, this concept will be expanded to encompass the goals of cost reduction for improved and ongoing profitability. The usefulness of ABC to pinpoint areas for emphasis by management will be shown.

HOW TO RELATE COST REDUCTION TO PROFIT IMPROVEMENT

When it is difficult to assign a logical place for a specific cost, you could ask, "Is this cost necessary at all?" On this basis alone, an arbitrary swath can be cut through the company's operations. This is especially true when cost-cutting decisions are left to a small group with a limited view of the overall direction of the enterprise. For example, production people can't wait to cut advertising and marketing expenses; sales people cannot understand the need for newly equipped warehouse space for a shrinking inventory, and financial control personnel have difficulty viewing increased expenses for dramatically new product or service development and introduction. Some of the areas where different individuals or groups will hold opposite views include:

- a larger vs. a smaller line of products
- more flexible vs. a fixed capacity production operation
- full scale cross training vs. specialized skill upgrading
- strategic vs. shorter-term pragmatic forecasting
- specialized vs. flexible equipment

- long runs vs. short runs utilizing quick set-ups
- supplier rewards vs. penalties
- employee motivation by financial vs. non-financial means
- providing increased base pay vs. decreased benefits

For all these choices, it is wise to consider them as options relative to increased profit contribution, not merely cost reduction possibilities. These choices are made easier where the controlling managers are keyed to profit improvement of the whole enterprise. In this way, individual preferences are subverted to the overall objective. What effect will each of the above budgeting and expenditure decisions have on improving the bottom line?

In this vein, some top managers are amazed when they receive individual project requests for funding that have little or no chance of producing dramatically improved profits. Yet, when the corporate cry for cost reductions is raised, dramatic profit improvement is the primary goal stated by top management.

CASE STUDY: RESISTING A SPECIFIC OVERHEAD ALLOCATION

As long as the allocation of overhead and indirect costs was made on the basis of a percentage applied to her direct departmental costs, Rachel, a section manager, found no reason to confirm, reject, or modify the cost of engineering recruitment services. These services were of major concern to design and production engineering, quality assurance, sales engineering and direct production operations.

Rachel's department provided for plant cleanliness and general appearance, contract maintenance as well as for janitorial services and supplies. She determined that the huge outlay requested (and preliminarily approved) for product design engineering services had no impact on supporting her particular area. However, in the past any such non-supportive expenditure was lumped in with all other overhead charges as part of a pro-rated percentage to be borne by the supported departments.

Under the new overhead application formula, overhead budgets were to be prepared and negotiated with the department these services were designed to support. In the negotiation, Rachel was able to prove that the requested additional funds for recruiting product design engineers had very little relevance to servicing her department's needs.

This meant the allocation now had to be spread over the six areas that did receive a very direct benefit from the proposed expensive recruitment effort. When this new allocation was shown to these remaining departments, a departmental management revolt cut the product design engineering recruitment budget by almost 24%. It is doubtful if such a commotion would have been caused by the simple allocation of an average overhead allocation which lumped together all requested costs.

For this reason, cost reduction can best be accomplished where the supported group has a meaningful input into overhead budgets. Such a program, described in Chapter Nine, increases the profit improvement awareness of all managers by expanding their perspective beyond merely reviewing their individual departmental costs. A prime opportunity for such innovative thinking exists where overhead charges are lumped into a gross allocation to all supported departments—without a detailed analysis of support enhancement.

SUMMING UP: Old-Style Cost-Reduction Techniques Won't Cut It Anymore

Cost-cutting requires a more diversified approach these days. In the past, cutting out bodies was always the first approach to any cost reduction effort. After all, direct costs drove all other cost factors. And, the magnitude of personnel costs made them stand out as the number one option to leverage cost reduction actions.

In the heat of battle, management wants action not analysis. So, moving quickly to reduce personnel was the first, and sometimes the only, effort before checking into any other cost-reduction possibilities.

At the close of the 20th century, however, direct labor costs have shrunk to 10–15% of total direct costs in many industries. Even a 10% direct personnel reduction will only cut between 1 and 1.5% of total costs. Thus, the simple cost-cutting ventures of previous managements no longer offer the same leveraging opportunities as before. Yet, reducing the direct workforce is still the first concern of most cost reduction efforts today . . . perhaps because such a strategy is both easy to perform and is highly visible.

In a manufacturing or processing firm, a wise approach is to segregate those costs which are production-related from those which are associated with absorbing past capital expenditures. In other words, a strategy to sell off excess capacity may prove to be more fruitful than expending effort and cash assets on management and sales efforts to use this excess capacity. This will also allow for matching direct personnel reductions to desired—not just existing—capacity. Chapter Nine will explore techniques for determining opportunities for cost reductions in manufacturing and processing industries, where unique capacity/cost relationships exist.

Remember, no one will question cutting fat, but future profitability is at stake where you cut into muscle, bone and nerves.

CHAPTER 2

TOP LEVEL STRATEGIES THAT TURN COST-CUTTING OBJECTIVES INTO PROFIT-IMPROVEMENT ACTIVITIES

During the Korean conflict, I was involved in an 8,000 man-hour effort at the Detroit Arsenal to improve the coolant for the M-1 tank's shock absorbing system. In the middle of our work, this system was replaced by a totally different weapon leveling device not requiring any coolant and the project was aborted. I remember the project leader commenting, "We should never work with a teaspoon before the earth mover has finished its job."

ELIMINATING FUNCTIONS TO CUT THE FAT

Companies today must have an overall strategy within which the details of profit improvement are developed. The strategic planners, reengineering practitioners, and the objective systems analysts are all seeking to develop new roadmaps for profitability planning and control. In order to get everyone "on the same page," these routes to improved profitability should start with questions about overall objectives, and culminate in agreed-upon answers to such sample questions as:

- "Why are we doing this?" compared to "How can we do this better?"

- What is the long term profitability (or cost effectiveness) effect of following this course of action?
- What resource re-allocation is required, and what assets must be acquired and/or discarded?
- What projects or processes should be aborted and when?
- What evaluation of success and/or failure should be used?
- What options can be simulated which will kick in at specific milestones in project management?

The above are but a small, partial list of strategic, overall planning considerations that blanket the philosophy of cost reduction for profit improvement. Inherent in this approach is the goal to cut the fat while saving and building the muscle mass. Cost reduction must lead to long-range, as well as short-range profit improvement, and should be management-controlled for long-lasting and anticipated results. As described in Chapter One, this is the strategy that boards of directors must demand from their top management selections, and which each echelon of management must relate to in their own strategic planning.

CASE STUDY: ANALYZING THE R&D BUDGET TO ELIMINATE FUNCTIONS

An off-shore manufacturer of components and clone products for notebook, and sub-notebook laptop computers had been measuring expenditures for research and development (R&D) by four main factors:

1. As a percent of forecasted and net actual sales currency generated by the past annual accounts receivable,
2. As a ratio of profits associated with ordinary income,
3. As a percent of budgeted expenditures for all manufacturing employee pay, plus capital investment for production and administrative support equipment, and
4. As a percentage change from prior modified average base figures for actual R&D expenditures.

Management used these four factors to set parameters around the total budget granted for individual R&D projects, as well as for the overhead required to support daily operations. The actual expenditure approvals were then allocated by a centralized R&D Department that was funded by a headquarters account.

Getting Started: The first attempt at reducing the cost of the R&D budgeting function was to decentralize the developmental work to the funding control and approval of the operating divisions, primarily the marketing and production areas. These groups would be spending their own budgeted funds for that R & D which would benefit their operations, i.e., new products and processes, advanced equipment and systems, etc.

Each project was re-reviewed for its contribution to the future profitability for the funding sources . . . the operating divisions. As a result, a new set of priorities emerged. The emphasis in the past had been on the centralized R&D Group's priorities, which related to the selection of projects on their individual estimates of return on R&D investment of skills and available technology.

Now it turned out that the actual highest priority was to reduce the time needed to get products to market. This became more important than (a) reducing the present manufacturing costs of today's products, and (b) applying funds to research projects by an estimate of future return on investment.

The reorganization of the funding process, through eliminating functions, not only changed R&D priorities, but also led to reduced funding for some projects after their merits were re-reviewed by the newly responsible operating divisions.

Establishing new criteria: The new set of priorities for R&D funding brought with them new questions about relevance to profitability. One such consideration was how to gauge true customer demand. Industry market research had shown that the ultimate customers for portable computers ranked their needs as follows:

- weight
- power source (battery) life
- quality of display (screen).

During an analysis of both manpower and total expenditures for current R&D projects, very little relationship to the above customer criteria was found. (Admittedly, research funding rarely has a direct line relationship to customer needs, but it should at least be given some priority for the limited funds available.)

About 25% of the R&D budget was limited to pure research projects which remained under the control of the headquarters committee of top level managers. However, future research funding was now reviewed under new criteria:

- Can the research be conducted under controlled contract conditions, off-site, with either an academic institution or a research contractor, whose facilities already contain the required professional skills and unique equipment? Thus, these manpower and material assets would no longer be required to be procured, retrained, modified and/or maintained on-site.

- Are research grants available from government, association or private foundations for projects in the field of public or national need? What is the value, on a per project basis, for a monopolistic control of the end-result?

With the new criteria for evaluating both the viability and priority for proposed projects, related management actions resulted in new ratios of R&D expenditures to sales, profitability and manpower. Because of this change in fund planning, related actual expenditures dropped dramatically. The new budgets for two successive years of R&D remained static, even though sales and profits increased by a cumulative 16% during this period of time.

FOUR WAYS TO GAIN CONTROL OVER MANUFACTURING COSTS

A new and broader theory of manufacturing cost improvement has been evolving in the last decades of the Twentieth Century. Marketing, design and logistical decisions are being integrated into manufacturing strategic planning. Isolation of these inputs, as was done in the past, is an imperfect approach that is being overcome in four major areas of production cost effectiveness applications—manufacturing systems design, skill reorganization and work place flexibility, manufacturing cost accounting, and producing quality products and services the first time.

MANUFACTURING SYSTEMS DESIGN

The physical plant is now approached as an integral part of the flow of forecasting on through to purchasing, capacity planning and simulation, production scheduling, materials handling and product distribution. Materials requirement planning, vendor certification and partnering, capacity scheduling, distribution channeling and warranty servicing are all part of a chain of activities controlled through simulation, selection of optimum operations and feedback controls.

The new systems are designed to integrate the objective of customer service to the total capacity and skills of the firm's operations. In so doing, the effects of optional manufacturing decisions are simulated, while cost savings opportunities are highlighted. The bright side of this is that the costs for installing these total operating systems has been dropping steadily . . . caused by new data handling storage and power inherent in electronic data integration, as well as by the volume of applications that have been brought into the implementation process.

SKILL REORGANIZATION
AND WORKFORCE FLEXIBILITY

The introduction of the machine tender (vs. the machine operator) approach to manufacturing operations has resulted from the introduction of robotics, numerically controlled and multipurpose equipment. In addition, the production unit has been expanded to encompass groups of employees with multiple skills . . . skills which are developed through cross training, as well as crew applications to modules of assembly requirements. This new flexibility allows for quicker responses to product design changes, as well as allowing for the downsizing of an economic batch being processed. (This is covered in more detail in Chapter 8.)

This flexibility permits the company to apply cost savings to previously uneconomic lot sizes, while allowing a much quicker response to changing market conditions. Heretofore, one of the major considerations to matching manufacturing supply to forecasted demand was the cost of inventory in process, or in the manufacturing and warehouse pipeline. Presently, the size of production batches has been drastically reduced by the application of quick changeover devices.

The cumulative effect of these manufacturing changes is to reduce the cost of matching manufacturing capacity to both forecasted and varying actual demand.

MANUFACTURING COST ACCOUNTING

The new manufacturing approaches, including activity based costing (A-B-C), aim to integrate business with manufacturing strategies. The major effect is to recalculate the true allocated costs, and thus the specific cost savings opportunities for the manufacturing manager. (These are detailed in Chapter Ten.)

The traditional approach of cost accounting has been to use direct labor as the basis for allocating all overhead and administrative costs. In this way, a heavy emphasis of allocated overheads resulted from their application to direct labor time expended. When labor accounted for 50% or more of manufacturing costs, this traditional approach was valid. With direct labor now accounting for about 15% of total manufacturing costs, this cost allocation base does not provide the data for optimal cost reduction strategies.

Direct labor can now be considered a fixed cost, and the time to produce a product has become the variable factor. Thus, cost improvement benefits come from reducing and controlling the time it takes to produce product against the fixed cost of the assets used for this activity.

PRODUCING QUALITY PRODUCTS AND SERVICES THE FIRST TIME

In cost reduction practice, anything done right the first time is far superior to multiple attempts at finally getting it right. To accomplish this in the manufacturing sector, complex monitoring and feedback devices are employed . . . many with optional choices already programmed into their routines. The theory is to find and eliminate defective parts and practices as early in the process as possible.

In addition, suppliers and sub-contractors are designated quality partners with the manufacturing facility, through vendor certification, in-house training and on-site assistance. In this way, product design, manufacturing process and administrative improvements, can be instituted in relatively brief periods of time. The cost reduction effects can be seen to drop to the bottom line without the hassle and delay of multiple and tiered approvals by disparate parties.

The theory is simple. Build quality into both the process and the operators' functions, as opposed to the 1950's approaches which were almost totally dedicated to separating "good from bad" product after it was supplied or produced. To accomplish this, machine operators have become part of the inspection process. In some cases they are now the incoming parts inspector, the in-process tester, the assembly sampler, and the final inspector of the results of the total manufacturing process.

Additional savings come from the application of advanced process knowledge, and commitment and pride exercised by the production employees themselves. The "we and they" concept is diminished. Now, it is quite common to hear, "We inspect, produce, and are responsible for our product's performance in the hands of the ultimate customer." Manufacturing employee pride and increased process knowledge are an integral part of new manufacturing quality systems. In this way, cost reduction applications come from many sources, not just those groups whose titles are synonymous with cost reduction activities.

OUTSOURCING ADMINISTRATIVE AND SUPPORT SERVICES TO CUT THE FAT

For decades the concept of make or buy has permeated most manufacturing analyses when seeking cost improvements. Initially, outside sources provided skilled personnel, additional capacity or manufacturing processes that were not available in-house. However, the analyses also involved selecting areas where the products or processes were less expensive when supplied from these outside sources. These analyses then related these potential cost savings to such factors as:

- reliability of delivery promises,
- financial stability of the suppliers,
- vendor ability to grow rapidly to meet forecasted customer needs,
- control of product or process secrets,
- data integration with the prime manufacturer,
- personnel communication, and
- a myriad of other perceived outsourcing concerns.

In the forefront of the manufacturing outsourcing approach has been the procurement function, through:

- integrating value analysis with the company's suppliers,
- coordinating vendor production scheduling and procurement with the prime user's mainframe programs
- contracting for on-site supplier process controls where only final or incoming inspection previously existed
- providing incentives for single sourcing and Just-In-Time practices that increase delivery performance while decreasing inventory investment as a hedge against both longer and/or unpredictable lead times.

All of these purchasing cost reduction practices are well documented in widely distributed trade books and industry periodicals. Thus, new procurement functions are becoming the objects of intense scrutiny as they relate to the strategic planners' unique question, "What is our core business?"

CASE STUDY: REDUCING COSTS FOR CREDIT AND COLLECTION SERVICES

A Southeast manufacturer of prosthetic devices was planning an expansion into new geographic areas where they had not done business before. This meant that their customer base would now be greatly expanded to include small practitioners, local clinics, walk-in medical centers, outpatient home care service companies, and health care distribution centers. Management's first thought was to create and staff a credit and collection department in their existing accounts receivable operation.

Their cost reduction consultant suggested they first review the scope of the business plan's objectives. The stated goal was to increase sales in order to increase return on invested assets. Thus, the cost of setting up any new departments, or increasing present department costs with expanded services, was considered as a straight line extrapolation from present practice. However, since there was no full-time staff currently fulfilling this function, what was the true cost to be factored into this new investment in next year's strategic plan? Considering this question brought forth the problem of whether outsourcing any new function would be a viable approach.

Before considering the cost advantages of using an outside credit and collection contractor, the company had to define those functions which it would be committed to funding. These included:

- designing credit application forms (1 time)
- examining credit policy with the existing customer base
- instituting ongoing accounts receivable analyses
- delineating risk factors with the firm's Comptroller
- issuing credit line advice on all new customers
- working with and/or serving on creditors' committees
- establishing agreements on security, warranties, collection, consignments, and reclamations
- handling bankruptcy filings.

The above functions were considered a cost of doing business, but were not directly related to the business of manufacturing and distributing prosthetic devices. Thus, the final decision hinged on the cost effectiveness of outsourcing (and improving) this credit and collection function. A strict financial analysis directed the company management to hire an experienced, local independent credit and collection contractor at a substantial savings in both start-up and continuing expenses for this needed function.

CASE STUDY: OUTSOURCING THE MAINTENANCE FUNCTION

This same Southeast manufacturing company studied the costs of both demand and preventive maintenance activities as they related to the specialized maintenance skills required to keep expensive equipment downtimes to a minimum. In addition to the fixed costs of the indirect maintenance labor budget, an annual indirect expense budget (as well as a capitalization account) was established to cover the estimated cost of materials to replace those used in preventive and demand maintenance activities. If material demand was less than anticipated for emergency and routine maintenance, and if preventive maintenance was actually only a fraction of that planned, a growing maintenance inventory investment became apparent.

Although the size of this investment grew quite rapidly until it was noticed, the reason for less-than-urgent action related to the usual management perception of this asset:

- "All the direct costs of maintenance procurement have been absorbed in the last period's Profit and Loss Statement. In addition, the indirect costs of maintenance materials' buying, warehousing, materials handling, picking and record keeping are fixed costs, irrespective of the volume and size of the maintenance inventory. Therefore, most of the present costs of the maintenance inventory (less the cost of cash) have been absorbed in a previous accounting period, or as part of the fixed portion of the budget."

- "Any excess items in the maintenance inventory act as an added insurance against expensive equipment downtime. Or, at the very least, the active inventory items will reduce the amount of purchasing replenishment required."

These arguments became the focal point of the cost reduction committee's discussions when the company embarked on an evaluation of two new preventive maintenance systems: (1) Local Area Maintenance (LAM), and (2) the Ratio/Benefit simulation of projected scheduling of maintenance materials and skills.

Since preventive maintenance is usually both predictable and time scheduled, it became the target for analysis of the true need to accomplish this function with in-company personnel and on-site maintenance materials. A cost analysis was undertaken to explore the option of reducing paid-for materials and fixed indirect labor for preventive maintenance.

To the surprise of the cost reduction study group, maintenance labor costs would actually increase using outsourced aid. However, this was greatly offset by the reduction of budgeted expenses for maintenance materials. The time factor of cash requirements was one of the main considerations in this analysis. The contractor was to be paid after the preventive maintenance services were completed. Thus, instead of paying for a huge and growing maintenance inventory when it is received and invoiced, materials would now be an expense paid for as the required materials were actually put in service.

In the first year of operation, a 21% reduction in the actual amount of direct expenditure for preventive maintenance materials was realized. The application of newer preventive techniques were also important factors. However, the major savings came from answering a basic strategic planning question, "What business are we in and, therefore, which services must we cost-effectively supply in-house?" Management realized that elimination of a function should precede any analysis to improve that service.

GOVERNMENT'S ROLE IN FOSTERING MEANINGFUL COST REDUCTIONS

The government's role in fostering and employing cost reduction strategies should not be overlooked in this discussion of strategic planning, objectives systems analysis, and selection of targets for cost improvement through expense elimination and control.

Probably every administration since Washington's has expounded fiscal responsibility—including elimination of unnecessary costs. In recent history, the Reagan Administration sponsored the Grace Commission, and the Clinton Administration has initiated the National Performance Review (NPR) to revolutionize the way government operates.

If past history is a guide, the cost reductions resulting from implementing the recommendations of these studies, will be negligible. Peter Grace, Chairman of the Grace Corporation, was the first to acknowledge that the Grace Commission's massive list of recommendations for billions of dollars of savings was yet to be significantly implemented 5 years after its submission. (In 1993, Mr. Grace initiated a fund-raising campaign to force cost reduction implementation.)

The NPR's charter is to focus on both effectiveness and savings as the primary criteria for their suggestions. Second-tier questions are to be presented. These queries will include:

- Does the program, as funded, work in accomplishing the departmental goals as established by the executive and legislative branches?
- Are quality services being provided, and, if not, why not?
- Does the funded entity encourage individual and group innovation for improvement?
- Are creativity and hard work rewarded?

I have labelled these questions, and this effort, a second-tier approach, essentially because what is required is a national consensus on the role of government. Past failures to restructure the national government will be repeated until the electorate defines and demands that the government stick to its core business. Until this is done, what is the value of working with a "teaspoon" where an "earth mover" is a first requirement?

In this regard, the politicians and bureaucrats believe they represent an electorate that desires efficiency of operations, as long as the cost reductions are "not in my neighborhood." At the same time, the electorate desires strong leadership and a well-defined set of goals by which to judge the effects of tax increases, service enhancements and cost reductions. The citizenry are supportive of leadership that promises governmental efficiency, as long as it doesn't mean a cut in their own services and entitlements.

There is a lesson in this for private industry leaders. Without a clear definition of the core business—agreed and approved by top management—long lasting and effective cost reductions may not be the end result.

For our national government, such an impasse can be overcome, where a national consensus agrees on the government's role in major areas of present-day concerns. For example:

Law enforcement: If urban crime is the Nation's number one concern, what is the point of sending well-equipped military forces to international hot spots, while our local police are undermanned and under-armed against the urban terrorists who control our neighborhoods? If the role of the federal government is to protect its citizenry, then the billions of dollars poured into local governments to fight crime has been an utter failure. Would a national police force be a more cost effective approach?

Would national law enforcement of local felony laws apply the best technology to a losing battle? Should we continue to rely on a fragmented State-by-State approach to law enforcement? "What is the best plan to protect our citizens?" should be the criteria for success, when faced with the usual arguments pertaining to States Rights, decentralization efficiencies, and the dominance of local prerogatives over the needs of all. The answers to these questions may only slightly modify our present course of law enforcement, but the role of government should be addressed before merely improving our present approach. An old Polish saying states, "You cannot put veneer on air; you must apply any finish to a base of wood."

Government aid: The economic well-being of our society is addressed through governmental efforts in the fields of housing, job training, stockpiling commodities, tariffs, and a myriad of other areas of national concern. Would more money or regulation help? Or, should goals, milestones of progress and controls measure the contribution of governmental efforts to aid our citizenry?

Billions of dollars are spent on stockpiling agricultural products in order to provide incentives for planting by our farmers. At the same time, senior citizens receive inflation-related increases for the purchase of food, while citizens at the poverty level receive food stamps to purchase derivative foods at prices jacked up by government subsidies.

Establishing and adhering to a cost effective national strategy may aid
our citizens far more than increasing taxes to expand these food products' programs, or relying on a program to reduce present expenditures
by a fixed percentage of projected national income. A consensus national policy should provide logical options for program planning both
to reduce redundancies and provide a measure of success (or failure) for
our collective cost effectiveness efforts.

WHAT INDUSTRY WOULD LIKE GOVERNMENT TO DO

In ascertaining the role of government in fostering a national industrial policy regarding cost effectiveness, the first obstacles are provided
by those who decry governmental intervention in the business of doing
business. This attitude was the dogma of U.S. business before the
crushing blows of foreign competition caused both the loss of domestic
market share and a corresponding 6% reduction of the U.S. manufacturing workforce in the last 30 years.

In the past, the cooperation of government with private enterprise
built our national road system as well as our aerospace industry. More
recently, government support has fostered breakthroughs in the electronics, advanced materials and biotechnology fields.

Since the U.S. is the world's leader in capital formation, the major
pressure exerted by industry on government has been in the area of tax
relief to encourage investment—especially in the area of research and
development for new products and processes. Two other areas of cooperative interest are (1) a desire for relief from the costs of the paperwork blizzard necessary for compliance with the sometimes conflicting
goals of governmental agencies, and (2) the application of pressure on
foreign governments to level the playing field in their nations, so that
U.S. companies can fairly compete with local producers.

FIVE ELEMENTS REQUIRED FOR A SUCCESSFUL NATIONAL INDUSTRIAL POLICY

It appears to me that industry would benefit most from a national industrial policy that:

1. provides support for efforts to introduce new products and services in cost effective time cycles,

2. reduces controls by existing, and perhaps redundant, regulatory agencies,

3. rescinds burdensome, existing taxing regulations in order to promote capital formation,

4. puts pressure on foreign governments to allow our products and services to fairly compete overseas, and

5. supplies aid in re-training America's workforce.

A stated national policy in just these five areas, could reduce many burdensome costs to industry, as well as the costs of operating existing government agencies. This would be an example of applying the "earth mover" approach to maximizing the role of government . . . an approach which should precede the "teaspoon" techniques which attempt to improve existing governmental services.

REDUCE COSTS WITH DISTRIBUTION PARTNERING

The 1990's saw the explosion of partnering arrangements between suppliers and their customers. This was triggered by both the quality improvement demands of manufacturing and processing industries, as well as the spread of Just-In-Time supply applications to product scheduling from source to ultimate customer. Certification of single source suppliers has now become commonplace, from training their personnel in international quality standards (ISO 9000 series as an example) to understanding the overall materials requirement planning system. Suppliers are now being recognized as an integral part of the overall supply chain.

This concept is being expanded to the distribution process . . . called third-party logistics. Companies are now delegating distribution activities from final packing through to customer delivery to outside specialists in the fields of traffic management, including air, rail, truck and ocean transport, and warehousing. This includes selection of carriers and insurance, and even accounts receivable collection. The end result is not only shorter and less expensive lead times for delivery, but also cost savings over and above staffing and maintaining a specialized in-house department performing these vital services.

An added advantage is that third-party services that bid for these logistics contracts, have also developed custom-designed approaches to meet the users' needs. These include new fleet management concepts, improved warehousing procedures, and other logistics management improvements . . . all provided as variable costs vs. the present need for funding forecasted fixed costs to maintain these services.

Distribution partnering also allows for incentives to cut costs as part of the contractual arrangement. This involves setting minimums for both the volume of business provided, as well as for the level of quality service (such as promised lead times for customer delivery) expected at that volume. The savings expected creates the base for an incentive payment, while missing the targeted volume and service level creates penalties for both parties. In this way, cost reduction is tied to both a volume and a quality expectation level, as agreed by both parties in the partnering agreement.

Sticking with your strengths: When a company recognizes that its strengths are in developing new products, and efficiently manufacturing and marketing them, does it pay to develop distribution expertise internally when such services can be contracted for with specialists? Such an analysis should precede asking:

- What warehouse configuration or location best suits our needs to provide customer service?
- Where should the fleet of tractor/trailers be located, and how much maintenance staff is required?
- How can we reduce the costs of material handling in our warehouse?
- What should be the skills of the new traffic manager that we are going to hire?
- How shall we measure and improve the performance of our distribution management function?
- Does our fleet management operation understand ISO 9000 series of quality standards, especially in regard to export shipments to European Common Market customers?

SUMMING UP: Zero in on Your Key Objectives

If you are to have the overall cost effectiveness from a directed program that cuts the fat while saving the muscle, you must ask the first questions first, such as:

"What business are we in?, and

"What are our objectives to maximize that business?"

Cost reductions that adhere to these objectives are a most efficient method of achieving the return on assets invested.

You can be at any level of the organization to use this common-sense approach to efficient cost reduction. "I'm not a part of top management" is no longer an excuse for a manager not initiating and continuing a cost reduction effort. Granted that a top-down approach works best if that top is the pinnacle of the organization. However, you shouldn't quit trying because upper management pays little heed to the need for providing overall cost-cutting direction.

The best cost-cutting ideas can come from anywhere. Many cost reduction programs start with:

- instigation from a junior member of management presenting the outline and a schedule of activities for installing an effective cost reduction strategy.
- committees that seek input from anyone with an idea.
- suggestions floated through the ranks to the top.
- examples from pilot programs initiated at any level in the organization, not necessarily originating from headquarter's group thinking (and approval).
- outside consultants' recommendations.
- acquired programs from observed or merged operations.

This Chapter has provided many examples of the advantages of an objectives-driven, cost reduction effort. The details of the techniques used will be provided in the following chapters. Remember, they are best suited to be applied in an environment of directed and agreed savings opportunities. In all situations, the final judgment relates to what drops to the bottom line on a continuing and accelerating basis. If you cut the fat *and* cut the muscle, the cost reduction effort may be meaningless.

CHAPTER 3

GAINING CONSENSUS FOR COST REDUCTION STRATEGIES TO IMPROVE ASSET MANAGEMENT

Techniques to improve asset management are related to the age-old business concept of improving return on investment. This ROI goal not only drives capital investment from start-up to expansion, but is also used to evaluate today's investment for tomorrow's future profits. Thus, cost reductions that cut the fat are evaluated as they ultimately contribute to this ROI ratio. At the same time, the firm must be actively engaged in improving the quality and value of products and/or services produced. In not-for-profit operations, a reduction in the expenditure for services provided generally reflects this same view of return on invested capital. Thus, the total package of this strategy relates cost reduction to both immediate and ongoing profitability.

SUCCESS CRITERIA SHOULD BE BASED ON COMMON ASSET PERFORMANCE RATIOS

In a growing business, where capital is aggressively re-invested from retained profits, as well as from outside borrowing and shareholder investment, an increase in the return on invested assets remains a most important goal of cost reduction activities. This is especially true for public company managements, where net worth per share is enhanced by reducing, or, at a minimum, maintaining the cost of invested assets relative to stable, increasing, and even declining earnings.

The ratio of significant importance relates profit to invested assets:

$$\frac{\text{GROSS PROFIT (before taxes)}}{\text{OPERATING ASSETS}}$$

This ratio can be modified to have more significance for a whole company (or an independent operating division) as the ratio of:

$$\frac{\text{OPERATING PROFIT}}{\text{OPERATING ASSETS}}$$

One of the positive effects of this ratio can come from a decrease in the cost of operating assets used to generate the operating profit. This is easier said than done, since, in many companies, fixed assets make up a majority of the cost of operating assets, and are the most difficult of costs to quickly be cut. Likewise, asset valuation (and verification) must be one of the first acts taken by managers looking for big savings in asset management, which is the main thrust of this Chapter.

By comparison, cost equations for analyses (comparisons) begin with the master ratio:

$$\frac{\text{OPERATING PROFIT}}{\text{NET REVENUES (SALES)}}$$

and then proceed to relate specific activities to this very same denominator, including such activities as:

- distribution and marketing
- gross value of good product produced as a cost of sales
- general overhead and administration
- direct and indirect labor
- average total direct cost by functional department
- design, development and research
- storage vs. processing vs. procurement to the same denominator, the investment in assets.

Thus, invested capital, howsoever derived, becomes, and should be, a significant factor in cost reduction analyses. Yet, when cost reductions are considered, this generally brings to mind:

- employee layoffs,
- streamlining of products and services,
- cutting the cost of carrying inventories,
- using robotics,
- applying computer-aided design and production (CAD, CAM),
- installing quality assurance techniques, such as:
  - certifying vendor capabilities
  - managing incoming statistical quality control applications,
  - applying design engineering reliability predictions of field performance and ultimate service requirements.

Of course, these activities should be encouraged for their ultimate contribution to profit improvement, but, simultaneously, analyses of asset ratios can be a very fruitful exercise in both defining opportunities and selecting criteria for cost reduction successes.

HOW TO ANALYZE ASSET RATIOS

Asset analyses begin with the master ratio:

$$\frac{\text{OPERATING ASSETS}}{\text{REVENUES (SALES)}}$$

They then proceed to relate specifically definable assets to this very same denominator . . . such assets as:

- current and fixed assets, considering allocation cost percentages from activity-based costing analyses
- depreciated land and structure values
- plant and warehouse market values
- overland and materials handling vehicles and equipment
- raw materials
- contractor supplied inventories on- and off-site
- work-in-process
- returns, warranty and repair materials
- maintenance supplies
- equipment employed in determining production capacity
- warehouse space available and utilized
- finished goods ready for distribution by location

The ultimate cost reduction projects relate to the application of cash as it is to be, or has been, converted to an operating asset. Where the budget may place constraints on use of the cash asset, analysis of return on investment opportunities provides managers with decision options that allow for an increase in the ratio of return on invested assets.

FORMING A COST REDUCTION COMMITTEE CAN BECOME AN EXCUSE FOR ACTION

During the 1950–70 era, a common excuse for non-action was to form a committee. In those cases, when a manager was asked, "What are we doing to get this problem resolved?", he would cite the status of the committee itself:

- "We just appointed the members, and they accepted their assignment to the committee yesterday."
- "Our first meeting is scheduled for next month."
- "We spent the initial time selecting the overall chairperson, and we also decided on sub-committees and their chiefs."
- "Initial generic goals were set, and we're waiting for approval from management."
- "Meetings will be held to allow inputs from non-committee members."
- "Personnel were assigned to gather necessary facts for the committee to consider. As soon as we know the size of this task, a deadline for completion will be set."
- "Our minutes are now being assembled for approval by the members."
- "Recommendations will follow the statement of the problem and its magnitude."
- "The final step has been taken. The report has been sent to a top management committee."
- "Approval of the report is imminent!"

The formation of the committee and its subsequent meetings formed a substitute for required action. Instead of the end result being implementation of an action plan, including (a) a schedule of expected savings, (b) specific assignments of authority and responsibility, (c) and a monitoring control, the company was presented with a report of the problem, which included an evaluation of the magnitude of potential savings and recommendations for implementation. Thus, the end result of the committee approach was simply an approved report. From this group of recommendations, management now had to assign both personnel and funding for the priorities recommended. At this point, action was supposed to commence (sometimes by the establishment of a new committee).

Although a company may never assign a new product cost accounting task to personnel untrained in this complex arena, it is not uncommon to form a committee with personnel who are only slightly experienced (or trained) in the techniques needed to get the job done. These include: running effective meetings, establishing attainable goals and prioritizing them, estimating and scheduling specific tasks, delegating authority according to the rules of accountability, listening and negotiating, project management, forecasting principles, cost leveraging, etc. It is as though no particular skills are required to be a cost reduction committee chairperson or, for that matter, a committee member. Obviously, this is not so! Yet, cost reduction committees are formed with high hopes, and with little direction other than the non-specific mandate, "Cut total costs by 15% and soon!"

WHY COST REDUCTION COMMITTEES FAIL

It is such a common procedure to set up a task force to initiate a cost reduction program, that a list of causes of failure may be as instructive as a mirror list of those better methods for achieving action. Following are some examples of why cost reduction committees fail and what can be done to avoid them:

HIGHEST LEVEL OF COMMITMENT IS NOT PERCEIVED

All who will devote time and effort to the cost reduction project must feel that positive results are expected and eagerly anticipated by the highest levels of management. It is difficult to sustain commitment to a program that is perceived as being low on the list of company priorities.

EXAMPLE: A Chicago company specifically desired four improved asset management results:

1. Reduction of leased office, plant and warehouse space that it didn't require by virtue of the new J-I-T applications at six operating locations.

2. Sale of all obsolete equipment, even that which may have a fuzzy future use ("You never know!") . . . equipment that was presently being retained in leased warehouse space.

3. Eliminate the purchase of redundant assets, such as equipment for a distant office that could be found lying idle in another company facility.

4. Reduce or eliminate the back-up equipment maintenance supplies held both in on-site storage areas, as well in centralized warehouses (to back up the maintenance inventories).

The committee's stated instruction was, "reduce the cost of assets not in use." This appeared in a loosely worded memo from the Vice President to the Chairperson who formed the committee. The expectations of management were stated as, "Cut present costs." There was no statement of urgency, or a requested schedule of progress to be demonstrated at presentations to top level managers. The feeling one got at the very first meeting was, "work on this when it fits into your present workload."

Actually, the corporate Board of Directors was demanding that the President improve asset management throughout the far-flung divisions as a major contribution to improving the Company's cash flow situation.

A motivated, dedicated, action-oriented group is difficult to assemble or mold, where the individual members perceive a low level of top management commitment. It is imperative that top management demonstrate—by both word and deed—their total commitment to both the resolution of the problem, arrived at through analyses, as well as potential solutions backed by realistic recommendations and constructive actions.

GOALS ARE VAGUELY STATED

Consider that team members may start out committed to the gains to be achieved by making the company operate at a more efficient level. Each member feels they were selected because of their experience, position and/or problem-solving abilities. They will view the cost reduction project from the perspective of their own skill levels, personal goals and aspirations. This is only human. These attributes will be evaluated against the stated objectives of top level management, who may charge the group with specific goals, short and long term expectations, financing back-up, ability to use available facility and personnel skills, develop a marketing strategy and a procurement plan, etc.

In this way, all data input, presentations of potential solutions, and the group's ultimate recommendations will have a base upon which to be measured, both for the commitment of the individual members and the viability of the proposals. Non-specific expectations usually result in data collection and recommendations that resemble the spinning of wheels—round and round and going nowhere.

Group consensus is gained through negotiation and compromise. It is imperative that this be achieved, because it is the future role of the committee members to install that which is proposed. The triangulation technique will be demonstrated later in this Chapter as a means of gaining consensus as well as prioritizing the committee's work towards stated objectives.

NO ATTEMPT IS MADE TO SEPARATE THE DOLLARS FROM THE PENNIES

One of the most fruitless efforts is where vast amounts of work result in minimal gains towards stated cost reduction goals. (Chapter Five will deal with techniques for overcoming this pitfall, by detailing specific tools for leveraging cost reduction efforts.)

FAILURE TO ANTICIPATE PROBLEMS

When the Cost Reduction Committee examined the data base of fixed assets in a Chicago firm's far-flung operations, they were amazed to find:

- exact asset descriptions were not standardized, so that like items were listed under varying descriptions ranging from old supplier catalog numbers to non-standardized narrative descriptions of parts vs. assemblies vs. complete operating systems.

- asset valuations were not indicative of market value or present operating condition, but, in most cases, represented depreciated values applied from straight line accounting methods. These values represented deductions of set percentage amounts from the original purchase prices. Barter values were non-existent. Thus, only a physical check of each piece of equipment could determine future use and value.

The problems with using the existing data were not forecasted by the group, until almost three months after the project's start-up. Thus, the funding and time required to perform a total overhaul of the fixed asset data base, did not exist. Optional approaches, which could have been considered at the outset, were now aggressively sought.

A simple sampling plan, which covered about 20% of the equipment categories, disclosed that 16% of the line items in the fixed asset inventory accounted for 88% of total dollar value of that inventory. It was determined that the application of CAFM (computer-aided facility management) software could be utilized to standardize descriptions, add visual images of the equipment and allow the Committee to analyze those very expensive and few fixed assets in light of the stated criteria for cost reduction.

The Committee figured that had this obvious data base problem been anticipated as an obstacle ab initio, 3 months of false starts in seeking solutions could have been avoided.

WORKING WITHOUT A TRUE SCHEDULE

One of the signs of disorganization is to see a group of dedicated, skilled and highly paid employees state that they will know where they are going when they get there. They usually also assume that they are halfway to completion when they have spent half the allocated funds.

Granted, estimating the time, effort, and cost to achieve an end result is a most difficult task. However, project management techniques, applied over the past half century, demand milestones, frequent progress reviews, feedback of data to modify future goals, and perhaps even a critical path which provides the benchmark for overall success. Cost reduction projects are subject to the same disciplines as any other projects that warrant a committee planning approach. The next time extensive time and costs are being expended on any project, see that controls are clearly established in the cost reduction project's planning stages.

INFLEXIBILITY IN THE FACE OF NEW EXPERIENCES

Cost reduction projects that the committee undertakes are usually planned in light of the group's past experiences. This becomes the initial benchmark for scheduling, funding and the application of people and their individual skills.

Cost and time parameters that relate to over- or under-estimating should be considered. At what point does the accumulation of actual experiences warrant a redirection from the initial planning estimates? Such an evaluation approach acts to limit or eliminate efforts in unproductive areas, while allowing for the re-application of funding and skills to more productive project areas. Again, benchmarks for success, established in the planning stage, act as the basis for both aggressive analysis and action by the cost reduction committee.

Prudent flexibility requires that the input of actual data be used to modify and improve the overall cost reduction plan on a timely basis.

ESTABLISHING UNREALISTIC GOALS AS A MOTIVATIONAL DEVICE

Setting realistic and attainable goals can act as a motivator. The recipient of a request for a logical objective will intuitively measure the personal effort required to achieve same, and, based on this subjective judgment, determine the ease or difficulty of realizing future success.

It is one thing to pursue a challenging yet attainable goal; it is quite another situation where the objective is perceived to be far too difficult to achieve in the time frame provided. Perceived unrealistic and rigid demands for accomplishment may act as a demotivator. Therefore, realistic goals should be set in terms of distinctive milestones for accomplishment. In this way, progress reviews, analyzing actual data vs. estimated accomplishments, will allow for modification of planned objectives, such that these new goals will demonstrate more realistic levels of future attainment.

How to make cost-reduction committees work: Take the opposite action to the failures discussed above and you have developed a positive cost reduction strategy. It is obvious that the reverse of these listed cost reduction committee shortcomings would produce far more effective results. Similarly, future success of the cost-reduction group depends upon how their work is perceived both by top management and all other levels which must make the results of their efforts a reality.

HOW TO GAIN A CONSENSUS OF PRIORITIZED GOALS

An important first step in establishing a framework for cost reduction plans and actions is the stated consensus of specific objectives. This specificity is even more productive where the goals are stated in weighted priority order. When the objectives are so stated, the recipients, be they individuals, organizational elements, or a formal cost reduction committee, will all have a specific set of consensus weighted goals. This aids in scheduling assets such as personnel, time, skills and, of course, funds.

Two popular techniques will be described that accomplish this. The first approach is popularly referred to as "triangulation," named for the shape of the simple matrix of combinations and permutations that is applied. The second tool is called the "Decision Tree."

Both will be demonstrated with examples that show how these methodologies work in the real world of both subjective and objective inputs by the goal setters. The process of establishing a consensus for weighted priorities, up front, eliminates the negotiating and compromising time spent at a later date, when conflicts can erupt in the allocation of limited assets to meet previously-agreed objectives.

ESTABLISH THE CRITERIA FOR SUCCESS

This is easier to achieve than it sounds to some of you who have had experience with recalcitrant inputters. Most participants in a cost reduction program could probably write these criteria down independently; and, when they are presented, find that there is a clear basis for mutual agreement. Thus, this approach may best be achieved by having these criteria drawn up by one individual, and then presented to a select group of peers for comment, modification and ultimate acceptance either by interoffice messaging, or at a meeting.

EXAMPLE: SHORT-TERM COST IMPROVEMENT GOALS SELECTED BY A DIVISION OF A CHEMICAL PRODUCTS' PROCESSOR

Agreed Criteria for Success: The greatest cost reduction emphasis shall be given to:

- that which promises the most return as measured in realizable profits that will drop to the bottom line, and
- that which can be accomplished within one year's time from the date of project approval.

HOW TO USE TRIANGULATION TO ESTABLISH THE CRITERIA FOR SUCCESS

The triangulation technique for gaining a consensus can be performed in four easy steps:

STEP ONE: LIST—IN RANDOM ORDER—THE SUGGESTIONS, IDEAS, ATTITUDES AND JUDGMENTS OF CONCERNED MANAGERS

This could be achieved by circulating pre-selected goals from the above-described procedure, where the criteria for success were agreed. Ask for written input of ideas to accomplish them. This may prove to be a more complete approach than having participants at a meeting call out their pet projects, by "shooting from the hip."

To encourage a flow of ideas, while seeking a diamond in the idea pile, it is best to have firmly stated those success criteria as the guiding factor. Of course, realistically speaking, availability of funds must also be considered in order to establish a parameter around the free flow of suggestions for cost improvement.

EXAMPLE: The following recommendations were part of a partial list submitted and then merged with like ideas, at this chemical processing company. They were listed in random order so as not to provide any sense of priority to the group that ultimately reviewed and commented on the list.

1. Reduce the quantity of products (or services) that are offered, such that only profitable products will be available for sale.

2. Invest in cost cutting activities for only those products that are presently known to be marginal losers.

3. Increase marketing and sales expenditures for high mark-up products, while reducing, or holding static, promotional costs for low mark-up items.

4. Review and introduce new products (or services) that project for high margins, while, at the same time, decreasing expenditures for projects designed to cut the costs of marginally profitable products.

5. Eliminate all expenditures for outside services that are considered discretionary. (Discretionary is defined as a cost which does not result in a figure that can be tracked to a specific increase in profitability on the bottom line.)

6. Contract for all services, including those presently performed in-house, where the resultant cost is less or equal to the present direct expense for these services.

7. Implement a program to reduce the possession of high-value inventories (raw materials, W-I-P, and finished goods) to a period shorter than the present accounts payable payment cycle time.

8. Immediately slash all departmental expense budgets, including manpower, direct and indirect costs, materials, administrative and supervisory expenses, etc., by a fixed percentage (10% was recommended).

9. Freeze all personnel hiring, even for replacements, except by explicit approval of the managing director.

10. Provide non-selective early retirement to all who qualify regardless of the incumbent's present worth to operations.

(Some organizations, using the triangulation approach, use letters A, B, C . . . to define the proposed random suggestions, so that the analysis of these ideas will not be prejudiced by any assumed ranking related to a numerical assignation.)

STEP TWO: APPLY CONSENSUS TO THE TRIANGULATION FORM

Triangulation is a graphic method of comparing cost reduction ideas, suggestions, opinions and recommendations. The mathematics behind this type of analysis need not be explained to confuse the participants. (It is based on combination and permutation formulae which both rank independent data inputs and weigh them in the same iteration.)

The selected group will be asked to compare two sets of ideas at a time, independent of all other listed suggestions . . . and then to continue to perform this comparison for all possible combinations. Each of the selected ideas should be described in enough detail so that the participant is aware of each suggestion's cost reduction ramifications.

Consider that if your company had the resources to implement all the worthwhile suggestions without prejudice to any other, there would be no need for this type of analysis. However, in most organizations, there are more problems to resolve than time, talent or funding available, so priorities and emphasis must be established.

The above comparisons may be performed independently; however, consensus is best achieved if the agreement is forged during open group discussion. It is amazing how such a consensus is really not so much a matter of individuals dominating the group with their own ideas of successful techniques, as it is a matter of applied group common sense and shared experiences. When the future problem solvers participate in the selection of techniques for successful accomplishment, the chances of that shared success are dramatically increased.

Figure 3-1 is a graphic presentation of what the usual comparison form appears like to the participants. As can be seen, each idea can be compared to every other idea by how the two-number sets are displayed.

Figure 3-2 shows a completed form, where all the recommendations for cost reductions have been compared to one-another (vs. the criteria for success) by the group on a consensus basis. An "X" is drawn where there is a clear superiority of one idea over the other in a set; the "X" being placed over the superior recommendation. A slash "/" is used to denote that the two ideas in the set are approximately equal when compared to the criteria for success against which they are both measured.

Figure 3-1　Triangulation Format for Recording Consensus Conclusions

```
1   1   1   1   1   1   1   1   1    1    1    1    1
2   3   4   5   6   7   8   9   10   11   12   13   14

    2   2   2   2   2   2   2   2    2    2    2    2
    3   4   5   6   7   8   9   10   11   12   13   14

        3   3   3   3   3   3   3    3    3    3    3
        4   5   6   7   8   9   10   11   12   13   14

            4   4   4   4   4   4    4    4    4    4
            5   6   7   8   9   10   11   12   13   14

                5   5   5   5   5    5    5    5    5
                6   7   8   9   10   11   12   13   14

                    6   6   6   6    6    6    6    6
                    7   8   9   10   11   12   13   14

                        7   7   7    7    7    7    7
                        8   9   10   11   12   13   14

                            8   8    8    8    8    8
                            9   10   11   12   13   14

                                9    9    9    9    9
                                10   11   12   13   14

                                     10   10   10   10
                                     11   12   13   14

                                          11   11   11
                                          12   13   14

                                               12   12
                                               13   14

                                                    13
                                                    14
```

Figure 3-2　Triangulation Format as Completed

```
1   1   ✗   ✗   1   ✗   ✗   ✗   ✗    1    1    1    1
✗   ✗   4   ✗   ✗   7   8   9   10   11   12   13   14

    2   ✗   ✗   2   ✗   2   2   2    2    2    2    2
    ✗   4   5   ✗   7   ✗   ✗   ✗    11   12   13   14

        ✗   ✗   ✗   3   3   3   ✗    3    3    3    3
        4   ✗   6   ✗   ✗   ✗   ✗    11   12   13   14

            4   4   ✗   ✗   ✗   ✗    4    4    4    4
            ✗   ✗   7   8   9   10   11   12   13   14
```

(continued)

Figure 3–2 (continued)

5	~~5~~	~~5~~	~~5~~	~~5~~	5	5	5	5
~~6~~	7	8	~~9~~	10	11	12	13	14
	~~6~~	~~6~~	~~6~~	~~6~~	6	6	6	6
	7	8	9	10	11	12	13	14
		~~7~~	~~7~~	~~7~~	7	7	7	7
		8	~~9~~	10	11	12	13	14
			~~8~~	~~8~~	8	8	8	8
			9	~~10~~	11	12	13	14
				~~9~~	9	9	9	9
				~~10~~	11	12	13	14
					10	10	10	10
					11	12	13	14
						11	11	11
						12	13	14
							12	12
							13	14
								13
								14

STEP THREE: TOTAL AND WEIGHT THE CONSENSUS SELECTIONS

Sum the "X"s and "/"s for each recommendation, and tabulate in the following manner:

CR Option	Frequency
1	5.0
2	4.5
3	5.0
4	3.5
5	5.5
6	7.5
7	4.5
8	3.5
9	3.5
10	2.5
	45.0

Weighted Ranking	Frequency
6	7.5
-	7.0
-	6.5
-	6.0
5	5.5
1,3	5.0
2,7	4.5
-	4.0
4,8,9,	3.5
-	3.0
10	2.5

The total number of comparisons should equal the result of applying the formula:

$$\text{POSSIBLE COMBINATIONS} = \frac{(N^2 - N)}{2} \quad \frac{100 - 10}{2} \quad = \quad 45$$

where N equals the number of ideas, options and/or recommendations that are being considered by the group.

STEP FOUR: EVALUATE THE WEIGHTED RANKINGS

As can be seen from the above tables of calculated values, recommendation #7 ("Implement a program to reduce the possession of high-value inventories . . . to a period shorter than the present accounts payable payment cycle time.") was ranked as more than twice as important a task to initiate, relative to the stated goals of the cost reduction program, as suggestions #4, 8, and 9. Other weighted rankings are also shown in the Tables above.

Through the use of triangulation, the consensus of the knowledgeable group has now been reduced to the specifics of desired, prioritized, and weighted actions for implementation. All parties will now be involved from initiation through selection, and on until implementation and evaluation. Thus, the consensus tool becomes the first step in forging a joint effort for effective cost reduction.

USING DECISION TREES TO GAIN CONSENSUS

A popular tool of the late Twentieth Century has been the decision tree. As a graphic display, it has focused creative thinking in a manner that invites participation. Proponents go further, stating that the identity of strategic alternatives ensures that no major options for reaching desired objectives are overlooked.

The concept of decision trees relates to the accepted cost reduction approach of defining the ultimate objective first, before proceeding to seek alternative solutions to processes, expenditures, plans and current actions (and their results obtained to date). The ultimate objective pyramid has been the diagram of choice for the proponents of decision trees as an analysis tool.

A generic example is depicted in Figure 3-3.

STEP ONE: DEFINE THE IDEAL OBJECTIVE

This step is similar to that described in the triangulation exercise earlier in this Chapter. However, the difference is in the creative and imaginative skills of the person or group that formulates this ultimate objective. The key to success in building this type of decision tree is in defining and understanding an ultimate objective.

Figure 3–3   The Ultimate Objective Cost Reduction Analysis Pyramid

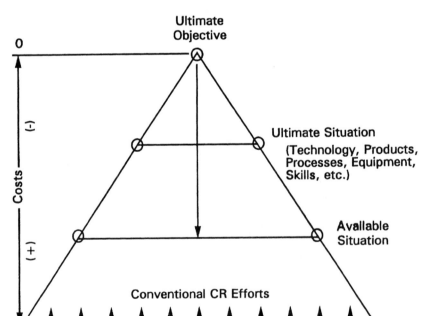

CASE STUDY: Overcoming a Cash Flow Problem—A major asset management problem in a New England electronics firm related to the value of their inventory as it related to their analysis of cash flow pressures. Two major problems were identified as the major causes of this problem:

1. High obsolescence of purchased materials and finished goods were an industry phenomenon. In other industries, purchased materials could be re-stocked with the original supplier at a markdown price. However, in the fast-paced electronics component industry, obsolete parts and assemblies were invariably reduced to scrap value if they could not be used as spare parts for products already in the field.

2. Suppliers moved materials to their customers, such as to this electronics firm, on a priority basis that related to the recent history of payments of outstanding accounts receivable. The size of the electronics manufacturing customer did not influence vendor production and distribution scheduling. But payment history could be a factor, especially when dealing with single-source suppliers with limited capacities for rapid expansion. This payment demand caused a severe strain on the electronics company's cash position, leading to heavy borrowing against committed assets. Thus, as the value of inventories declined due to obsolescence, so, too, did the company's ability to borrow funds against this previously paid-for asset.

The first approaches to this cash flow problem seemed obvious to management. Lower materials purchasing to the minimum forecasted levels of customer demand, while, at the same time, reduce cycle times in storage and production by applying the features of Just-In-Time methodology.

The first year's results were mixed. The use of single-source, product quality and service-certified suppliers—a major feature of the J-I-T approach—was already in existence. However, using the lower levels of the probability of forecasted sales, caused major problems in delivery to the electronics company's customers who, themselves, were original equipment manufacturers (OEMs).

New arrangements were sought from the company's existing customers. These concessions were to guarantee acceptance of scheduled production over the agreed minimum. Although some concessions were wrought, a majority of the electronics manufacturing company's customers declined to guarantee any purchases over a minimum, while bartering for reciprocal concessions from the electronics firm.

Compounding this situation was the fact that this request for guaranteed finished product sales, created a situation where the electronics company's competition did not ask for any such relief. The competition did, however, ask for more business from the electronics firm's customers, based on their superior sales terms vs. the competition. Obviously, new and imaginative directions had to be sought by the management of the electronics company.

Establishing the ideal objective: At a free-form meeting to discuss solutions, management decided that an ideal objective was to eliminate, or postpone, possession of material assets from suppliers on through to their customers. In this way, alternate cost reduction approaches to procurement, forecasting, production scheduling, finished goods stocking and sales promotion could be considered. The stated objective was to reduce the cycle time of materials' possession (and, of course, payment).

At the apex of the ultimate pyramid, the selected ideal objective was to reduce possession costs, at all stages of inventory, to nil. Everyone understood that the reference to reducing the costs of inventory related to the cost of materials, not necessarily to the size of the inventory. However, it was obvious that such a result could not be achieved in actual practice. However, this "ultimate improvement" approach was considered a far better start to discussing alternatives to the company's cash flow problem than randomly selecting projects from the base of the pyramid; projects which seemed quite promising at present.

STEP TWO: DEFINE THE ULTIMATE SITUATION REQUIRED TO ACHIEVE THE ULTIMATE OBJECTIVE

Given unlimited funds, along with a glimpse of future process and product developments, how might an ultimate objective be accomplished? This is not just a mind game, but rather a step to expand the horizons of the participants in seeking ways to accomplish the ideal cost reduction goals. In some cases, this Step becomes a wish list, but it also acts to uncover ideas that approximate those which would satisfy the ideal objective's requirements. Asking such questions may also accelerate funding and/or study into ideal systems sitting on the back burner awaiting approval.

CASE STUDY: The electronics firm ascertained that the first data link that was missing was information as to the time cycle during which materials were paid for from the accounts payable account vs. their payment as part of the sale value in the accounts receivable account. The difference in time is called possession time. Where payment is forwarded for materials before payment is received for shipment of the end product, this is a contributor to negative cash flow, especially where marginal profits exist due to competitive pricing policies.

When the time of possession figures were finally received, it was found that not a single line item of purchased materials was in the accounts payable figure at the same time as, or after being paid for from the accounts payable account!

It became apparent that what was required was a computer program to identify the opportunities to reduce possession costs. In addition, stocking, scheduling and payment practices with suppliers would have to be renegotiated and modified. The conclusion was drawn that the technology to accomplish the established ultimate goals was available.

STEP THREE (OPTIONAL)

Had the technology, data or equipment not been available in Step Two, the next step would have been to detail and work with a presently available level of support in order to move the analysis forward.

STEP FOUR: ADDRESS OPTIONS GENERATED BY STEPS TWO AND THREE

The analyst now must make specific recommendations that either accept the current status of skills and techniques available, or modify the requirements for success to meet the reality of the present situation. This conclusion should relate to that which is, or that which is achievable, in the short run of the goal's time frame parameter.

This type of decision tree examination usually leads to far more significant cost reduction analyses than the usual approaches. In a typical cost reduction plan, by systems or methods analysis, improvements are primarily sought by examining what is . . . actual history vs. expectations of positive results. Such random cost reductions, depicted as the base line of the ultimate pyramid in Figure 3-3, are rarely as productive or long-lasting and sizable, as moving down from the apex of the pyramid.

To fulfill the needs of STEP FOUR, detailed alternative practices, ideas, and recommendations, based on the decision tree pyramid analysis, form the basis of the subject matter in the following chapters. In these forthcoming chapters, techniques will be detailed to achieve these selected top level goals. But, all actions and expenditures should fit within the framework established by top management selection of the prioritized criteria for success. Both triangulation and the ultimate-ideal pyramid decision tree are examples of the techniques spawned by the philosophy that one should use an "earthmover," before considering the application of a "teaspoon" for applying both effective and efficient cost reduction activities.

SUMMING UP: Overcoming the Pitfalls to Successful Cost-Reduction Planning

It is important to gain consensus for the specific techniques required to improve asset management. This is because the techniques themselves eliminate some of the pitfalls which may lead to cost reduction planning failures.

Consider that managerial styles have a lot to do with successful applications. In some entities, consensus is not sought or even considered by the chief executive who commands and demands cost reductions of a fixed percentage by a set date. Lower-level executives have a choice to comply or depart, which leaves most with no other option than to grope and hack. In the short term, this type of forced consensus will cut costs, keeping the company viable, and perhaps many of these mandated actions can result in permanent improvement, essentially because they were long overdue.

Where the whole management team participates in both the process and the results, they become part of the solution because it is theirs. A management team approach results in the following:

- It encourages the gathering of many ideas from many sources with varied experiences.
- It assumes that problem resolution can be found in every facet of the firm's business.
- It provides both a forum and an "objective jury" for evaluating effects of cost reduction proposals, especially as they are weighed against both required priorities and emphasis relative to all other plans.
- It acts as a motivator for managers as it relates to their exposure to their peers' inputs, comments and criticism.

The primary disadvantage of the task force or team approach is that such a group of managers tends to achieve results more slowly than the demanding-compliance approach in an autocratic environment. However, this can be overcome with proper team management.

CHAPTER 4

HOW TO USE GROUP CONSENSUS TO SELECT AREAS OF COST REDUCTION/PROFIT IMPROVEMENT OPPORTUNITIES

After reaching a group consensus as to the goals of a cost reduction effort, each of the agreed goals must be addressed with specific sub-goals. These sub-goals must obviously relate to the condition of the enterprise at the time the study is conducted. Certainly, desperate times call for desperate measures, such that survival measures will dominate managerial activity in the short run.

However, worsening business conditions are probably the main rationale for motivating managers to implement a cost reduction program. These conditions are previewed by the warning signs of declining profitability.

HOW TO RECOGNIZE THREE WARNING SIGNS OF DECLINING PROFITABILITY

There are at least three telltale signs of profitability decay. Any one of these red flags can indicate serious trouble about to occur in the near future. And, the more warning signs exhibited, the more serious the trouble that can be expected. These warning signs are:

- slipping margins
- rising debt to assets and/or operating margins

51

- insufficient cash being generated to survive the slightest economic, industry or product acceptance downturn.

WARNING SIGN #1: SLIPPING MARGINS

A definite warning sign of profitability decay is where operating margins (net sales less operating costs, expressed as a percentage of net sales) are dropping faster than a 10% per annum rate, or where they are dropping to a point considerably lower than your competitors.

$$\text{OPERATING MARGIN} = \frac{\text{NET SALES} - \text{OPERATING COSTS}}{\text{NET SALES}} \times 100\%$$

You can take action in the short run to sweeten overall margins with:

- one-time sales promotions,
- short-term postponement of preventive maintenance expenditures,
- one-time extension of accounts payable payments,
- temporary service contracts combined with the use of overtime and planned shutdowns,
- temporary hiring freezes combined with the use of temps,
- elimination of specific advertising and PR expenditures, and/or
- delays in introducing new products or services.

Unless there exists the possibility of "permanitizing" these one-time gimmicks, the long term effect on operating margins may be negligible.

For this reason, it is important to understand that the basic bread and butter returns on ongoing operations must show a rate of return that is predictable, planned (forecasted), and either keeping pace with or exceeding past average returns. In growth companies, the rule-of-thumb states that if operating margins are not within 10% of recent highs, the company may be heading for trouble. A drop of 10% can often be attributed to a softening economy, or an unexpected disaster. However, a drop of more than that, caused by these abnormal situations, is usually difficult to justify as solely due to uncontrollable, but temporary, negative outside factors.

Managers should be examining the ongoing trend in operating margins, rejecting small blips, while at the same time, analyzing the true causes of continuing downward trends. To preserve profitability, or to return to it, requires constant vigilance, early detection of causes, and decisive, specific and timely corrective actions.

SOLUTION: Track operating margin trends, and develop plans and schedules for implementing them. Develop a management plan which provides for approximately the same desired end result, despite aberrations which are likely to result in the unpredictable future.

WARNING SIGN #2: RISING DEBT-TO-ASSETS AND/OR OPERATING MARGINS

It is common practice to utilize debt to finance present and anticipated future profit opportunities, be it through acquisition or internal growth. A red flag goes up where increased debt can be discerned to be solely useful for survival, or where it is obvious that a Ponzi-like scheme of paying off debt is creating new and larger repayment schedules . . . resulting in increasing the debt to operating margin ratio.

Borrowing should be justified, in the long term, as a technique to improve on or maintain current profitability, or as a short-term measure to allow an organization to return to profitability. To borrow for survival, until any of these positive events occur, makes for good business sense. Lee Iacocca's Chrysler experience is a noteworthy case in point where debt allowed for the introduction of a whole new line of innovative cars, vans and trucks. The failure of Pan American Airways is a contrary experience, where borrowing from every imaginable source—including their employees' union—could not ward off the inevitable demise.

A continuous downward trend in the operating margin must be met with both a survival format and a profitability plan. A lending source that does not require adherence to this dogma will also pay a severe penalty.

Debt is usually at an unacceptable level and rising when a company's basic products and/or services are no longer generating the operating margins they had once produced. Some managements may try to cover up this deficiency by borrowing more funds, in order to await a hoped for change in circumstances. What is the operating plan when these fortuitous circumstances do not occur? Are all failures due to circumstances beyond management's control? Can shareholders and directors be asked to sit by while the firm's economic future is solely based on hopes and dreams as an alternative to analysis and contingency planning? Of course not!

If revenues and ratios continue on a downward slope over a long period of time, debt payments that seemed manageable when the debt was incurred, become overwhelming. The very survival tool, the increased debt, now becomes a millstone around continuing operations. This is the downside risk that is generated when the funds for survival become the debt for destruction.

SOLUTION: It is essential that a borrower develop a contingency plan at the time significant new debt to margin ratios are contemplated.

It should be understood that creative accounting, while perhaps giving impressive short-term results, can lead to long-term damage as a potential consequence.

Debt payback schemes should not be treated as just another necessary evil imposed by the lending institution, but rather as a realistic forecast of possibilities.

EXAMPLE: The corner loan shark knows this as well as the banker at your sophisticated lending institution. The loan shark charges usurious rates, withholds interest from the principal at the time of the borrowing, and puts the borrower on notice of the dire consequences for non-payment of even a single installment. This loan shark wants a win/win situation, because he knows that he is the lender of last resort.

The usual situation is where the borrower needs immediate funds to cover pressing debts, and is overwhelmed by the consequences of non-payment. The borrower has probably only slightly considered any future problems of repayment to the loan shark. How many corporate debtors enter a borrowing relationship with the same mind set? Where is the downside risk plan, alternative actions scheme, strategic profitability plan, etc.? Or, is borrowing to survive the only plan?

WARNING SIGN #3: CASH GENERATION IS INSUFFICIENT TO WEATHER THE SLIGHTEST ECONOMIC DOWNTURN

Managers, especially financial managers, learn the vital significance of cash management relative to positive cash flow. By analyzing the status of the cash asset, they become cognizant of the importance of free cash flow per share. This figure is far more significant than the regular cash flow figures that are reported in the annual report.

This important number is derived by calculating:

FREE CASH FLOW / SHARE = CASH FLOW / SHARE –
CURRENT CAPITAL SPENDING / SHARE

(In non-profit organizations, this equation may be modified by considering the per share unit as either the total revenue category or the sum of respondents by collection category, i.e., corporate, individual, trust and/or beneficiary cells.)

The resultant calculated number provides a figure to be analyzed as a cushion against unforeseen and even expected cash deficiencies. The seriousness of the cash situation becomes apparent when the free cash flow figure drops to a negative value, especially on a monthly cumulative basis over an extended period of time.

There are two major exceptions to the above:

1. An exception would occur when the company is in the midst of a major expansion that is certain to preclude a return of major profits in the near future.

2. A long-term negative figure may be a part of the cyclical nature of the business . . . to be followed by a strong positive figure in the following months. For example, in the brewery industry, cans and bottles are produced well in advance of the summer selling season, because container production capacity cannot be as flexible as seasonal consumer demand for the dated end-product.

To gain management group approval for both cost reduction plans and the prioritization of the resultant effort, requires a management consensus. This consensus may be based on exception information on hand (red flags) that cry out for both:

*   corrective action, and
*   the measurement of a positive result gained from the allocation and timing of the use of company resources in performing the corrective action.

HOW MANAGEMENT CONTROL ASSURES PLANNING SUCCESS

There is a major business planning flaw that assumes reports, as well as statistical extrapolations from actual data vs. planned forecasts, will automatically provide the feedback necessary for corrective action. Management control is not merely a review of data on an exception basis, but requires the use of this data to:

*   predict trends to avoid upcoming catastrophes, and
*   employ appropriate action plans.

In cost reduction strategies, the reported numbers and ratios must be tied to financial red flags, and managerial reaction should be based on simulations of required and prioritized actions that return the organization to the expected profit and cash flow trend.

The above sounds simple to achieve . . . and it probably is in some organizations. However, the key lies in both the planning and control of cash and profits.

Management reactions to the crying need for cost improvement can be to:

- procrastinate
  "I don't believe we have to immediately act on this incomplete data."

- negate the conclusions
  "Even a fireperson doesn't have to answer every alarm bell!"

- suppress the data
  "Let's not scare those folks who will overreact to the data and these so-called red flags. Let's just keep it to ourselves until the picture looks rosier."

- contain the damage
  "What is the minimum reaction we can take until we are sure of our steps? In this way we can buy time for those major actions that are showing up as both imminently and desperately required at this time."

Or, consider that no action is also an action, just as no decision is also a decision. To be effective at cutting the fat not the muscle requires a clearly chosen path, hopefully by consensus rather than sheer mandate, as well as pre-determined action options based on ratios, reports, information and weighted opinions drawn from analyzed experiences.

You will be shown the techniques for both recognizing the warning signs and providing for alternative actions when actual experiences vary significantly from planned results. First, we must focus on gaining group consensus in the selection of areas for cost reduction/profit improvement opportunities.

INCLUDE THE DECISION MAKERS
IN THE DECISION MAKING PROCESS

In the arena of cost reduction, decision making involves a cycle of investment analyses, such as cost/benefit, profit or loss, short-term vs. long term, politically correct or the-rest-be-damned attitudes, as well as deciding on the salable vs. the inconceivable. To the pork-barrel Congressperson from your district, closing the local military procurement office is inconceivable . . . no matter who is doing the selling. No analysis by anyone can overturn this pre-set opinion. Only a barter for some other worthless project's safety can satisfy this Congressperson who is perpetually running for office.

For our purposes, let us assume that the normal manager is not running for political office every two years, has an average grasp of personal security needs, and is somewhat motivated to join in on projects for the good of the group, not necessarily benefiting one's self. He /she should be made a part of the decision making process from the initiation of the plan, on through to the measurement of results gained from controlling the project.

Problem solving philosophers call this the rationale mode, where all possible results (outcomes) are considered by a group . . . from which the group makes the most profitable selection. This analysis action weds the group to the solution through voluntary participation in the decision making process. Also, by weighing the forecast of the outcome, all members of the resultant consensus feel they have contributed to the conclusion. This is attained by having all inputs weighed against the opinions of the entire group. Management philosophers call this the "profitable solution."

The next step is to add restrictions to the free-form conclusion outlined above. This is the "bounded-rationale mode." These restrictions, that are added to the objectives for consideration, usually include the term "impossibilities." Some examples of impossibilities include:

- time limitations
- availability of personnel skills, and
- funds to be committed, which can be utilized for the exercise, regardless of the forecast of output vs. present actual input (cost/benefit or expenditure/savings ratios).

The next steps, that involve the participants, is where a schedule of actions is agreed. At this point the group decides on a planned series of related steps (called milestones in project management) as well as prioritizing their need on a time scale—similar to scheduling progress milestones. The participants pre-establish "go-no go" options, thus routinizing future decision-making as the cost reduction plan feeds back essential information of planned vs. actual data.

Throughout the decision making/problem solving process, the managers that participate are part of the solution, since they are part of the problem. No one is isolated from either the credit or the blame. The establishment of a participative environment allows for a more contributory attitude during the solution process. Where managements allow the weighing of all inputs against planned objectives with negotiated restrictions, a productive and contributory environment develops. This can be an essential ingredient when considering not just cutting the fat, but strengthening the muscle.

CHOOSING BETWEEN THE TWO DOMINANT APPROACHES TO CONSENSUS-BUILDING

There are two significant approaches to reaching a consensus . . . both of which are independent in scope and application. Proponents of each of these management techniques argue for the primal need of their approach over others. Yet, in my opinion, either can be applied—simultaneously or exclusively—with the main distinction being time available for realizing profitable results.

The two consensus approaches are:

- Mission statement development and disclosure to all levels of the organization.
- Benchmarking systems as a continuous measurement process.

HOW TO INSTALL A MISSION STATEMENT ENVIRONMENT

The concept of the team's efforts being directed to a consensus goal has been with us prior to the Industrial Revolution, and well before Alexander's legions dominated the Middle East, or Roman cohorts conquered Europe, or the Mongol Khan Dynasty's cavalry tactics controlled the known lands between the Danube and Yangtze Rivers. Granted, a dictatorial policy laid down by a tyrant seeking wealth, power, or immortality would be difficult for an individual slave to resist; yet, the results of objective-oriented group efforts—from construction of the Egyptian Pyramids to the planning and completion of the Los Angeles Subway System—make for models of consensus achievements. The main difference lies in how this consensus is achieved.

Yet, establishing, applying and upgrading a universally accepted and applied mission statement, remains an uncommon practice in corporate America. Generic terms are often displayed, as developed by either public relations or corporate advertising gurus:

- "Service is our #1 one business."
- "Quality improvement guides us."
- "Constant productivity improvement keeps our price down."

- "We listen to our customers and employees."
- "Working for you on the cutting technological edge."
- "Safety is our prime consideration."
- "We serve the public with affordable services."
- "No improvement is too small for consideration."
- "We provide value in selection and price."
- "Buy low and pass the savings on."

Questions remain after these mission statements are expounded. What do middle and first level managers think (and do)?:

- "How does that specifically affect the way I operate, or how my performance is judged?"
- "Who agreed to this? What is my input regarding modification or other improvements to the specificity of the mission statement?"
- "Since the end-result of this top-level strategic plan is the announced budget, is all I need to do is work within the mandated funding limits in order to have my contribution judged positively?"

In order to effectively cut the fat not the muscle, dedication to a consensus mission statement, translated into the language of all management level practitioners seems to be an essential ingredient. Providing for that management objective to be a consensus goal will undoubtedly sustain and encourage continuing participation at all levels of the organization.

To measure each initiative, the company requires a usable mission statement, says Howard D. Putnam, former CEO of the Country's most profitable airline, Southwest Airlines. He feels that each manager's proposals must be judged against the criterion, "Does it fit the company's mission?" (He also believes that this mission statement should be stated in 100 words or less, which, by itself, could be a challenge in multi-product and multi service entities.) He concludes that measuring up to a mission statement allows an organization to discard peripheral or useless operations, and concentrate on the core business activities. This, in turn, allows the corporate entity to bank the resources required to respond to both unexpected crises and radically changing and unanticipated events.

Putnam also believes that a contributory and multi-talented management team can be assembled from a pared-down executive staff. In this way, the mission statement can not only be re-initiated and/or modified by this new group, but individual mission requirements can be performed by fewer, multi-skilled personnel. He feels this also contributes to consensus objective setting, since fewer less-than-valuable inputs must now be considered to arrive at this consensus.

After the initial mission statement is tentatively adopted, in order to arrive at conclusions for cutting the fat not the muscle, Putnam believes that the next step is to decide where to cut the management bureaucracy. This is done by reviewing each senior management position to determine which functions are absolutely necessary to meet the consensus mission objective.

This is followed by asking these self-same senior executives, "How many of these absolutely necessary functions can be personally handled by you?" This exercise is designed to isolate those managers with multiple skills, as well as to provide a basis for hiring future managers with multiple talents and experiences.

Another advantage is that this new core of managers can develop a new and better mission statement, which will include contingency planning for those unlikely occurrences that may crop up. Putnam says that consensus mission statements by the evolving management team will encompass unlikely events as well as those that an entrenched group considers likely.

By working from a consensus mission statement, the organization can set a profit goal. In many entities, the profit goal is a residual of setting the budget for expenditures, while relying on the forecast of revenues by those responsible for selling the services or products. Even flexible budgeting allows for this type of profit planning exercise. By establishing the expense budget relative to the revenue forecast, this practice permits each organizational element to have a mind-set for having permission to spend up to this limit.

In mission statement applications, the profit objective establishes the level of expenditures required to meet this goal. Each management concept of doing business, at all levels, is then matched against expenditures required to meet this consensus goal. In turn, this becomes the expense justification in a goal-oriented environment.

Some examples will make this point:

EXAMPLE #1: A processor of juice and juice products sold a nationally advertised product from regional production facilities. These facilities were combined with regional purchasing and distribution centers. Many cost reduction schemes had been employed over the years, most of which were related to cutting costs by combining operations, centralizing procurement, building a fleet of trucks, improving product scheduling, expanding centralized warehouses and the like. A consensus mission statement encouraged all managers to reconsider their goals in light of this publicized statement. It was found that many of the centralized cost savings were minimal compared to the savings that the middle managers now proposed, such as:

a. contractual manufacturing of containers. The company was in the juice supply business, not in the business of expensively manufacturing juice containers.

b. use of co-packers for required additional capacity, instead of the prior mandated use of overtime in company-owned facilities. This change had to be negotiated with the various unions, but turned out to be a far cheaper exercise than paying premiums for forecasted on-site use of overtime labor. Inventory costs were also reduced by installing a just-in-time system of receipts from these co-packers (suppliers). This reduced waiting inventories that had been produced heretofore in so-called economic runs, when in-house production and procurement services were scheduled solely to use available personnel and plant capacities.

EXAMPLE #2: An overland transport company maintained a huge fleet of trucks, supported by rebuild and maintenance facilities. Scheduled preventive maintenance and most demand maintenance was conducted at company-owned facilities, where warehouses maintained costly maintenance, operating and repair (MRO) supplies. These supplies were a growing consumer of cash as well as an asset that was requiring larger and more costly storage facilities. A cost savings program, with limited success, involved standardizing all newly purchased tractors and trailers.

After all managers contributed to the company mission statement, whose objective was to become the lowest-cost provider of quality transport services, a profit objective was established by which to measure all cost center requests for funding. The first suggested changes required the preventive maintenance function to be upgraded through a mandated logistics plan which reduced demand maintenance, similar to that used by the airlines. At the same time, the demand maintenance function was budgeted out to local managers to negotiate, on a local as required basis, with truck mechanics at local garages. In addition, most lower level fleet managers found success in giving greater minor repair latitude to the individual driver as part of their participation in a cost vs. delivery performance incentive program. The end result was a much smaller preventive maintenance inventory than that required to be on hand for both scheduled and demand maintenance.

The additional costs of demand maintenance, when being supplied by local garages, was more than offset by the reduced inventory of demand maintenance items in the company's central repair facilities, as well as by the profit incentive plan budgets that were activated at the point of the demand expenditures. The mission statement's emphasis on profits—not merely cost reductions at existing operations—was the main catalyst for these improvements. At the same time, the consensus approach allowed for many more participants in the profit improvement process.

SIX STEPS TO PREPARING AN EFFECTIVE MISSION STATEMENT

The steps to achieving a consensus mission statement environment are:

1. Determine it is worth the effort.

2. At each level of management, beginning with the top level, encourage participation in drawing up a draft mission statement. Supply this statement to the next levels of management, for them to expand, personalize and otherwise modify the goals to meet their specific, local needs.

3. By consensus, adopt and publicize the consensus mission statement.

4. Establish a profit plan, and request all management levels to meet this plan by drawing up expenditure budgets that conform to the mission statement approach.

5. If possible, establish incentives to meet the approved goals set in paragraph #4 above.

6. Monitor, modify and reward. Consider the "daizen" approach to constant improvement as one of the extended goals of the consensus mission statement approach.

Consider the mission statement approach as a cost reduction plan that can quickly and inexpensively be adopted. However, it is a cut the fat approach that is centered on self-improvement based on self-analysis. The next section of this chapter covers a technique that expands the performance appraisal and idea contribution concept to encompass ideas from other companies, including competitors, and even foreign organizations.

CONTINUOUS IMPROVEMENT THROUGH BENCHMARKING

In the late 1980's, the concept of benchmarking exploded on the management scene. It is based on a business activity that had been carried out for years, i.e., measuring your company's performance against that of other companies in a similar field. For years, industry associations and related publications published data on ratios, averages, trends and forecasts for groups of firms, as well as by commodities and services provided. Many a purchasing manager has been confronted by their industry's lead time supply analyses; many a financial manager has been compared to industry norms for credit, collection, cash flow and return on investment; while many a materials controller has been confronted with industry turns ratios for work-in-progress, raw materials and finished goods.

Benchmarking has been compared to ongoing competitive analyses, with the added activity of using the data and observed creative ideas to augment a formal internal improvement program. Benchmarking started as a quality improvement tool, and was quickly expanded to include the identification of superior practices wherever they were found. Instead of just copying these innovative practices, these variations become the base for local modified applications, through communicating both the theory as well as the actual practice. Thus, today's benchmarking activities encompass a whole range of activities from investigation, through absorption, to modification, improvement, local implementation and on to communicating the new practice to other organizational elements. However, unlike the consensus mission statement approach, previously described in this chapter, benchmarking begins with a formal procedure to investigate the "outside world's" practices, followed by relating (adapting) these practices to the internal world of your very own organization.

As such, benchmarking has become a continuous measurement process against comparative performance measures. However, critics have called it a systematic approach to "shamelessly stealing," and even "banditry," since access to competitive operations was never a simple procedure in the recent past. But, the world's industrial leaders have watched the Japanese approach to shared improvement in their "kaizen" concept of shared product development and information sharing, which is funded and sponsored by both industry associations and the Japanese Productivity Board. (Many of their practices of economic cooperation are considered illegal practices in the U.S. as competition destroying techniques.)

The practices that lead to superior performances are called enablers, and are an important part of the practice of benchmarking. Thus, benchmarking allows for two major activities:

1. measuring of competitive performance, and
2. determining the theories behind these superior practices.

W. Edwards Deming (the father of Japanese quality improvement practices) stated it best when he said, "Adapt; don't just adopt. It is a hazard to merely copy. It is necessary to understand the theory of what one wishes to do." Taiichi Ohno, when VP, Manufacturing at Toyota, developed Just-In-Time (kan ban) concepts by examining the shelf stocking practices at U.S. food supermarkets, which he proceeded to adapt to the practice of the supply and flow of materials at Toyota's assembly plants. Likewise, the Xerox Corporation gave credit to their creative adaptation of benchmarking practices when they received the Malcolm Baldrige National Quality Award in 1989.

In the early 1980's, benchmarking was viewed as a product comparison discipline. Design engineers compared quality performance and reliability with function and price. These comparisons were against the products and services provided by the "leaders," but especially those provided by the competition. Reverse engineering became the key term, wherein products and services were examined back from the end product through tear-down and testing of technical characteristics. At the same time, the "marketeers" were evaluating, by comparison, the market strategies that gained the competitive edge for their competitors' products and services.

It was the advent of processing comparisons that led to the explosion of interest in the benchmarking approach. This phase required observation experience, as well as data and knowledge sharing not only between domestic companies, but between foreign equivalent organizations. In addition, benchmarking practices now target any company that has developed a system, process, or creative modification, in order to determine the adaptation of the creative improvement process itself . . . no matter the relevancy of the source company's services or products to the investigating entity.

Gregory H. Watson describes strategic benchmarking *(Strategic Benchmarking,* John Wiley, 1993) as the next step. This includes the "systematic process for evaluating alternatives, implementing strategies and improving performance by understanding and adapting successful strategies from external partners who participate in an ongoing business alliance. Strategic benchmarking differs from process (and product) benchmarking in terms of the scope and depth of commitment among the sharing companies." This is a broad range statement of consensus required for internal improvement as defined by the new benchmarking strategies.

Thus, consensus should not only be sought in the internally oriented mission statement process, but also in the externally oriented benchmarking process. A major advantage of benchmarking is that consensus can be driven by the profitable experiences of others—as well as by their failures, if disclosed. Also, the continuous improvement nature of the benchmarking process, through the use of ongoing comparative analyses, allows the consensus to shift emphasis without seeking out whom to fault by piling on self criticism. After all, the competition is mostly external, and a consensus is required to perform the Alice In Wonderland tactic of running to keep up with the trees.

PARTNERING AS A CONSENSUS TOOL IN BOTH PURCHASING AND BENCHMARKING PRACTICES

A significant development has been attributed to both the purchasing and benchmarking fraternities. This process is called partnering. In the purchasing world, this involves supplier certification and training, single sourcing, contractual purchasing and vendor logistic supply, including control of internal supplier stocking and scheduling practices. In the benchmarking world, this involves sharing process and product knowledge through observation, inspecting and sharing experiences through data collection on-site, or through information access while processes are actually being performed at a distant site.

Partnering may involve actual sampling of the partner's processes to validate the procedures which enabled the partner to achieve the superior performance of services or product reliability. For example, while Aqua-Chem Corp. was developing its version of the reverse osmosis process utilizing fiberglas laminated tubes, all of its on-line tests were being monitored by the Dow Corporation, a major licensee and subsequent reverse-osmosis installer for shipboard units which converted sea water to potable drinking use. The Union of Japanese Scientists and Engineers routinely distributes quality data as provided by the various corporate donors who are under exclusive contract to both use and redistribute this data to its members.

Both sampling and on-site data collection overcome one of the major early drawbacks of the benchmarking activity. Estimates of both performance and data to support the performance could never be as significant or accurate as actual data collection through direct observation, or through sampling. Extrapolation from an estimate or guess can be both fruitless and expensive if wrong. A good benchmarking system requires both accurate measurement and relative monitoring of changes. The use of valid, comparable data is vital to success for adaptation to local needs.

Partnering is sold to suppliers by sharing the results of analyses, such that cost-cutting becomes a profitable venture for both the supplier and the supplied. Increased profits are a more important initiation incentive tool than merely cutting costs to a customer. And, the final incentive to cut costs lies in the promise of remaining the single source supplier . . . a reward for partnering cost reduction practices with the customer concern.

WEDDING THE CONSENSUS MISSION STATEMENT TO BENCHMARKING

The mission statement provides the company with the necessary selected objectives to initiate the benchmarking process. This is achieved by isolating those consensus areas of concern that should be benchmarked. Some companies use the Pareto Principle (described in Chapter Seven) to select the critical few products or processes, some use triangulation procedures such as those delineated in Chapter Three, and some perform an analysis of key business factors, selected by senior management consensus. These key business factors are derived through input/output analyses . . . measuring the dollar value of inputs of personnel, materials, indirect costs for administration and the like against the outputs that contribute directly and materially to the success (profitability) of the business.

The mission statement is specified at each level of the organization. An example will make this point:

EXAMPLE: HOW A MISSION STATEMENT MAY BE DETAILED FOR ACTION

Through a key function analysis and a triangulation exercise, a series of areas for emphasis were singled out in a food products company. One of these key functions was the delivery expectations of its customers vs. the perceived service that could be provided, and was assumed to be provided by the competition. This latter assumption was based on customer comments such as, "They do better!" MISSION STATEMENT #4 addresses this issue.

MISSION STATEMENT #4

Products will be made available to the customer within 3 working days after receipt of order. (The original mission statement requested prompt reaction to customer order requests.)

Definition: A customer order is received when either voice recorded by telephone or faxed to our sales offices, written and picked up by our sales representatives, arrives by fax or mail at either our, or the sales representatives' offices, or is orally transmitted in any meeting between a customer representative and any member of our company.

Confirmation: Written confirmation must be delivered to the customer within 24 hours of this order receipt.

Delivery: Delivery will be made within 3 days of this receipt of customer order. Custom accessories will adhere to posted longer delivery times, which must be maintained as advertised.

Performance Measurement: Customer delivery performance will be measured by total line items delivered on-time vs. ordered, dollars shipped vs. dollars back-ordered, and a tally of delivery cancellations caused by irregular occurrences. The delivery performance incentive system will cover all company direct, indirect and administrative employees, and will include the first level of management in each department. The 50/50 sharing system (IMPROSHARE, service mark of Mitchell Fein) will use the past unmeasured and uncontrolled performance as the base, so that both the company and its employees will equally share in delivery performance improvement.

Required Actions: Stocking practices must forecast a supply and re-supply of each product based on demand patterns. A safety stock must be calculated that allows for just-in-time purchasing and scheduling, supplier and consignment stocking where possible to negotiate, lead time reductions by stocking standard-built frames, and adherence to extended delivery promises for customized products. These customized products must be "standardized", so that only true customization need be estimated for delivery. Logistics must pre-determine methods of shipment, and notify and contract with external carriers within 24 hours of order receipt. The traffic department must notify in-house transport within 1 hour after order receipt and confirmation about pick-ups and delivery requirements that are external to normal procedures.

When the cost of conducting the above mission statement proved to be larger than expected, the company included MISSION #4 in its request for analysis by the benchmarking group (which was originally an informal committee that met infrequently, but became a permanent two-man task force after initial successes were reported). In this way, the mission statement's practices were reanalyzed by an external investigation promulgated by the benchmarking group.

SUMMING UP: Group Consensus on Cost Reduction Objectives Leads to Successful Group Implementation

The warning signs of possible slippage and decay must be brought to the attention of all. This is an approach which is significantly different from the usual . . . where only the CEO, the Chief Financial Officer, and a select few senior executives begin to worry, in order to prepare for the Board of Directors' penetrating questions. The warning flags, such as slipping margins, rising debt to asset ratios, and increasing negative cash flows, can best be addressed as, first, the management group's problem, and, second, as a target for a consensus selection of possible cures.

The mere distribution of pertinent data, statistical extrapolations, forecasts, planned vs. actual comparisons and experienced opinions do not in themselves provide the total basis for corrective management action. Management control is exerted not merely by a review of information, but by a concerted consensus-derived effort to alter the negative course of events. The red flags must be understood and interpreted by management levels that are empowered to recommend as well as act, to stem these negative flows. Thus, consensus isolation of problem causes, as well as developing a plan for corrective action, become a major goal in attempting to cut the fat not the muscle.

This approach requires involving the decision makers to be intimately involved in the cost reduction, decision-making process. Todays two dominant techniques that provide for this are: (1) consensus mission statement development and (2) benchmarking.

The consensus mission statement environment is installed by the 6-step process heretofore described in this chapter. The main features of this process involve the consensus adoption of the mission goals, initiation of a profit plan to develop the budgetary expense controls for each department, and the "monitor, modify and reward" approach to continuous improvement. This self-analysis, self-improvement approach can be installed both quickly and inexpensively. The gauge of progress in cutting the fat is the company's own subjective view of itself.

The benchmarking approach is driven by an evaluation of the advances of creative innovations and continuous improvements at other organizations, and even in other societies. The whole process has been formalized . . . from improvement opportunity selection, through off-site observation and data collection, and on to internal adaptation and communication practices. Almost 1000 articles have been written on how to apply benchmarking to your organization. However, primary factors in the successful applications of benchmarking practices, are relevant to both the consensus selection of areas of cost savings opportunity, and in the consensus agreement of actions and controls required when adapting new and innovative ideas from a dedicated observation of external operations.

A key to success, when dealing with outside organizations, is the concept of partnering. To the purchasing function, this involves single sourcing, supplier certification, off-site scheduling of procurement, quality controls, work flow and delivery timing, and a whole range of training and communication practices. To the benchmarker, partnering involves determining mutually acceptable gains from information trade-offs. Where both parties can point to positive gains from partnering, this becomes the basis for consensus-achieved success.

One of the techniques for assuring success is to wed the consensus mission statement approach to the benchmarking application. In this way, the internal group has agreed to the major targets for improvement, and has set the guidelines for a directed benchmarking process. By seeking advantages for your benchmarking partners, this establishes the proper motivational environment that can aid the partnering drive for successful acquisition of creative information to be adapted to local cut the fat opportunities.

Re-engineering need not include re-inventing the wheel. However, consider consensus approval a vital ingredient that has always been an accepted informal practice. This chapter provided some formalized approaches to using the consensus concept towards profitable cost reduction and profit improvement ends.

HOW TO ANALYZE EXPENDITURES AS INVESTMENTS TO MEET CONSENSUS GOALS

Consider that a consensus-agreed cost reduction philosophy establishes goals, which, in turn, aid in the selection of techniques to achieve them. This was the theme of the previous chapter, where profit targets were used to set expenditure budgets. In this way, expenditures become an investment to meet these agreed goals. Specific analysis procedures are described that investigate the use of current expenditures as investments to achieve these goals.

USE EXPENDITURE ANALYSIS TO MATCH COSTS TO GOAL ACHIEVEMENT

The specific techniques available to you are listed below. These can help the manager select action alternatives to accomplish agreed goals:

- graphic decision trees
- simulation of effects of action alternatives
- downside risk (vs. upside gain) forecasting
- input/output ratio analysis
- Kepner-Tregoe problem-solving rationales

- Pareto Analysis (Chapter 8)
- leveraged time management (Chapter 9)

A basic feature of all of these analysis techniques is the cost discovery process.

STEP ONE: INITIATE THE COST DISCOVERY PROCESS

This is where true costing, with believable and validated data are "discovered." The results are usually surprising to a manager who is inured to receiving calculated cost add-ons for:

- corporate overhead and administrative services,
- carrying costs for inventory,
- unit cost variances from volume discounts,
- single source R & D procurement charges,
- contractor claims based on contractual provisions,
- actual vs. budgeted variations, and
- fixed, mixed and variable designations.

From an environment where cost add-ons are an accepted, but not a questioned practice, the discovery process turns all managers into cost sleuths. It is no longer acceptable for a manager to state, "They add on these costs based on some top management acceptable formula; and, my job is to work with the results, not question the formula."

In the cost discovery process, all costs are considered an investment subject to analysis. Heretofore, the major investment cost was labelled "depreciation," and was related to a capital project expenditure (investment) recovery formulation. The usual justification for capital expenditures was that they would result in future lowered costs, increased quality and safety, etc. The measurement of this gain vs. the monetary investment is supposed to be based on cost reduction gains during the tax life of the investment (the depreciation schedule).

This latter measurement is called the capital investment "post mortem" analysis, and is conducted for the purpose of improving the capital investment approval procedure. Obviously, those whose past capital investment requests never seem to come to fruition, will be viewed in a harsher light when new requests surface. In this way, the more accurate prediction of savings is rewarded when weighing forecasts of savings associated with capital project requests.

The new wave of managers is now required to look beyond depreciation cost analysis, and to be able to question, justify, request modification and improve all costs charged to, allocated or directly incurred by his/her cost center. This is the basis of the discovery phase in cost reduction, which is designed to answer the following questions:

- "How does this cost, however allocated or directly charged, impact the profitability of the process, product or service?"
- "On a cost vs. benefit basis, should this cost (investment) be increased, decreased, modified, or eliminated?"
- "Can this investment (cost) be postponed, or should it be accelerated?"
- "What additional input information would be useful in order to reach any of the above decisions?"

Using the Discovery Process for Construction Projects

A major application of the discovery process appears in civil engineering construction projects, where contractors dispute with the owners and the general contractor on total cost claims. The contractor must prove:

- cost impacts caused by actions or requests by either the owner or the general contractor
- the reasonableness of the original bid vs. subsequent add-ons and engineering change orders
- that adequate records were kept on actual costs incurred
- deviations in the receipt, storage, and distribution of materials, including indirect supplies
- a failure existed in carrying out contractual provisions, as well as being able to specify losses attributable to these deviations
- claims of mark-ups were not justified
- malicious intent existed, and/or
- the risks and insurances were ill-defined or not noted and covered.

In the above situations, it is common practice to build the cost discovery process into the very first stages of a construction project, so that disputes may be settled as they arise, instead of coming to a head at the conclusion of the total (and usually very lengthy) construction process.

The discovery process is a vital part of any introduction of an activity based costing (ABC) program. This will be covered in detail in Chapter Seven.

The Case of the Missing Savings

On a very cold day, near the Lake O' The Woods in Northern Minnesota, a warehouse manager was describing his efforts to cut the size of his inventory. At a particular juncture in the discussion with the company's management consultant, he was asked, "Are you interested in cutting the size or the cost of this inventory?" Stunned by this apparently obtuse question, the warehouse manager responded, "Aren't they the same thing?"

To a whole host of warehouse, materials and purchasing managers, who may be untrained in inventory cost analysis, that may appear to be a logical response. Isn't size directly related to value? If not, where are the true savings from Just-In-Time applications, if size reductions do not directly equate to inventory cost reductions?

Asking and answering pertinent questions are very important to providing an understanding of the concept that cutting the size of an inventory is not necessarily directly related to cutting a related cost of inventory.

Using Analytical Questioning in the Cost Discovery Process

The consultant continued to probe with the following questions:

- "Do you know how the carrying cost of inventory is calculated and applied to your warehouse inventory? And, were you ever involved with performing this analysis?"
  "For example, if we cut the inventory in half:

  a. which half of this warehouse can be eliminated? Or is storage space a fixed cost not directly related to the size of the inventory stocked?"

  b. which half of the materials handlers (and their fork lift trucks) can we eliminate? Or is their numerical requirement a direct function of material moves required (transport empty and transport loaded) not directly related to the size of the inventory handled?"

  c. which half of the pickers, packers and counters can we send home? Or, are their activities more directly related to orders or line items processed, not remotely related to the size of the inventory in the warehouse?"

- "Will a smaller inventory require less warehouse supervision, fewer reports or data inputs, reduced incoming inspection, less home office administration, etc.? Be specific . . . what group of people is being made redundant by reduced supervisory requirements to manage a smaller inventory?"

- "If the inventory is cut in half, will the company reduce its borrowing by an equivalent amount, or use these released funds for a better business investment? Or, does the release of funds com-

mitted to inventory have no trackable relationship to the borrowing strategy of the company?"

An inability to answer these questions logically reduced the frus-
trated warehouse manager to suggesting that the cost of auxiliary services might be cut. To this, the consultant queried, "You mean we can
perhaps reduce the cost of heat, light and power into this warehouse if
we reduced the size of the inventory by 50%! I suggest the reverse is the
case, i.e., we could probably cut the cost of air-conditioning and supplied heat if we doubled the inventory, since, in such a situation, there
would be much less air to heat and cool!"

It was obvious that a cost allocation discovery process, including
management training in understanding and properly applying variable, fixed and mixed costs would have helped.*

Thus, the cost discovery process begins with a knowledge (or training) of cost generation and allocation for all cost center managers. Simply mandating cost-cutting, without providing the necessary skills,
knowledge and array of cost reduction techniques, can never be as rewarding as preparing (and where necessary training) managers in cost
generation, allocation, modification and, of course, reduction.

STEP TWO: DESIGN THE COST ANALYSIS DECISION TREE

When confidence in the cost figures has been either confirmed or
re-instituted by the discovery process, it is now possible to use any of
the applicable cost analysis tools available. In this instance, I have
chosen to demonstrate the use of a generic/specific decision tree which
utilizes:

- the consensus approach to analysis (and subsequent actions required) based on the consensus objective,
- the concept that expenditures can be viewed as an investment in
  achieving these goals, and
- cost reduction not as a process "performed with mirrors," but
  rather an exercise that drops trackable results to the bottom
  line.

Figure 5-1 depicts a cost relationship diagram that follows classic
analysis patterns. Note that the objective is listed as increased profits.

---

* A detailed description of the formulations of add-on carrying costs to inventory valua-
tions can be found in my book, *Managing Inventory for Cost Reduction,* Chapter Eight,
"How to Determine and Use the True Costs of Inventory," pages 275–308, published by
Prentice Hall, 1992.

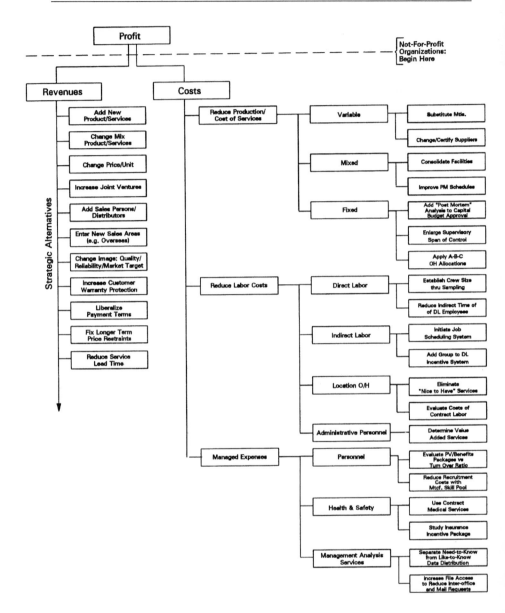

Figure 5–1. Diagramming Cost Saving Opportunities

(A not-for-profit organization can begin at the second level where increased revenues and decreased costs are the goals.) For the profit seeking organization, it is most important to initiate the analysis at the increased-profits step, in order to focus the analysis participants on all costs as an investment to increase profits.

A major advantage of using an organized, decision tree technique is to ensure that no major cost improvement options, which need to be considered to reach the desired objective(s), are overlooked. At each level, randomly supplied and considered options are reviewed as the analysis progresses.

Note the questions that are raised at each point in the diagram in Figure 5-1. The very first one relates to the simple equation:

$$\text{REVENUES} - \text{COSTS} = \text{PROFIT}$$

Obviously, the following options exist when an attempt to increase or maintain profit levels are analyzed:

1. Increase revenues while holding costs at the same level as heretofore,

2. Maintain revenues at the current level while decreasing costs,

3. Increase revenues while decreasing the ratio of costs to revenues required to achieve this increase, and

4. Decrease revenues while decreasing the ratio of costs to revenues below the current ratio level.

All four of these management options may also be considered where the goal is to either control a declining profitability trend, or do all that is necessary to maintain the current level of profitability.

None of the above are departures from current thinking in your organization. Presently, everyone knows these options. However, an organized approach to considering them may best be shown in a diagrammatic look which focuses a management group on viable alternatives to achieve a consensus objective. This also puts cost reduction in perspective regarding forecasted revenues and the ratio of costs to these revenues, both being studied as a vital requirement to achieve a profit increase objective.

Since the thrust of this book is to cut costs, the following step-by-step analysis will emphasize the cost side of the diagram. However, remember that increased revenues may mask ongoing cost inefficiencies. This is especially true where costs are viewed as expenses budgeted to match and support projected revenues, not as investments for increasing profitability.

STEP THREE: ESTABLISH ALTERNATIVE OVERALL STRATEGIES

The major cost factors, defined by a "Cut the Fat" Task Force in a consumer appliance manufacturing concern, were listed as shown in Figure 5-1. A cost discovery process, described in the first part of this chapter, was first conducted so that all parties to the analysis had a realistic faith in the cost figures then derived. Three major categories were chosen, which became the basis for the decision tree analysis. (Be advised that a specific company was chosen to demonstrate this approach, because decision trees are custom-fitted to individual needs, both by existing account information and the prejudices of experienced managers.) It is quite difficult to provide a one-size-fits-all generic decision tree.

This company settled on three major cost areas for analysis, even though there are obvious overlaps in the definitions for these unique areas. The company felt that redundancy was far superior to ending up with undetected omissions of vital cost reduction opportunities.

Thus, the resultant three analysis areas were:

1. Overall costs of products and services provided, listed by classification of variable, mixed, and fixed costs. (In the federal budget, this would be akin to breaking out entitlement from annual legislated expenditures.) The breakout should be determined by both data accessibility and potential cost improvement actions.

2. Labor costs included all categories of personnel that received payment for full time services, for which there was a description appearing on the table of organization, and whose costs were regularly budgeted in the annual fund approval process. The reader may more readily recognize such descriptions as: factory overhead, supervisory and management personnel, support and support service manpower, etc.

3. Managed expenses are those which relate to specific categories of mandated costs for:

    - joint venture contractual obligations,
    - special skill services,
    - one-time costs associated with unique expenditures, such as validating and modifying warranty claims,
    - research and development charges to canceled projects,
    - public relations expenditures, such as for speech-writing or association travel
    - special task force expenditures, where personnel are drawn from the present work force,
    - outside consultant fees,
    - start-up projects, etc.

An important check point is where the total company costs are consumed by the assigned cost analysis categories (or combinations of these categories).

STEP FOUR: SELECT AND SCHEDULE TASKS TO ACHIEVE THESE GOALS

The column at the farthest left of Figure 5-1 lists the consensus choice of actions that could realize the selected goals. In this appliance company, this list was chosen by the consensus technique called triangulation (described in Chapter 4). Only the top weighted choices are shown here.

A prioritization process, similar to the Pareto Analysis (described in the next chapter) was used to both schedule and fund the improvement process. The company used the term "Emphasis Analysis" to describe their priority scheduling process. Management realized at an early stage that not all improvement efforts could either be funded and/or performed at the same time. Thus, it was necessary to prioritize the efforts of the group before beginning the process.

At the particular time that the various managers met to determine the priority of the individual cost reduction projects that were selected, a general demand existed to shorten the turn-around time for products returned under warranty. These products were replaced immediately by good product that was either in stock or scheduled to be produced. The major concern was for the inventory that was in limbo, which consisted of the returned product awaiting performance testing, modification and possible return to usable service parts and/or as remanufactured product.

Yet, when this highly visible individual project was listed against all other potential projects, it ranked very near the bottom of the rank. The primary objective was to increase profits, an objective against which all costs (investments) were being measured. As long as the customer received the fruits of the warranty insurance (product replacement) in a reasonable period of time, the cost savings from accelerating the return of the warranted materials, were greatly diminished. Thus, the priority for this cost improvement project dropped against other potential investments for profitability.

CASE STUDY: USING THE DECISION TREE TO DEFINE STRATEGIC OPTIONS

A closer look at the decision tree process is evidenced by the detailed look at specific costs at the third level of the decision tree of a Texas producer of materials handling equipment, primarily used in the furniture trade. Figure 5-2 lists strategic options derived from their annualized, rolling three-year strategic plan.

The managers in this company selected these strategic options from a menu of alternatives. This was a task they chose to accomplish

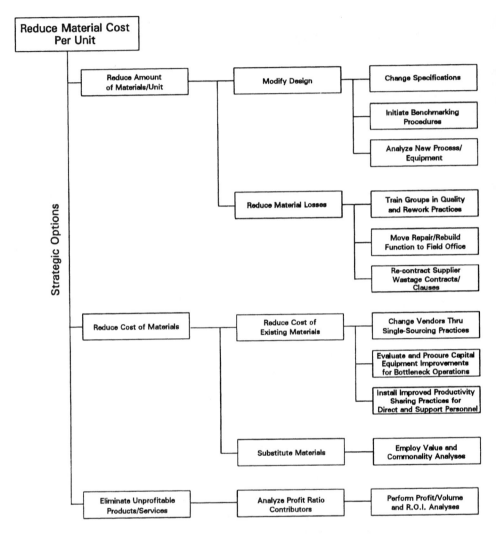

Figure 5–2   Consensus Objectives Tree

before the decision tree analysis began to select, prioritize and schedule specific cost improvement tasks. In this way, recommendations of the management group were made within consensus-designed parameters. Three strategic options to reduce material cost per unit were chosen:

1. Reduce the amount of material content per unit of product.
2. Reduce the cost of materials used.
3. Eliminate unprofitable products and/or services provided.

These options were exploded to the next level of chosen actions:

1. REDUCE THE AMOUNT OF MATERIAL CONTENT

    Two major management actions were determined:

    *   Modify the design.
    *   Reduce material losses in purchasing and processing.

2. REDUCE THE COST OF MATERIALS USED

    *   Reduce the cost of existing materials used.
    *   Consider substitute materials.

3. ANALYZE PROFIT/VOLUME RATIOS TO SELECT AREAS OF COST REDUCTION OPPORTUNITIES ON A RETURN ON INVESTMENT (OR ASSETS) BASIS

Seek cost reductions for selected products; selected for their impact on the profit/volume ratio.

Note that selected projects to reach these goals (see right hand column of recommendations in Figure 5-2) are directly related to the chosen few management actions. Thus, both the goals and the actions to achieve them are pushed through the selection, recommendation and prioritization process by the consensus of company management. In this way, the decision makers are part of the decision making process for cost improvement to increase profits.

CASE STUDY: MAKING REDUCED ASSET POSSESSION A PRIMARY GOAL

Having cash to spend on a management-discretionary basis, and not just to keep the creditors happy, creates a whole new array of cost reduction opportunities. To illustrate this point, consider the decision tree goals of a financial controller, as her struggle for cash (drive for liquidity) spilled over into an area of operations that consumed the majority of the company's cash. Inventory, listed as a "Current Asset," constantly showed this asset as equal to 65% of all the current assets.

The Financial Controller had attended a seminar where she was struck by the relationship of possessed assets to cash drain. The main thrust of that seminar was lease vs. buy as a financial option. During the course of the two days, a diagram was shown relating accounts receivable to accounts payable, depicting seasonal cash flow requirements as a result. When possession of the inventory asset was at its lowest, cash flow was most positive for that period of time. She could have guessed at that conclusion without spending two days in a conference room.

However, she had not considered the vital affect of possession time on cash flow. This led her to return to her company full of questions relating to financial possession vs. on-site, physical possession. Like all managers in her company, she had embraced the Just-In-Time concept as a sure road to reduced costs for the single largest asset of all current assets on the balance sheet of the company. Now, she realized the road to cost reduction success lay in the reduction of a possessed asset, not merely in the size (value) of this asset.

She realized that the closer she could have the company bring accounts payable together with accounts receivable could have a direct and major effect on total cash flow (and the costs associated with this asset).

Her decision tree established a major objective to reduce possessed inventory, not necessarily the value of the inventory on-site. This involved two major actions to be adopted by the management group, especially the procurement, stocking and scheduling personnel:

1. A lead time analysis was conducted of the minimum time that an assembly or component needed to be in-house. This was the time from acceptance at the receiving dock, until that assembly or component was part of a shipment that became an account receivable. She was looking for those line items that could be paid for as an account payable during the same time frame (30 days) as that line item became part of an account receivable (shipment). A total of 26% of the value of the materials inventory qualified.

2. For the remainder (74%) of the inventory value, action steps were initiated to reduce possession time. These steps included:

   - partnering contracts for vendor stocking
   - consignment designations being applied as a condition of single contract sourcing with selected (qualified) contractors, and
   - re-negotiation of payment terms in exchange for volume purchase agreements.

The above implementations affected another 39% of the value of line items in the raw materials and work-in-process status.

The financial controller reported her significant savings along with her management approach as follows:

1. **Philosophy.** Establish the strategic goal vs. the opportunity as portrayed by managerial options. Do not consider the lines of the organizational chart as a limiting factor, since processes are functions which should be viewed independent of arbitrary boxes on a wall chart.

   The closer accounts payables move towards accounts receivables (in accounting time frames) the more efficient use of capital invested must result. Consider that materials (inventory) are a conversion of the cash asset. Any excess conversions result in a less-than-desirable cash flow situation. Conversely, any reduction in possessed assets will positively affect cash flow, where such a reduction does not negatively affect the production or sale of our product.

2. **Practice.** Analyze costs, in descending array of cost reduction opportunities, in order to close the gap between receipt of payment (accounts receivable) and payment (accounts payable) for services, payroll, materials, as well as capital invested in fixed assets of plant, equipment, warehouses, etc.

3. **Technique.** Develop a schedule for purchasing, manufacturing, receiving, warehousing and material transfer. These schedules will attempt to minimize payment time relative to the receipt of these materials and services. The objective is to reduce cash invested prior to collection in a product that is sold and becomes an account receivable. To do this requires the separation of fixed, variable and mixed costs in order that the strategic goal is realistically attained, i.e., savings can be tracked as they drop to the bottom line. (In the past, there were reported cost reduction savings that were actually greater than the bottom line profits of the total company!)

4. **Control.** All analysis efforts must result in a forecast of savings that are trackable. Since the company has more problems to resolve than time, talent or assets available to solve all of them, projects must be selected, scheduled and controlled based on the size of the expected effect that will be seen on the bottom line. Wherever possible, a consensus should be achieved from philosophy right on through to the control of this ongoing effort.

The savings, based on the manager's leadership of this project, were significant, primarily resulting in an increased cash flow during the first reported year—an increase of as much as 16%. This figure was in comparison to the best seasonal increase in years past at an equivalent revenue volume and product mix.

APPLYING CONSENSUS QUALITY IMPROVEMENT THROUGH THE USE OF FISHBONE DIAGRAMS

Two important themes permeate the quality improvement field:

1. Make it right the first time.
2. For every effect there are many interrelated causes.

This second point has been demonstrated world-wide through the application of cause-and-effect diagrams, which are usually called "fishbone" diagrams. These diagrams are both:

- a means to graphically portray situations that are too complex to explain in simple narrative terms, and

- a method that allows for consensus evolution of both the explanation of the problem, and guidance towards a possible cure.

These types of decision trees were popularized in the early 1970's as a talking point for quality circles, a 1970's phenomenon in Japan, the U.S. and Germany. The diagrams were simple drawings of symbols and connecting lines that related effects to possible causes. Where a rejected product or process was examined, a whole host of variables could be contributing to that result, either independently, or in combination with other causal variables.

Where the use of multi-variable analysis was used in both the design of experiments and in reliability analysis, it was found that a great deal of time was spent determining the variables, and very little time applying the multi-variable and field reliability formulas. Essentially, these formulas simulated situations that changed specific variables and combinations of them, while holding all others as fixed. In this way, the causes of product or process failure were isolated, described and measured against their effect on the resultant problem.

However, most of the time spent in using these formulas was in collecting the variable data which listed the probable causes of the quality problem. This discipline led to another advantage, i.e., "good" effects provided knowledge of those "right" actions that must be continued to consistently continue to produce "good" product.

In the 1980's, the fishbone decision tree process was expanded to encompass the total cost improvement effort. In those cases, the effect was profit, and the causes were all costs required to increase this desired resultant. This process relates to:

- decision tree analysis
- consensus derivation of the problems to attack, and
- the study of quality effects in cost reduction.

It was found that the best way to allow for inputs from all sources was to establish the ground rules for analysis that were both easy to understand, and would encompass all of the cost elements to be considered. This reduced the sometimes wild and free-form ideas that had to be considered in an open brainstorming session, but were, in time, rejected as highly improbable causes to be investigated in order to improve the end result. (Who can ever forget the suggestion that related rough toilet tissue as a major cause of employee friction, or the personnel manager who believed that the best employees were not recruited because the CEO didn't personally go out on field recruiting trips.)

By pre-selecting categories for causes to be investigated, the four major sub-divisions of causes in a manufacturing or processing operation were established: manpower, machines, methods and materials (named the 4 Ms). In a service organization, such as one selling insurance, the major sub-divisions of causes could be: organization and personnel (including skills and training), operating procedures, software programs, and forms.

Step #1. Decide on a consensus effect, such as "increase quality yield from vendor." In the quality fishbone diagrams, this would be called the desired "quality characteristic."

Step #2. In the categories of major causes described above, list these as offshoots of the line that leads to the desired characteristic. See Figure 5-3.

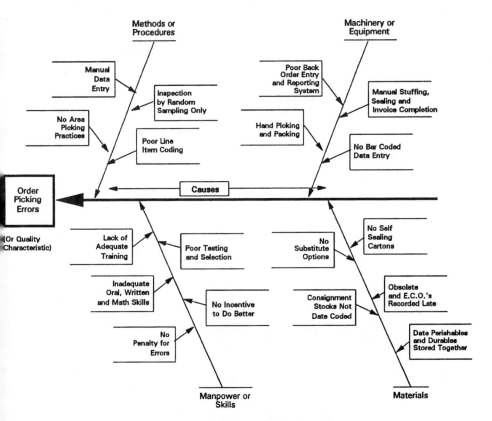

Figure 5–3   Wishbone Example

Step #3. Add the minor causes, clustered around the major cause categories. Consider these minor causes as influencing factors that are the variable causes that call out for improvement.

Step #4. Decide on a schedule of improvement actions that take into account a priority basis for ameliorating those causes that have the greatest positive effect on the desired result.

KEY RULES FOR MAXIMIZING USE OF THE FISHBONE TECHNIQUE

Some other rules will help gain better inputs from a group:

- To insure participation, use a format for listing the proposals from the group that is both highly visible and easily understood. Use an overhead projector, large flip charts, enhanced local computer screening, image portrayal, etc. People tend to be more participative if their ideas are exposed to view in a meaningful and easy-to-understand descriptive way. This also allows for modification and improvement of the recommended causal factor.

- To assure that everyone concerned is allowed to contribute, the group leader must encourage a "listening" attitude by all in attendance. In addition, don't consider the group's input as the final list of causal factors. Publish the list, and ask for input by those who either could not attend the brainstorming meeting, or who weren't invited to participate.

- Wherever possible, name the contributor. Give credit, not just for ego satisfaction, but also to encourage individuals to add more than just a summary review of causal factors. Recognition can be a motivator for those who only came prepared to "give lip service to another one of those gimmicky, new management ideas."

- It is important to encourage the participants, many of whom have never before been asked to contribute. Junior members of a group may also be quite reticent in the presence of higher ranking corporate officers. On the other hand, here is a chance to shine for those who may not recognize their ability to make positive contributions. It is vital that the leader assure that there be no unsubstantiated criticism of anyone's ideas. Fear of ridicule is probably the major cause of non-participation in the disclosure process.

- Organize a separate causal diagram for each result desired. This is not a set-in-cement rule. But, it has been found that when a group of causes overloads the diagram, it is possible that the group is attempting to effect more than one desired result.

- After the diagram is completed—which is assumed when the group's contributions diminish or vanish, or are reduced to the far-fetched groping recommendations that clearly would have little effect on the desired result—assure that the listed causes are understood by all. Repeat them; modify the language; and apply the "why?, what?, where?, when?, who? and how?" questions to be certain that the group understands.

- Have the group consensus select the most likely causes. Circle them on the fishbone diagram, or isolate them on the computer screen. This does not mean that the non-selected ideas are summarily rejected. However, focusing on consensus chosen winners shortens the potential improvement process. The non-selected few are kept as insurance, to be used when the more likely prospects fail to improve on the desired result.

- It is important that the list of causes focus on solving the problem, not just on the initial causes of the problem. In this way, the group focuses on improving the future, not just overemphasizing that which "should not have been done." This is not a call to disregard history, but it is part of the human condition to emphasize blame rather than seek improvement.

These diagrams have been used to seek cost improvements in such diverse areas as marketing, research, office procedures, traffic and distribution management, loss detection, information collection and distribution, warehousing, manufacturing, processing and quality improvement. In government practice, the fishbone analysis can be a useful tool to match causal factors to the level of service that an agency believes is both mandated and desired as an "effect" characteristic.

The major advantages of using the cause and effect fishbone diagram process in the consensus process is to:

- allow for an organized analysis of the cost or other factors that impinge on the desired result to improve profits

- apply a visual aid, which allows a group to ascertain if all pertinent factors (causes) have been considered

- allow for merging or standardizing existing and proposed improvement schemes with each other

- develop a training aid for the decision-making and problem-solving curricula.

SUMMING UP: Cost Improvement Insights Gained When Treating Expenditures as Investments

The key to implementing the themes of this Chapter is to apply techniques that relate improvement goals to specific action alternatives. In this way, you can be assured that cost factors can be viewed as they impinge on profits or cost improvements, therefore, as investments to achieve these stated goals.

The first logical step is to exercise the cost discovery process. In this stage, realistic and true costing emerge as the basis for facts and factors for management consideration. A prime example of the use of cost discovery is shown in the application of carrying cost factors to inventory acquisition and storage values. Such an example of the misuses of applying variable cost factors, through the allocation of fixed percentage charges, was detailed in the beginning of this chapter.

Similarly, the overhead allocation process should be a prime analysis target, and will be one of a series of important considerations when Activity Based Costing (A-B-C) is covered in Chapter Seven. So, too, true costing bears investigation and re-application where variable, mixed and fixed costs are randomly co-mingled.

The best understood and simplest approach to the cost discovery process relates to prioritizing the effects of cost reduction options, to produce positive profit alternatives. In any array of cost factors, a small percentage of significant costs produce the improvement opportunities for quick, meaningful actions that drop results to the bottom line.

The cost discovery step allows for the application of the simulation process. "What if . . ." techniques abound, but have less of a positive cost reduction effect where they are not preceded by a cost discovery process. So, too, cost leveraging, whose flagship technique is Pareto Analysis (covered in Chapter Eight) will bear lesser results if not preceded by cost discovery.

Some of the most effective cost reduction consensus tools are decision trees, which graphically illustrate both the scope of the present status of costs vs. profits, but also allow for group participation in fashioning positive action alternatives.

The basic management options (goals) are first considered. This allows managers to think beyond the obvious, which is especially important where prejudiced solutions are lobbied for before all possible alternatives have been considered.

Based on the decision tree exposition of true costs as contributory investments to reach profit goals, three selections are made by the management group, namely:

1. those cost reduction actions which will have the largest desired impact on the end result (goal),

2. matched by a time schedule for funding and implementation of these selected projects, and

3. a progress control process which will track results that drop to the bottom line.

This procedure is invaluable when separating the popular from the best profit improvement solutions. This becomes evident where the management group relates improvement potential to strategic options. In this scenario, popular solutions must meet the same acceptance procedures as all other alternative proposed actions will receive in the decision tree process. The use of profit/volume analysis typifies this objective approach to selecting specific cost reduction applications.

Another major advantage to using decision tree analysis results where all managers, not just financial controllers, are involved in selecting projects to increase cash flow. In this Chapter's example, a case study of increasing positive cash flow by improving purchasing contracts and delivery procedures, wedded the cost reduction concept to the installed Just-In-Time application.

How to Conduct Organizational Realignments to Foster Cost Reductions

It is important to consider the organization structure as a housing for the procedures of work flow. Thus, when the work procedures are proven cumbersome, it logically follows that a review is necessary to determine whether these procedures are forced to follow the organization structure, or whether the organization structure could best be redesigned to meet the requirements of the necessary flow of work and related procedures.

CHANGING PROCEDURES TO REDUCE COSTS

A leading example of this type of thinking was the 1990's trend that allowed the user to order materials directly from suppliers, specifically in those cases where contractual arrangements were previously established by the purchasing group. In this way, the user came in direct contact with the supplier relative to the procedures of placing orders, expediting delivery promises, overcoming delays, conducting quality and quantity inspections, assessing warranties, returns, cancellations, and stocking levels, modifying procurement terms, authorizing product or service re-design, and even modifying payment schedules.

Previously, it had been a cardinal rule that all contact with outside suppliers had to be conducted through the purchasing department's personnel. By changing the procedure to allow for direct communications between the action parties to a buy—as long as they conformed to the terms of the prior negotiated contract—significant savings in time and cost have been documented at every application site.

The rules that govern both procedures and organizational analysis are basically simple. But, applications are made most difficult by the forces of human inertia and personal prerogative. Organization structures are most commonly changed, or at least approved, by top, not middle managers. Therefore, the initiation of an organization analysis as well as the applications of the recommended results, must receive the topmost approvals in any organization. To a much lesser degree, forms and procedures may be analyzed with little or no prior approval, except where additional budgetary funding is required.

In the last half of the Twentieth Century, major changes have been effected as a result of the changes made necessary by computer information flow requirements. Data collection, storage, merging, manipulation and distribution have developed procedural requirements that cross the lines of organizational authority and responsibility. The most notable example has been in the electronic data interchange (EDI) concept, where a network (ring, interlock, or link) of users is tied to a central information collection and distribution center. Whereas in the past, it was common to have a mass of inter-office memos flowing between departments, now, controlled information access and entry can be performed without approvals, memos, concurrences or other paperwork that justifies organizational prerogatives.

Department B can peruse its total of current vendor overages, a comparison to last year's norms, company-wide ratios; all of which data is current and available without the necessity to resort to a formal written request to any other departments.

IT'S NO LONGER ACCEPTABLE TO STATE, "THAT'S NOT MY JOB!"

Organizational allegiances, like nationalism, are a major cause of conflict. For decades there was a rule that one can keep their nose clean if they "remember which flag is to be saluted." Thus, stating that a task is being refused or delayed, while awaiting prior written approval, became the ultimate in the costly tactic of procrastination.

An outgrowth of the above occurs where one organizational element uses the failure of another company group as an acceptable excuse for their own non-performance. Instead of pitching in to correct the situation, even though the solution is outside of their normal activity, it is far easier to use the other party's failure as an excuse for inaction or their own failure.

CASE STUDY: HOW ONE COMPANY CURED AN ONGOING CUSTOMER SERVICE PROBLEM

An example of the above occurred in a California small appliance supply warehouse. Orders were constantly shipped short, some by the wrong carrier, at the wrong time. A whole host of wrong order picks (line item errors) were not noticed at the packing area, which resulted in wrongful billing and constant customer complaints. In addition, many products were action tested—tests which related to shelf life warranties—just prior to shipment. Yet, the rate of field-received defectives was on the increase.

The Company initiated bar-coding of orders, which were coded and exploded into line item requests to be re-assembled at the packing area. These pick slips also segmented the task by both product type and type of storage area, i.e., bulk, shelf, palletted, bin, drawer, etc. In this way, line item verification was automated. While the volume of picking errors decreased only slightly, errors in shipped orders dropped dramatically. The bar-coded order installation was justified, more for the increase in customer satisfaction than by the reduction of costs caused by internal errors.

A training program was initiated for all warehouse personnel, with emphasis on the costliness of avoidable errors. This training program was recommended and partly funded by the sales group, whose commissions were significantly affected by picking, packing and shipping errors. At each and every training session, where input from the attending warehouse personnel was encouraged, the trainees commented on the numerous errors that were attributable to the supplying manufacturing group.

It took a while for an entire cadre of company personnel to realize that they were trying to ameliorate a company-wide problem by attacking the known causes in obvious organizational blocks—one block at a time. Through the use of a cause and effect fishbone (described in Chapter 5), a task force analyzed order fulfillment procedures independent of the error source by organizational element. It was found that employee motivation and attendant supervision were two major areas that were not improved by merely adding the bar-coding technique and providing some much-needed skill training. As long as the ultimate error was made by a human, motivation of that individual seemed the key to solution.

To eliminate the salespersons' constant complaints about the operation of product performance inspection, picking, packing and shipment, the sales department was placed in charge of the finished goods' warehouse. In this way, it was no longer the "stuff that they shipped," but it became "our error in order fulfillment." Electronic techniques and an incentive system were added to the warehousing operation, both methodologies that were familiar tools to sales personnel. Direct access to funding for delivery improvement was also initiated. Sales personnel were cross-trained in both warehousing skills and internal picking problems. Both of these were none-of-my-business situations before; now they were sales problems.

The biggest breakthrough occurred when the task of final inspection was transferred to the sales group. Two results were immediately evident:

1. The acceptance of finished goods product was no longer solely the domain of the manufacturing inspection team (the supplier). It was now the function of the sales department (the customer). As the representative of the ultimate customer, the sales department's motivation to conduct inexpensive but error-free inspection was increased.

2. The accounting department added the final motivational factor by requiring that all products, shipped from the manufacturing facility to the finished goods warehouse, actually be sold to the sales department. This was already the case for product that was bought from external suppliers, such as spare parts. By becoming an independent buying authority, pricing and profit were added to the sales procurement function. This put real meaning into the make or buy activity at both the warehouse and manufacturing level. Manufacturing now had to compete on a cost and quality basis with other suppliers considered by sales.

Sales became the true customers' representative. Instead of merely having a critic's role in attempting to affect internal costs and procedures, the sales group now assumed an active role in promulgating improved and cost effective manufacturing and warehousing procedures.

HOW FORECASTING ACCURACY WAS IMPROVED BY ASSIGNING PROPER RESPONSIBILITIES

A dramatic change occurred in the forecasting procedure. Previously, if the forecast was higher than proved to be the actual order input, inventory grew in the warehouse. When this occurred, the cost of carrying this excess inventory was not charged to the forecasters (the sales group), but was assessed as a charge against the warehousing activity. Under those conditions of operation, the warehouse collected the costs of each line item's inaccurate forecast vs. the actual order input.

Under the adopted organization change, the forecaster and the warehouser were one and the same entity, bearing the burden of excess inventory carrying costs as well as those associated with unacceptable stockouts vs. customer demand. This organization change led to a dramatic modification of the forecasting activity, as well as decreases in the resultant warehoused inventory value. Finished goods are now stocked at levels which provide reasonable and calculated safety for actual order input both over and below the sales forecast.

HOW STOCKOUTS WERE DECREASED BY REALIGNING THE ORGANIZATION

Another major cause of excess cost was the stockout situation, where the sales forecast fell well below actual demand. In the new circumstance, where the finished goods warehouse was the sales responsibility, shortages and back order control costs acted as motivators to make the forecast more responsive to history and experienced judgment. Now, the most accurate mathematical forecasting techniques were sought by the sales group, including control approaches not used before. These objective techniques were then modified by a more conservative and motivated experienced sales staff viewpoint.

The combination of adding more accuracy to the extrapolation of history, with the addition of more conservative experience factors by the sales group, led to increasing inventory turns in the warehouse by 19%. The manufacturing requirements planning (MRP) system absorbed the improved forecasts, such that stockouts dropped by 26% in the first year of the new organizational alignment.

You may be tempted to say, "If everyone did his or her job, these problems could have been alleviated under any organizational relationship." This is probably true in some situations. But, where inertia to continue past practice overrides management's calls for cost improvement, and where the ultimate security blanket of procrastination is the driving force behind current inactivity in problem solving, drastic realignment of authorities and responsibilities may be the recommended cure.

The conclusion that should be drawn is that functional reassignments can create the motivational drive that may be lacking in the present situation.

MAKING A JUST-IN-TIME SYSTEM WORK IN AN INCOMING GOODS WAREHOUSE

Flushed with success in cutting material carrying costs in the finished goods warehouse, this same appliance supply company went on to attack another ongoing problem that caused excessive costs. In attempting to implement a well-planned Just-In-Time application, they applied the proper principles of supplier partnering, vendor certification, single sourcing, on-site inspection, subsidiary detail scheduling, vendor and consignment stocking and a whole host of attendant procedures. However, the initial savings proved negligible when compared to the promises made vs. the results achieved. The cost of the supply operation remained fairly static.

Closer scrutiny of the relationship of installed procurement procedures vs. in-place organizational prerogatives disclosed a friction between two competing groups. Both the procurement and the raw materials warehousing groups saw the promise of a proper J-I-T application.

In actual practice, however, any slight discrepancies in either scheduling or quality by any supplier became the exclusive problem of warehousing management. Procurement was happy to set up the system of inspection and receiving coordination, but backed off when there was any hiccup in logistics supply caused by a whole host of recurring negative occurrences, i.e., from traffic management failures to the problems associated with expediting the entry of engineering change orders.

The pressures on the raw materials warehousing group multiplied when additional complaints and comments came directly from the product processing group:

- "Where are the goods I need to keep my people and equipment working?"
- "If there is a problem, why not let us know as soon as possible so that we can react responsibly?"
- "You people accept too many supplier excuses!"

It was determined that separation of the buyers' contact from the supplier, after the formal relationship was established, was a significant contributor to the failures encountered. The warehousepeople had user's needs for good performance, and required a continuum of aid by the purchasing function. The existing situation created an environment of "if we are all responsible, then no one of us is singularly or totally responsible." Split responsibility when dealing with their suppliers was considered a prime factor in producing the failures in supply.

Another cardinal rule of management is that you can delegate authority to perform a task, but never the ultimate responsibility for its performance. This principle is carried forth in the doctrine that planning without controls—like analysis without follow-up action—is busywork at best. When the purchasing group developed the J-I-T relationships with certified vendors, the basis of this relationship was delegated to the warehousing people to carry on with the newly formulated supply function. The procurement function then assumed more of an auditing function. They reviewed the history of the contractual relationship, offered commentary, and changed the rules where they saw fit. In other words, purchasing personnel developed the plans and oversaw the results. However, the warehouse supply people were the recipients of poor continuing practices until the purchasing auditors changed the way the game was to be played.

The company changed the relationship of the two major groups involved in the supply function. A new Supply Group was formed which consisted of three major arms of activity: (1) procurement and (2) receiving and inspection (including on-site inspection). In addition, (3) minimum warehousing, required under the J-I-T plan, was also added to this group. In this way, all activities of re-supply were under the same company umbrella. A great deal of finger pointing and procrastination ("That's not my job!") disappeared.

Measurable success was recorded in the first six months of operation under this reorganization scheme. The reader may again say, "Cooperation could have been achieved under the existing organization." Agreed! But, in some cases, the individual's motivation to cooperate can be reinforced by the specific designation of a manager's authority and responsibility. This is also a case of individual employees' perceptions of what constituted the team. Cost reductions can be achieved through expected normal cooperation, or can be accelerated by organizational changes that re-focus and encourage individual participation through renewed motivation.

HOW TO INVOLVE THE PRODUCT DESIGN GROUP IN THE FIRST STAGES OF ALL COST REDUCTION EFFORTS

Those involved in Total Quality Assurance programs know this quite well. It is a common circumstance to augment the design and development function with added product introduction duties. In today's drive to both:

1. build quality into the design phase, and
2. carry forth these quality improvement concepts into the production phase,

the design of processes, the specification and procurement of new equipment, and the development of inspection procedures can now be totally vested in the design engineering staff.

In this way, the design engineering group assumes new functions as the product managers for all new designs, responsible for releasing these functions to the normal channels for procurement and production, only after these functions have been initiated and successfully handled in pilot operations.

Reorganization of responsibilities and authority can be a motivating factor in achieving cost reductions. To respond by stating that, "They didn't do their job!" is no longer an acceptable excuse for avoidance or procrastination in the face of costly ongoing problems.

HOW TO PRACTICE ASSET CONSERVATION IN A FAST GROWTH ORGANIZATION

A phenomenon on the business scene is the fast-growth company that makes up its own rules as it grows from the garage to the coliseum in size. As sales explode, so do profits, which are related to present income vs. recent current expenditures during this dramatic growth period. Whether the company is taking advantage of a unique market niche, revolutionary new processes, a monopolistic new service, or a sensational new promotion, sustaining this dramatic growth relies heavily on supplying the ravenous demand.

All efforts to organize and install systems for improvement, especially cost reduction efforts, are relegated to a very much lower priority. Success seems to be solely measured on delivery performance. The stock market views the growth of accounts receivable, as well as the reinvestment of current profits from earned surplus, as the keys to fantastic price/earnings ratios. It is considered a wise conclusion that, at the present rate of accelerated growth, tomorrow has got to be much better on this fast track.

Cash flow, coupled with the increasing demand for greater liquidity to meet this rapid growth, dominate the thinking processes of the financial members of the company. They are told that dramatic sales increases will generate cash, as well as secure new credit lines that will overcome any temporary shortfalls.

However, two new cash drainers come to the fore during this period: (1) capital expenditures, including major equipment procurement and new facilities construction, and (2) abnormal growth of accounts payable for both needed research and development costs and increasing material purchases. The company is now in the unique position of utilizing most of its current assets (cash generated and collateralized assets) for this planned and expected dynamic growth. All other management priorities are doomed to postponement, or, worse yet, to a total lack of any consideration whatsoever.

Capital construction takes place even though present use of existing capacity is not examined, even for obvious improvements. This is evidenced by straight-line extrapolations of input, e.g., present personnel, materials, and depreciation costs vs. output of revenue-producing goods and services. When one assumes the ratio of input costs to the output of revenues will remain the same in the immediate future, this had best be related to a situation where the fat has been cut out. Otherwise, extrapolating the present ratio merely sets in cement the inefficiencies of present operations as acceptable practices in the future.

As covered in Chapter Three, the budgetary process that follows this line of reasoning, further establishes these present inefficiencies in procedural cement. This is how these existing inefficiencies become the basis for future spending ratios. Past inefficiencies in the use of capital for present capacity are extrapolated into future uses of capital to expand capacity. These become management expectations which are lower than they should be, thus adding to the problem.

At the first major demand downturn, debt service to finance these new facilities becomes a major factor in cash erosion. Then, profits are affected negatively, since expenditures for debt service were planned to be covered by the ever-increasing demand for the company's product or service—a demand which has now faltered.

HOW ACQUIRING COMPANIES ASSUME POSTPONED COST REDUCTION OPPORTUNITIES

In a similar situation are those acquisition-minded companies who plan their growth through intelligent acquisitions of assets and profits. As long as the expected profits keep coming in, the acquiring management team exerts little energy to examine cost effective practices in the acquired company. If the old management did not routinely seek cost improvements, it is now probable that the acquiring management will be hard pressed to begin an analysis of cost reduction opportunities in the short run . . . other than the obvious simultaneous cutting of fat plus muscle in their drive to justify the acquisition.

In a worst case scenario, the acquired company starts to drain cash from the acquiring company, putting both entities at risk by virtue of negative cash flows and more conservative creditor funding.

CONSIDERING SHORT TERM COST REDUCTIONS AND SUSTAINED PROFITABILITY SIMULTANEOUSLY

The major current asset on a manufacturing company's balance sheet is usually inventory, equalling as much as 50–60% of the Current Asset account. To calculate the potential savings that could be derived from this asset reduction, many companies determine the optimum possessed inventory level. This becomes a better base for improvement schemes than merely demanding that management "do better than the industry turns ratios" (frequently dubbed as the "DO BETTER" exhortation approach). Again, it is a fallacy to extrapolate past inefficiencies as a basis for improvement, or for the purposes of merely maintaining the status quo.

The acquiring company may go to extremes in effecting cost reductions at the acquired company site. Without prior knowledge of cost effectiveness opportunities, a slashing-cost reduction program may be the immediate answer to the acquiring company's dilemma. Thus, certain obvious expenditures are selected for mandated reductions, without regard to their role as investments in future profitability. These actions are taken to show that the new management acted decisively to quickly reduce the entitlement costs of current payroll.

The cost reduction targets are obvious; and, the immediate savings are trackable right down to the bottom line. It doesn't take a management guru to slash costs without regard to long-term future profitability opportunities. In fact, attempting to consider any long-range factors will probably be discouraged, as well as be considered a frivolous view of the present dire situation.

At the point in time where sales level off, or even decline, management reacts with many panic actions, including, "Cut the payroll and save the company!" Assuming the slowdown in demand is temporary, and can best be met with a drastic cut in those obvious people costs, management seeks the quick-and-dirty solutions vs. performing any gross analysis of costs and their contribution as investments for future profits. The justification for immediate and drastic actions is simply stated as, "The chicken coop is afire; this is no time to evaluate procedures for improving egg production."

Thus, across-the-board, mandated layoffs become deep cuts in hours and skills of available capacity, creating new problems.

For example,

- indirect and overhead slashes on a straight percentage ratio basis may cause imbalances in services delivered.

- Trouble can develop where plant maintenance personnel cuts are indiscriminately made, especially where no viable preventive maintenance system is in effect, or where the age of present equipment demands a greater, not lesser, amount of maintenance time and skills.
- Another example of action gaining priority over analysis exists where installation of a new and more approachable data base may be postponed indefinitely, creating an unusual demand on the present patchwork data system.
- Some effects of across-the-board personnel cuts may produce other imbalances, i.e., instead of selective, planned cost reductions, savings in short run expenses may cause great harm to longer term profitability opportunities.

The problem with seeking a better solution than across-the-board cuts is in the time frame allowed. Top management is demanding action . . . NOW! They are impatient with any employee who asks for time to study some alternative mix of expenditure reductions. Instead, arbitrary doctrines are set in effect:

- freeze the budget at last year's limits, line item by line item
- decrease, eliminate, or postpone funding for previously approved projects
- despite the urgency of some personnel and skill requirements, an immediate deep freeze is placed on all hiring either to fill existing vacancies or to fill new job descriptions
- dictatorial demands are sent out to decrease inventories through mandated purchasing volume cuts
- a call for immediate elimination of any perceived and actual task redundancies . . . called a reduction in overlapping
- immediate direction is issued to consolidate geographical areas and warehoused inventories
- fire sales are mandated of obsolete, unwanted, and overstocked items in both indirect supplies and stock materials
- price cuts across-the-board are authorized to provide buying incentives, or at least to accelerate the time frame for taking possession by the customers
- reductions in travel costs are requested, as well as for communication, and all outside costs of contractor personnel, including cancellation of all outside non-essential contractor services
- elimination of long range planned projects, thus shifting emphasis to one-year projects, i.e., those that can yield a return on investment in that short time frame.

By practicing the above strategies, fire fighting becomes the order of the day. In this way, those managements that did not have the motivation or skills to preserve the cash asset through planned cost reductions (fire prevention) in the good times, now become the champions of cost reduction, at any cost, when cash flow is no longer fueled by rapid growth. Thus, one of the major causes of the problem (present management), now have a chance to become the company's saviors. Managers who do not run a tight ship in the good times are asked to manage a slashing offensive against cost inefficiencies, mainly brought about by their very own lack of positive actions in the recently aborted go-go surge period.

IMPLEMENTING SOLUTIONS FOR THE FAST GROWTH COMPANY'S MANAGEMENT IN THE "GOOD TIMES"

Management should be authorizing the analysis of objectives and actual practices of all facets of the company, as an ongoing technique at every phase of the growth cycle. Do not treat cost reduction as a secondary problem to be attacked when the necessary time and skills are available. Make cost reduction part of the growth process. This is an ideal place to reinvest accelerating profits. It is as important as the time spent in considering the purchase of new equipment, processes and technical expertise during the fast growth stage. Cost reduction should also be considered as an investment for future profitability, and, as such, should be given the same priority as any other capital re-investment for the same profitable end result.

Some cost improvement steps that could be taken at any stage of growth are:

- seek to employ skills and techniques that are not now available in the company to perform overhead cost analysis, install productivity incentives, simulate designs, initiate marketing analysis, install commonality analysis, explore field quality reliability, initiate strategic benchmarking, introduce supplier partnering, analyze service acceptance evaluation, etc.
- initiate a review of all practices, at all levels, on a cost and priority basis for cost improvement
- institute an ongoing training program, for all levels of personnel, on how and what to seek out as an improvement
- establish a recognition or monetary reward for positive contributors

- analyze specific capacity vs. forecasted and actual demand on an ongoing basis
- review the time consequences of all approved work procedures vs. the control achieved over specific affected areas of concern
- relate all recommendations to results that will ultimately drop to the bottom line by improving cash flow, releasing both fixed and variable costed assets for other profitable uses, and taking actions that will lead to liquidating inventories; or relate to improved employee motivation, increasing the quality of services and goods to the ultimate customer. Of course the list is endless.

Directed analysis followed by planned installations have a much greater impact on future profitability than random and sporadic cost reduction activities.

It is important to consider that the management skills and efforts that were necessary contributors during the rapid growth era, may not be the exact same skills required to manage a slower growth into the next phase. In the period following rapid sustained growth, the emphasis will shift to a more specific and conservative view of expenditures as investments for future profitability.

At some point in time, fire fighting should become an exception activity during the ongoing, planned approach of fire prevention.

SUMMING UP: How the Present Organization Works Can Be a Clue to Introducing Major Cost Reduction Motivators

As a housing for the flow of work procedures, the organization may also be the cause of excessive approvals, personnel pressures and data distribution. As such, analyses of work flow, conducted independently of the present organization structure, usually produces opportunities for cost reduction.

It is important for entities—both corporate and governmental—to have employees consider themselves a part of the whole. This unchains a great resource of constructive criticism conducted across and between formal organizational lines. It is no longer considered acceptable for an employee to state, "That's not my job!". Thus, all improvements are sought from all personnel at all levels and in all organizational boxes.

To overcome present and past prejudices, training on how and where to look for cost reduction options is imperative. Of course, this must be preceded by the presentation of the new management approach to making the entire group part of the management team.

The best approach may be to realign functions. In this way, authority and responsibility are coupled for a most effective resolution of ongoing and costly problems. Your problem is now part of your responsibility. Numerous examples of this approach have been described in this Chapter.

The fast growth company presents a special application for analysis of organizational principles in motivation. Where the major drive is to meet unprecedented demand, little attention is usually paid to internal improvements in service, product or procedures. Thus, when any major slowdown hits the fast growth company, instead of implementing parts of a planned existing cost reduction program, management slashes costs in an across-the-board fire-fighting blast. Imbalanced effects occur where the baby is discarded with the bathwater. Little if any consideration is given to any costs as investments in future profitability. Analysis is regarded as footdragging.

The answer for a fast growth company is to consider ongoing cost reduction analysis as important an investment as the acquisition of new equipment, new skills and new plant capacity.

This same approach applies to acquiring company plans for acquired companies. The introduction of an ongoing cost reduction program should be considered as an essential part of asset and profit preservation.

The obvious answer is to have an ongoing cost reduction program that is constantly evaluating equipment, procedures, skills, motivation and capital assets. It is management's responsibility to provide the environment for this approach, training in techniques, expressing goals, providing recognition, funding qualified projects and the like. In this Chapter, the one-shot approach was shown to have significant flaws, that is, when compared to the advantages of a planned, approved, communicated, long-term, and ongoing managerial encouragement to cut the fat not the muscle.

CHAPTER 7

LEVERAGING COST REDUCTIONS TO INCREASE PROFITABILITY

There is an old management axiom that proclaims there are more problems to resolve than time or talent available to solve them all. Thus, applying equal amounts of time, talent and funding to all areas of cost reduction opportunities may very well be an exercise in futility. There are opportunities to reduce costs by small percentage amounts that require a less than average effort, when compared to the effort needed to augment all management actions spread over all areas of opportunity.

Leveraging is the recognized management technique to utilize available management skills, funding and time, for significant gains that are achieved for minimal efforts. The main requirement is to be able to identify selected areas for cost reduction opportunities to utilize the leveraging principal.

HOW LEVERAGING HAS BEEN APPLIED
BY SUCCESSFUL STRATEGISTS

This approach has been applied since Biblical times, as when the few outflanked the many at Jericho with a well-placed, directed effort. This application of the organized significant few conquering the massed multitude is also seen in the description of the Roman cohorts defeating vastly superior forces through the application of wedged maneuvers of groups of 100 shielded warriors. Alexander the Great used small mobile groups to outflank the vastly superior forces of Darius in Asia Minor; and, Ghengis Khan, with his outnumbered cavalry, performed miracles of warfare in building the largest land empire ever. In more recent history, conquistador Hernando Cortez performed this same military leveraging maneuver in the 16th Century against Montezuma, when a few hundred Spaniards defeated an Aztec army the size of imperial Spain's total military force at that time.

For today's manager, strategically applying limited resources of both skills and time, when seeking cost reductions, can be a very positive approach to making significant gains with limited effort and assets. What is required are detailed analyses which adequately present the cost inequalities that exist in almost every circumstance. Specific examples of these types of leveraging analyses will be described in this chapter.

ORGANIZING DATA IN
A CHAOTIC ATMOSPHERE

A prerequisite for applying leveraging principles is the organization of data, both past actual and projected assumptions. However, the Newtonian solutions that have dominated management thinking for five hundred years are under fire by those who have stated that the business world is not amenable to standardized prediction and control. Advocates of the chaos theory (non-linear thinkers) press for creative thinking as far more relevant to cost reduction than Newtonian linear thinking, where solutions are extrapolated from past actual data.

In leveraging terms, the chaotic, non-linear approach states that a very small force may have an astronomical affect on future events, similar to the straw that finally breaks the camel's back. Conversely, large forces may have a very insignificant impact on the course of events.

EXAMPLE: For 15 years, I have provided two and three-day seminars to hundreds of business leaders in various African nations, with little effect on these countries' economies. Yet, on six consulting assignments with a precious metals mining company, an agricultural combine, a chemical processing giant, a maker of vehicle tires, a quasi-government research agency, and a multi-government construction project, I have single-handedly effected savings in three African nations equivalent to one hundred times my consultancy remuneration.

EXAMPLE: On a micro basis, a President of a food packaging company in the Southwest gave a New Year's cost reduction exhortation talk to 245 employees. Little change resulted, if any at all. Yet, in March of that same year, he had a 30-second verbal exchange with a key executive in the narrow executive office hallway. The result was a specific modification of three shifts of crews on fourteen production lines, which cut 6% of the ongoing operating costs out of an annual total of 42% of the entire operating budget. The 30-second discussion was not planned or even sought. But, the discussion was specific, reasonable, and resulted in a conclusion that cried out for immediate implementation.

SEEKING ORDER THROUGH LEVERAGING

It is possible that these self-same significant solutions may flow from traditional problem solving/decision making processes. However, these techniques assume much more universal order than the non-linear proposers will accept. The main claim to improvement by the linear thinkers is that information is the raw material with which managers must work; and, the most effective way to improve managerial problem solving and decision making, leading to significant cost reductions, is to improve the use of this available or extrapolated information. The base data is then used to develop the techniques that lead to cost reduction solutions, based on the following premises:

- Systematic processes for gaining solutions also prevent potential problems from occurring or reoccurring.

- Gathering data is the first step in analysis, preceded by (1) stating the objective(s), (2) defining the criteria for success, and (3) establishing the parameters of expenditure to meet (1) and (2).

- Current data produces continuous improvement (which the Japanese call, "kaizen"), which is best realized when there exists a policy of intensive cross-training, involvement of many more managers and their employees, and the introduction of both financial and nonfinancial motivational techniques.

- It is essential to bring together diverse groups of personnel (simultaneous engineering), including key suppliers, in order to examine product, process and/or procedure improvements.

- Data is used to measure and thus reduce the time required to make changes (time-based management) when considering: product or process improvement, introduction of new procedures, accommodating customized requests both internally proposed and from your customers, and reducing possession time of assets, especially inventory.

In all of the above approaches, data collection and summarization is an automatic, mandated requirement. Thus, cost reduction proposals are based on the assumption that events of the past will continue until altered by today's management personnel working with the presented data to bring order out of chaos.

DATA-COLLECTION PROCESSES USED FOR PRE-SELECTED COST REDUCTION TARGETS

In a product manufacturing environment, cost reductions are analyzed by pre-selected areas of opportunity, such as:

- external influences, including competition, corporate and product image, governmental controls, and forecasted economic trends
- money availability, including its present and future cost (debt service) and uses for profit maintenance, improvement and expansion, as well as for survival
- product and process control, including status of proprietary positions, adaptability to other processes and/or products, acquisition plans, divestiture and licensing strategies
- organization flexibility, including relative support and co-existence among and between departments (formal vs. informal structure analysis), function and personnel skills inventories, mandated and volunteered communications, adherence to the rules of delegation, responsibility and authority, teamwork and coordination of efforts (project planning)
- financial controls, including those relating to budgets and expenditures, capital approvals, fixed vs. step vs. variable cost analyses, loss control, pricing reviews, allocation of overheads (activity based costing), credit and collection policies, return on investment strategies, and profit planning techniques
- facility, equipment and methods analyses, including capacity planning, competition process and equipment comparisons (benchmarking), space utilization, materials substitution (value analysis), contractor utilization (partnering and certification), equipment flexibility, sitting time reduction, quick change set-up and teardown, operator on-line quality inspection and feedback, crew analysis (simulation and multi-man analysis), incoming and outgoing materials management procedures (logistics manage-

ment), materials handling and storage (movement and possession analysis), and input/output analysis

- personnel motivation, including skills inventorying, financial incentives (such as IMPROSHARE), cross-training, performance measurement, teamwork development (empowerment and job ownership), and developing recruitment and promotion criteria

- asset control, including sales to production forecasting, purchasing and scheduling controls (materials requirement planning), possession analysis as this relates to cash flow and return on investment, single sourcing, quality assurance policies, data collection and report design.

The above is a partial list of techniques applied in the linear, Newtonian approaches (the set of scientific analysis principles that were in use from the 16th Century forward) to cost reduction. In these cases, data of past actual occurrences is extrapolated, usually in a straight line, into future expected information to improve profitability. From this potpourri of analysis and action options, you can select those that suit your skills, interests, and scope of knowledge.

AVOID BEING TRAPPED
BY SHORT-TERM THINKING

Many managers are measured specifically by the financial results of their efforts, such as where profit centers are reviewed exclusively on the return achieved on invested capital. Obviously, this type of measurement motivates managers to maximize their efforts by reducing invested capital to forecasted output, rather than on increasing profits over longer than the budgetary time frame.

This attitude is especially significant where applied in companies competing for foreign market share, which requires the domestic producer to compete with a World of subsidized competition. It is here that planning the longer-term stream of profits is crucial to the company's competitive position, as well as future success. Thus, where managers regard that which they control merely as financial investments, they will primarily work to invest only in improving present (known) operations, developing these operations as cash cows, and divesting or rejecting any products or processes that do not meet present return on investment criteria. "If its not broken, don't fix it" strategies dominate, substituting future improvement for today's rewards.

This discussion of linear thinking demonstrates the reliance placed on extrapolating from data as a precursor of future expectations from cost improvement applications. Leveraging is one of the powerful and recognized tools that must be used to augment this approach. The manager is urged to select the significant few areas of opportunity which then provides the analysis data for seeking significant cost savings.

The data basis for this linear approach is now discussed in the arena of linear vs. non-linear proponents. Are we limited to improving on a forecastable cost model? Or, should today's managers look upon techniques that respect the theory of chaos as the dominant prognostication, and, therefore, the basis for applying the techniques of leveraging? From my 35 years of experience, I believe the latter to be a more fruitful approach.

APPROACHING CHAOS WITH CRITICAL, NON-LINEAR THINKING

John Smith of The Futura Partnership, states that, "Chaos is the anomaly! . . . One does not have to define, identify or organize chaos . . . therefore, chaos provides the opportunity to avoid investigation as being out-of-order . . . and thus does not need an organized assessment . . . Chaos is the real rule of order!"

If, however, a manager believes that chaos is an aberration from the expected order of things, he will apply the universal problem solving approach which decrees, "It's broken; fix it!" Techniques of management are established to determine the scope of the aberration and fix it, so as to return to the "normal" order of the situation. This approach assumes that cost and performance data will provide the feedback to show a return to the planned and established order of events.

However, if you assume that chaos is the normal order, then what is the validity of using past data to fix a situation and then to use feedback reports to ascertain the existence of an improvement or a return to normal? Consider how many savings reports are generated by managers to justify funding for their department's pet projects, where the projected savings are never documented as ever dropping to the bottom line.

Ralph Stacey in *The Chaos Frontier* (Butterworth-Heinemann, 1991) places great emphasis on when the chaotic event takes place, or is to take place, as well as how long a period of time the particular chaos exists. He continues with a discussion of determining the event's impact over a period of time. All of this leads to a division of chaotic events into classifications of changes, from Closed Change, through Contained Change, to Open-ended Change. By illustrating the levels of change, he has defined the need for, and the management actions, that are required to bring about profit improvement through cost reduction in a world of chaotic events. In this way, defining the level of chaos control to be achieved provides the manager with the leverage of choosing the few, or only, tool(s) to use in a defined classification of a chaotic situation.

Dr. Edward de Bono (*I Am Right—You Are Wrong,* Viking Penguin, 1993) calls out for critical thinking as an antidote to the philosophy, "If it ain't broke, don't fix it!" (the maintenance concept). Without competition, he claims, this postulate might work. However, since your competitors are looking to do things better, not just fix existing problems, they are examining new procedures, designs and processes. Assuming a linear, static world also assumes that what you are doing today will be sufficient tomorrow, i.e., after it is fixed.

In the real world, managers must fix what is broken, while, at the same time, apply critical thinking to all aspects of the business. Thus, it is essential not only to fix deviations from normally expected situations (maintenance thinking), but this approach should be expanded to include (in de Bono's words) "opportunity thinking, initiative thinking, enterprise, improvement, and all those types of thinking in which we set out to think about things which are not wrong."

If we assume that improvements will be continuously resulting as part of the normal evolution of industrial progress (kaizen), we may miss the opportunity of the "breakthrough" as described by Dr. Joseph Juran in all his quality assurance writings. If we continually improve surface travel vehicles and ships, would we ever have considered airborne and inter-galactic flight? Eventually, of course.

HOW LEVERAGING BUILDS ON ACCEPTED MANAGEMENT THEORY

Leveraging is a traditional method of analysis; actually but one step in the problem solving approach. It usually takes place after the following steps have been completed:

1. Agreeing or mandating an objective.
2. Determining criteria for success.
3. Establishing parameters of expenditure.
4. Gathering data as it relates to the above.
5. Analyzing these data by placing them in logical groupings (cells) for study.

Leveraging is a problem solving analysis tool (step 5 above) that is applied to the information and data gathered in Step 4.

Thus, if we remain with the traditional linear approach to problem solving, leveraging is an analysis tool in the traditional chain of steps in a maintenance procedure. Traditional managers are taught the linear approach in order to analyze a situation to remove the cause of the problem. This will obviously solve the existing problem—in most cases.

However, breakthroughs occur where managers use creative thinking, such as in value analysis, where one looks at the design of the product or process and asks, "I know what it is, but what is it supposed to do?"

Edward de Bono states, "Our traditions of thinking have always preferred analysis to design." This assumes that traditional analysis of "what is" will produce something better if we find the cause of the problem and remove it. Therefore, the usual conclusion drawn when a problem is resolved, is that the cause must have been removed or overcome. Dr. de Bono goes on to conclude that the traditions of problem-solving and removal of causes are valid as far as they go, but they are only part of the thinking required, since progress does not come just by fixing problems.

In all of this, consider that both linear and non-linear thinkers can agree with the leveraging analysis approach, but they disagree with the route used to get to the point of bringing data to the analysis stage.

Consider that leveraged actions may also stem from the brainstorming approach, sometimes called the "Rationale Mode." A manager can decide on a cost reduction approach by assessing all possible outcomes in order to select the most profitable. As will be seen later on in this chapter, since information is usually gathered at random, this then requires the analysis mode (cell grouping) to efficiently isolate and highlight obvious areas for applying leveraging, i.e., pinpointing areas where small specific actions may lead to large or significant cost reductions.

THE USE OF LEVERAGING IS NOT LIMITED TO LINEAR THINKING

Linear thinkers can readily produce the causes and predict the effects of problem solving, followed by a structured analysis and eventual decision making. Managers can predict the manpower necessary to run a production line, or staff an advertising task force for a client. Past history provides the base.

Non-linear thinkers begin by asking the purpose of the production line, or the very need for the agency's task force. By either determining the problem to be resolved (the cause), or assuming chaos requires a creative approach, both sets of management thinkers begin with the steps that set the parameters for fact gathering leading to cost reduction analysis.

In order to practice the leveraging approach, it is required that the gathered information be grouped in selected order (analysis cells). The most profitable approach is usually the one that requires a small significant effort to secure a large cost reduction. Therefore, any "free form" approach, to selecting a problem to resolve, sets the parameters of fact gathering; but does not generally select the analysis technique which we are covering in this chapter . . . leveraging. This was the conclusion reached by Tom Peters in both *Thriving on Chaos* (Alfred A. Knopf, 1987) and *Liberation Management* (Knopf, 1992).

During the 1950's and 1960's, statistical planning models were developed to simulate the variety of effects which could be achieved by decisions that impinged on the economic strategy of a nation, right on down to the lower level decisions required for a single company's make-or-buy decisions. In a stable world, these models were very helpful in predicting the future, considering that almost any group of factors could be required for event-forecasting within acceptable three standard deviation limits. The recurring problem was in the validity of extrapolating from past actual data to predict the future.

During this time, the introduction of multi-variable analyses to problem-solving suggested an answer. In this approach, a whole range of factors were independently varied by measured fixed increments while holding the rest of the contributory factors in a fixed position. This allowed apparent causes and their effects to be isolated for solution.

THE IMPACT OF THE BUTTERFLY EFFECT

When followers of the chaotic theory investigated this approach, they concluded that, in a chaotic system, information for prediction loses its value. They declared that the existence of the "butterfly effect" allows microscopic differences to go unmeasured. In a multi-factor analysis, these minute differences do not cancel each other out. Instead, they have a cumulative effect that grows at exponential speed, like feedback produced in a microphone.

Simply stated, the butterfly concept concludes that a single butterfly in New South Wales, Australia, by flapping its wings, can cause a disturbance that, when ultimately magnified, can cause major weather changes in the El Nino air mass off the coast of California. This is similar, they state, to minute changes in personnel in a factory atmosphere which can ultimately change the company profit picture. Moving these few people to other areas of operation may cause dramatic changes, for better or worse, in the overall operation's performance.

Thus, the butterfly effect may cause unexpected, but major changes, in a management system that appears to be running smoothly in a world of chaos. A statistical planning model, that extrapolates the future from a supposed predictable past, most likely overlooks the butterfly effect at work. Tranquil conditions may mask unusual, unexpected and perhaps irrational changes, presaging major disruptions due to the butterfly effect.

MAKE BETTER USE OF COMPARISON DATA RATHER THAN SIMPLY DEMANDING MORE DATA

In the area of cost improvement, non-linear thinking casts doubt on the value of gathering more and more information prior to making a decision. Yet, our management information systems are driven by the concept that gathering more data at a faster clip will assure management success in decision-making. Will this be a viable approach in a chaotic world of unpredictable incidents?

The answer seems to lie in the ability of managements to use feedback data. Management control requires:

1. A review of what actually and factually occurred compared to what was predicted and expected (within acceptable statistical limits).

2. A statement of the effects of measurable variations from expected performance (causes), and

3. A measured reaction, on a timely basis, for the next plan-do-review cycle.

In this way, managers will begin to recognize cost improvement opportunities, both for immediate and short-range solutions, as well as for long-term growth and breakthrough gains. Old, cold historical reports, merely showing financial planning variations, do not provide managers with such an opportunity. Both unexpected and expected events are merged to produce an average variation report. Breakthrough management actions, as well as short term problem solving, will more likely come from an acceleration and improvement in the management control information loop.

With the rules for managing chaos in place, a new degree of freedom can be taught to middle and lower level managers. Instead of waiting for long term strategies to emerge from "mahogany row," decision making for cost improvement can be driven by the delegation of authority right on down to the lowest supervisory levels. These are the managers who receive the first reports of their department's actual vs. planned activities. Information can be acted upon within the parameters of overall policy, instead of constantly and continuously awaiting approval for recommended actions.

Within the strategic vision provided, top management can press for cost reduction initiatives at all levels, instead of having their total activity based upon demanding and approving actions at all levels. In turn, this type of management not only encourages individual initiative, but also encourages decentralization of the attack on cutting the fat. Employees will feel trusted, not merely like directed cogs in a giant gearbox of requests for approval and concurrence . . . prior to receiving authority to take constructive action.

The aid a company management can give to all of its employees is not only to provide pertinent and timely data, but also to provide analysis tools and a listening environment. One of the least expensive and simplest analysis tools to explain (and train) is the analysis tool of leveraging.

HOW TO USE THE COST REDUCTION OPPORTUNITY CURVE

One of the oldest and most popular leveraging tools is the Pareto Curve. In cost reduction activities, it appears as an analysis procedure entitled the Opportunity Curve. In materials control activities, this same curve was labelled A-B-C by the post-World War II materials controllers (Dickie et al) at General Electric. Within the U.S. Air Force Air Material Command, this leveraging exercise is named Hi-Value/Lo-Value Analysis. Other titles for this leveraging exercise include Emphasis Analysis in scheduling activities, and partnering prioritization in the purchasing arena.

An Italian economist, Vilfredo Pareto popularized this approach to analyzing Gross National Product (GNP) data in his landmark paper, "The Theory of Maladjusted Statistics" in 1896. In analyzing the contributory factors to the GNP in various industrialized nations, he noted that a small change in a significant area of a nation's economy could have a significant effect on the total GNP. At the same time, a major change in an insignificant area of the economy barely changed the GNP. In the U.S., a 5% drop in auto production (or purchases) can have a far more destabilizing effect on the GNP than a 50% to 75% drop in the sale of lawn mowing equipment.

The Pareto Theory states, "In any series of elements to be controlled, a selected, small fraction in terms of numbers of elements, always accounts for a large fraction, in terms of effect." Out of the total number of problems and opportunities that confront the manager on a daily basis, a small percentage of them will account for a large percentage of potential cost reductions.

Figure 7-1 depicts the usually drawn Pareto Cost Curve. This analysis is also referred to as the 20-80 curve, since 20% of the total items under consideration usually account for about 80% of the total costs being reviewed for cost reduction opportunities. Other commonly used definitions refer to the "significant few" vs. the "insignificant many" items or opportunities that exist. The concept is the same, i.e., a small reduction of costs in a significant area of total items to be reviewed will yield a significant result.

Therefore, this becomes a fruitful avenue for leveraging management activities, especially when one considers the opening sentence in this chapter, "There are usually more problems to resolve than time or

Figure 7-1   A Sample Generic Pareto Curve

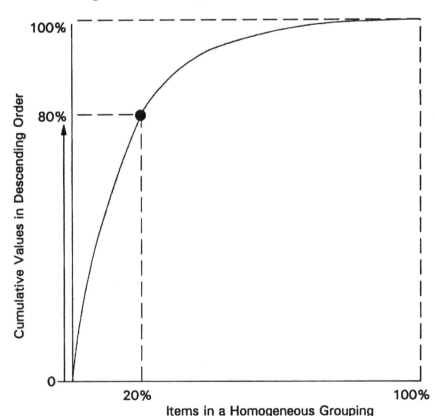

talent available to resolve all of them." Leveraging through the use of Pareto Analysis is both a cost and time saver in directing improvement activities.

Telling "them" where to work is at least as significant as merely demanding action without providing the tools for analysis. "Cut costs!" is an exhortation. In cutting the fat and not the muscle, aiding in data stratification can be viewed as an aid to analysis. "Sell more!" is merely an exhortation. Analyzing marketing strategy relative to position, product and potential penetration will more likely produce a positive effect on future sales (and efforts). Management must provide analysis tools, not just authoritarian mandates requesting that everyone "do better!" Even Henny Youngman understood this. When asked, "How's your wife?", he responded with, "Compared to what?"

Figure 7-2 is a valuable interpretation of the Pareto Curve. The Opportunity Curve indicates that a small 10% cost reduction in a

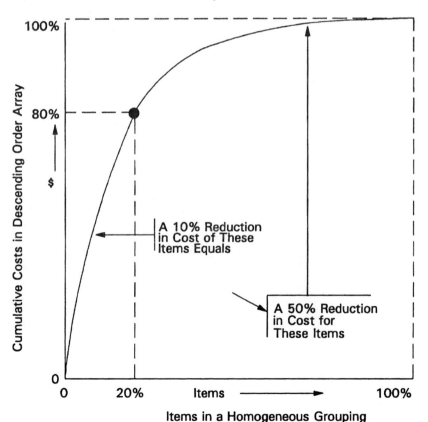

Figure 7-2   The Opportunity Inequality Curve (Also Called the 10–50 Curve)

significant area of the total cost curve, can have the same effect as a
40–50% savings in an insignificant area of opportunity. This is not a
call for neglecting cost improvements in less significant areas of opportunity. Rather, it is a call for the prioritization of management
time, skills and departmental money to leverage out into areas of
more significant potential savings than would most likely result
when treating all cost reduction opportunities as equal.

THREE EXAMPLES OF PRACTICAL PARETO ANALYSES USED IN COST REDUCTION

1. **Setting up a cost tree:** Figure 7-3 depicts a simplified product cost
tree prepared by the financial controller for each of the product man-

Figure 7-3   Schematic Pareto Cost Estimate Analysis

MODEL #16032 L

ESTIMATE – $1,635.   *ANALYSIS TYPE* – Component –
                                                         ALL COSTS

1st LEVEL	1A	$863.		
	1B	275.		
	1C	186.		
	1D	180.		
	1E	131.	TOTALS	$1,635.

2nd LEVEL

1A		*1B*		*1C*		*1D*		*1E*	
1A1	$320.	1B1	$116.	1C1	$51.	1D1	$76.	1E1	$85.
1A2	210.	1B2	81.	1C2	36.	1D2	63.	1E2	19.
1A3	116.	1B3	69.	1C3	21.	1D3	41.	1E3	18.
1A4	51.	1B4	9.	1C4	19.		$180.	1E4	3.
1A5	50.		$275.	1C5	19.			1E5	3.
1A6	48.			1C6	18.			1E6	1.
1A7	36.			1C7	6.			1E7	1.
1A8	32.			1C8	6.			1E8	1.
	$863.			1C9	6.				$131.
				1C10	4.				
					$186.				

3rd LEVEL

1A1   *1A2*   *1A3*   *1A4*   *1A5*   *1A6*   *1A7*   *1A8*

agers. Like most cost analyses of this type, the cost tree begins with the end-product, followed by the estimates and actual costs for indirect support services and applied overheads, as well as for the direct materials, labor, depreciation, and all other mixed and fixed costs that are charged to this product. These costs are accumulated from the roots up, but are usually shown as cascading costs down from the crown of the tree.

Many assumptions are made relative to volume forecasts, location of processing, inflation, debt service, etc. But, at some point, a representative cost is required in order to both provide an analysis tool and to determine a selling price. The cost tree provides the compromise results of operating and cost personnel inputs.

You will note that, at each level in the diagram, the costs are listed in descending order. This is usual, since the Pareto Curves are cumulative depictions of descending value elements moving up along the "y" axis (also called the coordinate or vertical plane). The horizontal axis (ordinate or "x" plane) consists of the elements or items related to the cumulative descending order of values represented on the vertical axis.

Figure 7-4 indicates that, at the second level of the product cost tree, nine of 33 items of cost at that level (27% of the total cost estimate) represent 70% of the total cost. Thus, the opportunity curve provides an option to effect a small savings, say 10%, in a significant cost area, which can be equal to a savings (or loss) of as much as 50% in an insignificant area of cost savings opportunity. This provides direction for management breakthroughs, creative thinking and choice of options relative to such limited resources as funds, manpower or specific skills.

Figure 7–4   Pareto Analysis of the Second Level of Costs

2nd LEVEL PARETO   (27% of items equals 70% of Cost)

RANK	ITEM	COST	CUM
1	1A1.	$320.	$320.
2	1A2.	210.	530.
3	1A3.	116.	646.
4	1B1	116.	762.
5	1E1	85.	847.
6	1B2	81.	928.
7	1D1	76.	1,004.
8	1B3	69.	1,073.
9	1D2	63.	1,136.
Σ	Σ	Σ	Σ
33	1E8	1	1,635

2. **Breaking down costs:** An analysis by type of cost incurred can be of equal value when seeking to cut the fat by finding leveraging opportunities. Figure 7-5 illustrates this kind of cost analysis. This can be quite valuable when conducting an Activity Based Contribution Analysis (see next Chapter) or a value analysis (what does it do? vs. what is it?). In both of these investigations, it would be appropriate to isolate the significant opportunities from the less significant, especially where limited skills and personnel hours are available for the task.

Note that this Pareto leveraging analysis defines 13% of the total items for three purchased materials equaling 57% of the total cost estimate. Likewise, 21% of the items equals 70% of the total cost. Obviously this leveraging technique indicates significant areas of concern or opportunity, where small savings can be leveraged into large percentage cost reductions. Of course, this is quite obvious in a simple 23 element cost analysis. When the cost tree lists 2,500 to 10,000 cost items, this Pareto effect is not as obvious to a casual observer of cost elements when performing a random analysis.

3. **Drawing a cost-times-usage curve:** A Canadian company, producing industrial pressure vessels in Ontario Province, found that even with the installation of their Materials Requirement Planning system, they still had too much inventory and too many stockouts. This seemed to be a situational dichotomy to management, until they reviewed their total line items on a cost-times-usage, descending-order curve. (See Figure 7-5). It was discovered that the most expensive cost-times-usage items (called "A" items in inventory management) were accounted for by 12% of the discrete part numbers, but equalled 84% of the total value of inventory on hand.

Like most companies employing an MRP system, the management group believed in the reported numbers without questioning them on a sampling basis. This created an enormous opportunity for savings. This opportunity was based on two existing fallacious assumptions:

a. all stockouts can be overcome by attacking them as though they are equally felt and equally resolvable—regardless of whether the stockout occurs for an "A" or "C" item; and

b. across-the-board stock reduction mandates are simple and effective routes to reductions in the cost of carrying materials.

Consider that stockouts occur by line item, irrespective of their positions on the cost times usage Pareto Curve. Thus, if all line items are treated equally, a company is more likely to have 3–4 times as many stockouts for "C" items than for "A" items, since there are 3–4 times as many items in this category. The leveraging factor discloses that, with very little additional cost, "C" item stocks, purchasing quantities or

Figure 7–5 Elements of Cost Pareto Leveraging Analysis

MODEL #16032

ESTIMATE – $1,635

CODE –	M	=	Material – Other than in P.I.
	P.I.	=	Purchased Item (P.I.)
	D.L.	=	Direct Labor
	I.	=	Indirect Labor
	O.	=	Overhead, Burden or Other

1st LEVEL	*1A*		*1B*		*1C*		*1D*		*1E*	
	$680	P.I.	$94	D.L.	$56	D.L.	$158	P.I.	$100	P.I.
	100	D.L.	80	O.	44	M.	12	I.	12	M
	45	I.	52	I.	30	O.	6	D.L.	10	D.L.
	27	O.	49	M.	30	I.	4	O.	6	O.
	11	M.	——		26	P.I.	——		3	I.
TOTAL	$863		$275		$186		$180		$131	

1st LEVEL PARETO   (22% of Items = 69% of Cost)

RANK	*ITEM*	*CUM*	*RANK*	*ITEM*	*CUM*	*RANK*	*ITEM*	*CUM*
1	1A (P.I.)	$680	6	1B (O.)	$1212	11	1C (M.)	$1458
2	1D (P.I.)	838	7	1C (D.L.)	1268	12	1C (O.)	1488
3	1E (P.I.)	938	8	1B (I.)	1320	13	1C (I.)	1518
4	1A (D.L.)	1038	9	1B (M.)	1369	14	1A (C.)	1545
5	1B (D.L.)	1132	10	1A (I.)	1414	15	1C (P.I.)	1571
						23	1E (I.)	$1,635

safety stocks can be increased by as much as 50% to reduce 75% of the stockouts. At the same time, "A" item inventories need to be reduced by a mere 10% to equal this planned increase in the "C" item stocks.

Thus, leveraging analysis can indicate the opportunity for a sizable stockout reduction, requiring a small savings in a significant few "A" item inventories. At the same time, these savings can more than offset increases required in "C" item inventories to significantly reduce stockouts. This materials leverage is not available to inventory controllers who treat all materials requirement planning (MRP) inventories, purchasing policies and possession costs as if they are equal.

After five months of applying cost and stockout reduction strategies to meet the real stratified needs of inventory asset control, stockouts were reduced to an infinitesimal percentage factor, while at the same time, the total materials cost on hand balance dropped $6 million (Canadian dollars), or about 8% of the previous value.

Compare the above with results that are usually obtained in the same circumstance, solely as a result of a mandated directive to "cut material costs across the board, while at the same time reduce stockouts to nil!" When all items are treated as if they are equal in cost effect and in relation to stockouts, the existence of leveraging data is missed. The use of Pareto Analysis highlights both the opportunities and the action options. In many cost reduction programs, this type of analysis tool is provided for managers at all levels of an operation.

APPLYING LEVERAGING PRINCIPLES TO VALUE ANALYSIS ACTIVITIES

Purchasing and design functions are in the forefront of the value analysis impact on procedures, processes and products. In the office environment, much progress has been made utilizing these principles of analysis to eliminate unnecessary paperwork and procedures that add cost but not value to service-type operations.

Consider that in today's information explosion context, almost everything you may wish to know can be made available through a network of terminals in an electronic data interchange (EDI). But, "like to know" is different than "need to know," and significant data should be separated from insignificant information so as to emphasize cost reduction opportunities. This approach should minimize the gut-feel approach, which concludes, "I know what is significant, but pennies saved add up to dollars in your pocket." This is true where one has an infinite amount of time and talent to apply to cost improvement. Leveraging allows for prioritization of scarce personnel skills by directing effort to areas where small gains can result in significant savings.

Value analysis (as well as value engineering) principles have been with us for over half a century, yet they are still conducted as one-shot analyses at most companies. Successful applications, annually documented in *Purchasing* magazine (Cahners Publishing, Boston) are the result of ongoing analyses, sitting task forces and top management attention.

The most successful applications are those where the savings of material, personnel, time and design are shown to be significant cost savers over a period of time. Therefore, prior to applying value analysis to a procedure, product or process, it seems logical to select the area for the application of this effort. Does cost leveraging analysis, like Pareto Analysis, precede the structured work performed by a group as they plod through the steps of a value analysis? Why not set the priorities of value analysis for the few significant areas of cost reduction opportunities, before spending significant effort in the less significant opportunity areas?

APPLYING LEVERAGING TO JUST-IN-TIME APPLICATIONS

The logistical goal of just-in-time (JIT) applications is to reduce the sitting time of the material asset from receipt through assembly, as well as in the finished goods warehouse.

Figure 7-6 depicts, in a simplistic manner, the lack of a direct relationship between input, output and materials on hand. This is a cost reduction opportunity which can be turned into cost savings through directed (leveraged) analyses. It seems obvious that those relationships which are most costly, i.e., in terms of the ratio of input/output to possessed assets sitting between these events, should receive the highest priority by those responsible for instituting a JIT system.

Figure 7–6   Input/Output Analysis in Just-In-Time Application

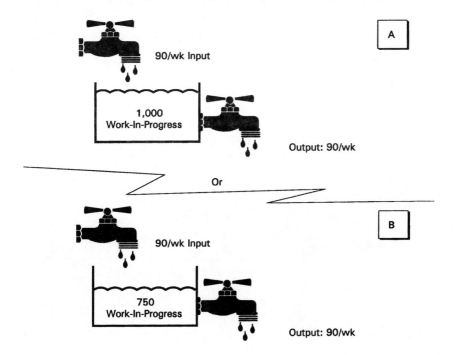

Two other examples of leveraging are depicted in Figures 7-7 and 7-8. In Figure 7-7, the asset possession analysis is carried down to the individual operations or groups of operations in a department. In this case, all inventory behind an operation is measured in terms of time, that is; the time to be worked on in the operation it is supporting. Theoretically, the supporting inventory should be zero. This is mostly achieved in automated assembly operations where the activities of the robotic equipment is programmed to provide sequential operations in a time-phased module.

However, for most of the readers of this book, seeking immediate cost saving through inexpensive techniques, the measurement of the sitting inventory, as a time factor of the capacity of the operation it supports, will provide the necessary base data for determining the significant few areas requiring priority sitting time analysis.

Figure 7-8 is a graphical presentation of machine and skill balancing, appropriately named during World War II as "bottleneck" analysis. In this situation, sequential operations are aligned with one another in terms of their capacity to produce. This is not derived from actual performance, but is related to the capacity to produce, which comes from a performance capability analysis of equipment, manning crews, as well as through estimating personnel standards of performance for various process and product mixes. Using past actual production data may be meaningless, since this information includes wait and down times

Figure 7–7   Diagram of Input/Output Relative to the Sitting Asset

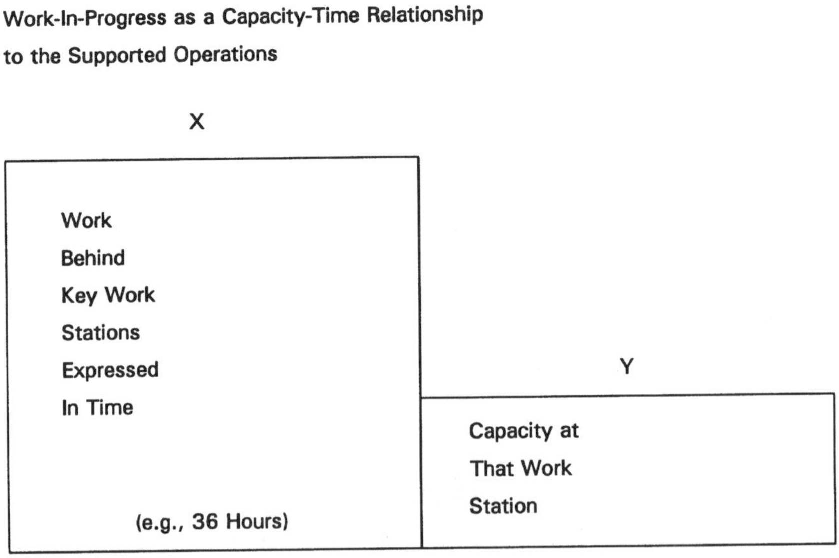

Work-In-Progress as a Capacity-Time Relationship
to the Supported Operations

Figure 7–8   Diagram of Input/Output Relative to the Sitting Asset

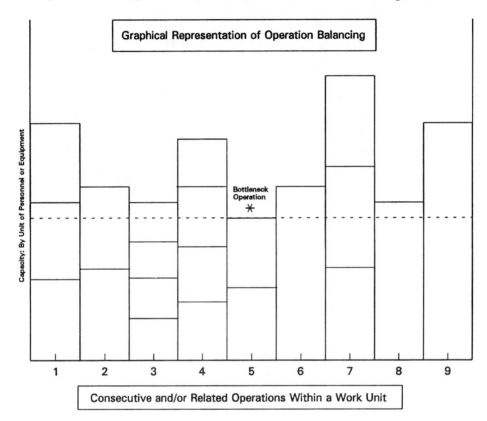

caused by either planned attempts at balancing operations, or individual employee or supervisory efforts to reduce work-in-process.

There is no need to add manpower or equipment to improve operations #1–9 less #5, since their capacities exceed the bottleneck capacity. The bottleneck operation must be addressed first to have an effect on input in man and machine hours vs. output in terms of the value of units produced.

Other cost reduction opportunities relate to the following management philosophies concerning sequential related operations:

a. The faster capacity operations in a single center, or a series of faster operations in a unique geographical location, produce inventory for all the slower operations.

b. By design, or by concerted performance reaction of the whole group, the slowest operation(s) determine the rate of output for the entire group. In Figure 7-8, no cost reduction can have the same immediate effect as improving the performance of operation #5.

c. The object of this work is to:
    (1) increase output with the same input,
    (2) decrease the amount of assets required to produce at the current level, such as eliminating a unit of capacity (person or piece of equipment) from operations #1, 4 and 7, or
    (3) employ a combination of (1) and (2).

A simple sitting time formula can be applied, which establishes ratios to be improved through specific, directed scheduling techniques:

$$\text{WAITING TIME RATIO} = \frac{\text{THRUPUT (MEASURED AS LEAD TIME)}}{\text{ACTUAL TIME ON OPERATIONS}} - 1$$

A short-cut approach is simply to sum the hours of operation as depicted on the operation sheets. This figure becomes the numerator. The resultant number is then divided by the actual total time it takes to progress through the entire sequence of operations. The difference in the two time values is a measurement of sitting time, while the ratio, resulting from the formula shown above, becomes the benchmark for measuring improvement from the present situation.

In Just-In-Time scheduling practice, cost reductions come from recognizing the existing inequality in related capacities and balancing the application of resources in order to achieve improved ratios of output to input. Bottleneck analysis is one method of leveraging, where the most significant operation creates the opportunity to make small significant improvements to achieve a disproportionately larger result of reduced costs.

HOW TO IMPROVE TIME MANAGEMENT WITH LEVERAGING

A major asset that is commonly overlooked in cost reduction pursuits is time. Yet, improved time management is a recognizable, though not easily measurable, cost reduction technique. The reason for this is that unless you can prove that saved time is used for another profitable purpose, the positive results achieved are difficult to classify as cost reductions.

The cost reduction aspects of improved time management will be covered in detail in Chapter Nine. However, the subject is introduced here because the leveraging concept is put to use in time management to overcome the plaintive cry of overworked managers, "I don't have time for time management!" This is probably true where all aspects of the manager's tasks are treated equally, without regard to potential payback as a limiting factor in the effort/time commitment ratio.

This is an easily identified problem for many managers, who are concerned with time spent vs. payback. The two main approaches that are simply applied, and set up a leveraged analysis, are:

(1) personal commitment analysis, and

(2) subjective goal ranking.

Figure 7-9 is a sample list that was prepared by a financial officer in a prominent New England firm. The "PLAN" column (his personal commitment) was prepared prior to the annual budgetary period (April to March). The "ACTUAL" figures were derived from a combination of time diarying and activity sampling (to be described in Chapter Nine).

Granted that priorities do change within a year of activity, it is obvious that this cursory analysis did show a marked difference between planned and actual time spent on projects. The differences in actual use of time from planned use also related to the priorities of the projects as they evolved during the period under analysis. However, as a rough guide to time use vs. plan, the financial manager felt that improved time management planning was definitely required in the upcoming year.

The key here was that the time management effectiveness was not measured against some nebulous past time usage, but against the important management tasks that were planned. Leveraging demanded that the tasks be prioritized in order of importance as they related to results expected by the enterprise. Thus, three out of the ten projects were denoted as "high priority," and two as "priority" . . . such that 50%

Figure 7–9   Plan vs. Actual Time Management

	This Year	
	Plan	*Actual*
Financial Planning and Relations	10%	2%
Credit, Collections, and Insurance	10%	17%
General and Cost Accounting	20%	4%
Budgetary Planning and Control	20%	31%
Tax Preparation	5%	6%
Internal Audit	5%	1%
System and Procedures	10%	0%
Fund Management	10%	21%
Data Processing	5%	1%
Financial Counseling	5%	12%
Training	0%	2%
Other	0%	3%
	100%	100%

of the tasks required improved planning and a greater concern for time management to achieve these prioritized goals.

To assure that he was not planning in a vacuum, the financial manager compared his independently prepared priorities with those of his manager. There are few more discouraging situations than to have goal setting and prioritizing at odds with your superior. The oft-heard laments are, "I didn't know you really wanted that!", and "Was that expected of me . . . and, when you say?"

Figure 7-10 is an example of the list of tasks for the following year as ranked, independently, by the financial manager and then by his boss. Obviously, an in-depth discussion of relative priorities was called for between the two managers, a review that, in reality is ongoing, and in this case lasted for the entire ensuing year. Alignment of priorities is a major step in both focusing and leveraging your management of time. The ranking achieved by a consensus of goals should provide the leveraging factor for prioritized planning of your time expended vs. agreed goals to be achieved.

PLANNING TIME CONTROL

The steps in planning time control to utilize the leveraging concept are:

Figure 7–10   Comparing Your Goals with Those of Your Manager

Your Ranking		Your Boss' Ranking
1	Introduce new labor control procedure	4
7	Put in new government contract cost controls	3
3	Change physical inventorying verification	6
8	Weigh L.I.F.O. change and gain approval	2
2	Eliminate parallel system in receiver verification	8
5	Prepare better graphics for divisional presentations	7
9	Recruit and/or train your potential replacement	5
10	Rearrange your office layout	10
6	Reduce number of people reporting to you to four	9
4	Close E.O.M. reports within 2 days; quarterlies in 3	1

(1) Find out how you are presently using your time by categories of work. (A detailed description of a 5-minute per day technique is explained in Chapter Nine.)

(2) Match these against your job objectives, which should be evaluated in conjunction with your boss' objectives for you.

(3) Develop procedures to reduce or eliminate time spent on lesser or unimportant tasks.

(4) Add the saved time from #(3) above to the time to be spent on more important tasks.

(5) Keep checking, on a regular basis, to assure that your goals are being achieved. If not, revise your goals or time expenditure.

As has been the theme of this Chapter, separate the significant from the insignificant, so that, by leveraging, small savings in significant areas can be more effective than across-the-board actions. This should lead to a more efficient approach to achieving improvements than are usually obtained from treating all data and inputs as equal.

SUMMING UP: How to Effect Large Savings for Relatively Minimal Effort

Strategically applying the limited management resources of time, talent and funds, when seeking cost improvements is a fruitful pursuit to gaining significant savings from the use of minimum effort and assets.

The first step is to organize data in appropriate cells. In the problem-solving world this step is called leveraged analysis. Prior to taking this step, you should consider the new approaches to solving problems, such as the non-linear breakthrough techniques that have come to the fore. These approaches have been developed as a response to the theory of chaotic events vs. the linear thinkers' tranquil theory of order that is simply out-of-control. For our purposes, both the Newtonian linear, as well as the non-linear, chaotic theorists all could use leveraged data inputs to measure base data and improvements therefrom.

Leveraging is a grouping of data for analysis that allows the manager to seek out the few significant factors that are potential sources of significant improvements. Consider that analysis techniques do exist, such as multi-variable analysis and simulation and linear programming—each of which can assimilate all available data, actual and extrapolated forecasts, and then merge these inputs with experienced viewpoints in order to develop viable management options to improve profitability. Leveraging is a short-cut for quickly moving forward to expose the better options.

The maintenance concept, "Don't fix it if it ain't broke" has seen its day. Cut the fat approaches require creative thinking as well as anticipation of problems, such as recognizing that your competition is also trying to solve the same problems as you are coping with today. Even the continuous improvement (kaizen) and value analysis concepts can gain from applying the leveraging concept during the analysis phase; this, by allowing the manager to move more quickly to significantly more favorable outcomes.

A very popular leveraging approach is Pareto Analysis, which when viewed from the aspect of the opportunity curve, allows instant recognition of where management talent, time and funds can be used most effectively to achieve cost reductions. A prime example of the use of the opportunity curve was shown as it related to the analysis of a product or process cost "family tree".

Other applications of leveraging principles surface when:

- auditing a materials requirement planning system,
- instituting a Just-In-Time application,
- determining make-or-buy solutions,
- analyzing contributors to off-quality situations,
- making partnering decisions for single sourcing,
- performing bottleneck analysis and sitting time studies,
- balancing capacity planning for internal scheduling with external suppliers.

There are also many applications of leveraging to time management, such that substantial time use savings can be achieved with a leveraged placement of management thinking. Managers can better evaluate their actual time use with their plans for using this valuable asset. In turn, comparing your goals to those desired by your manager can be a very fruitful effort, if the outcome is weighted by the results to be obtained from the effort expended through the use of leveraging.

Consider the leveraging concept as an extremely useful tool for moving quickly and inexpensively towards gaining significant savings with minimal effort.

C H A P T E R   8

CUT THE FAT WITH TRUE COSTING TECHNIQUES

The compilation of direct costs for services and product has long been known to be quite accurate, and can be made even more so through the expenditure of some additional data collection costs. At the same time, the applications of indirect and overhead charges, primarily through percentage allocations, have been close approximations at best. In fact, the major drive in the mid-Twentieth Century was to assure the total absorption of these indirect and overhead charges as they were added to the direct costs of products or services.

During the middle of the Twentieth Century, Profit/Volume Analyses were the rage. P/V analyses changed the way management looked at fixed and semi-fixed costs. In fact, it was the introduction of P/V studies that made cost accountants and general management personnel aware of the applications of semi-fixed, or semi-variable costs when attempting to define true costing for this analysis tool.

ANALYZING THE COST VS. BENEFIT OF TRUE COSTING

There are very few pure variable costs; direct materials' costs are a prime and perhaps a solitary example. But, almost all other costs that were considered either fixed or variable proved to be purely neither. The vast majority of fixed costs were fixed only within set volumes, and most variable costs contained fixed elements . . . also within specified volume limits peculiar to a specific company or group of operations.

However, even with the vagaries associated with approximating the fixed and variable portions of costs, the P/V tool still proved that analysis of true costs could be a valuable cost reduction tool, as well as a better guide to improving pricing and profitability strategies.

The latest revolution, leading us closer to true costing, takes advantage of computerized cost breakdowns, activity sampling, and the simulation of forecasted events. Activity Based Costing (ABC) rose to popularity in the early 1980's as a technique to both measure and improve the application of indirect and overhead costs. Competing in the bidding wars with local and foreign competition requires a true cost knowledge of each process that absorbs indirect and overhead costs; sometimes referred to as contributions or allocations. No longer is the gross application of a percentage value for indirect and overhead charges a simple and acceptable costing method.

In this chapter, you will be shown both the cost-cutting advantages resulting from performing profit/volume analyses, as well as opportunities to cut the fat through the use of activity based costing. Only those portions of these techniques that relate directly to cost reduction options for the manager will be covered. Obviously, more accurate costing applications have many other uses in:

- modifying marketing plans,
- pricing policymaking,
- tax reduction strategies,
- the timing of equipment procurement relative to forecasted cash flow,
- facility location and layout,
- methods improvement in both support and supported operations,
- as a superior tool when bidding for work,
- determining training or pooling of skills for crew applications, and
- as a prelude to the acquisition of external operations, such as contractors and/or other outside capacities.

SEPARATING FIXED COSTS
FROM VARIABLE ONES

No true costing process generates as much interest and apprehension as when separating the fixed portions of total costs from the variable portions. However, this single, significant process activates inquiry into areas of cost improvement that have long been masked by the indiscriminate merging of these two distinct types of costs.

Three examples of the importance of this separation for determining true costing are span of control, material add-on costs, and purchase order costing.

HOW SPAN OF CONTROL IMPACTS TRUE COSTING

For many years prior to the 1970's, when employees were first empowered to make vital decisions at their workplaces, a concept of span of control stated that supervisors, especially those on the first level, could effectively manage only 6 same-skilled employees performing like duties. Group operations and the team approach have pretty much destroyed this dogma, so that it is no longer mentioned or even relevant to today's operations in both the office and on the factory floor.

In its wake, direct employees now perform some indirect work, such as:

- inspection of both incoming and their own work,
- initiating methods improvements,
- attending productivity meetings,
- providing temporary supervision of their peers,
- data entry,
- expediting and scheduling work,
- materials handling inter- and intra-departments,
- receiving both formal and informal training at the workplace, etc.

If a company is to aggressively cut direct labor costs, it behooves those managers responsible, to determine that portion of direct labor input which may be diluted by the indirect labor content expected of those bearing the title, "direct labor". Cutting the fat without harming the muscle may be more effectively achieved by seeking ways to maximize existing direct labor skills and time use as direct labor services.

Two techniques for effectively and inexpensively acquiring this information will be described in the next section of this chapter.

HOW TRUE COSTING AFFECTS MATERIAL ADD-ON COSTS

When Just-In-Time techniques appeared on the scene, an army of material controllers and purchasing personnel hailed the achievement of dramatic savings in the carrying costs of inventory. These carrying costs were traditionally used to improve decisions regarding the scheduling of batches of work, the use of personnel and equipment, and control of the cost add-ons of warehousing, materials movement, and picking, packing and shipping activities. However, many of the claimed savings did not drop to the bottom line because of the lack of understanding of the differences between the fixed and variable portions of inventory carrying costs. Thus, a 20% per year carrying cost reduction was a phantom carrying cost saving in many companies. This was especially true when the reported savings emanated from those eager to justify the costs of the J-I-T installation. (A detailed analysis of cost factors in materials control practices is contained in Chapter Eight of *Managing Inventory for Cost Reduction,* N. Kobert, Prentice Hall, 1992.) Consider the following:

- The cost of storage is barely diminished when less materials occupy the same space as when there was a surplus of inventory in the same space. Depreciation costs for both plant and warehouse will remain constant until the building is sold, leased out, or demolished. J-I-T programs allow for the options to reducing these fixed costs, not the automatic savings associated with less inventory investment. Less usage of a fixed cost element does not diminish the cost. In fact it spreads the cost over less product, until a positive real estate action is taken.

- The costs of heat and other air conditioning will usually increase as less space is occupied, since these costs are now required for heating and cooling more space than when the stored materials inventory was larger.

- Materials handling is usually dependent on the number of moves, either transport empty (TE) or transport loaded (TL). Personnel and equipment are required to move materials as needed for assembly, to and from incoming inspection, from receiving dock to point of disbursement or storage, etc. All of these transports are costed by moves, not the size of the inventory sitting on shelves, pallet racks, or in bins. Thus, when a fork lift driver moves to a stack of three pallet racks (one TE), then removes one pallet and carries it to the first operation (one TL), this work is performed independent of the amount of material stored at either the place where it was picked, or the area to which it is moved. In fact, to reduce inventory on-hand, many companies have gone to smaller, more frequent deliveries from their suppliers, thus increasing required moves. Logically, one can see that materials handling costs either will remain the same, or may even increase as more receipts are received! Therefore, to achieve the goals of J-I-T, it is imperative that the ancillary costs of materials handling be factored into the savings calculation so that procedures for movement can be improved.

- The one cost that is definitely reduced is the cost of money to fund a smaller vs. a larger inventory. For this reason, the cost of money is considered an opportunity cost, since any reduction in materials costs should provide the opportunity to use these released funds for other purposes, at the very least to reduce debt service.

HOW TRUE COSTING CHANGES PURCHASE ORDER COSTING

Cost analysts cringe when someone from their company declares, "A purchase order costs $14.72!" To which the usual comeback is, "If we reduce the number of purchase orders by 1,000 next year, through blanket ordering, consignment stocking or vendor storage, will we show an additional $14,720 on the bottom line?"

You probably could save the variable costs of purchasing, which are minuscule, by placing less orders. However, the major purchasing costs are fixed, such as for buyers' salaries, office support personnel, travel, negotiators and contract enforcement personnel, certification trainers, value analysts, etc. Consider that the staff required to manage a modern purchasing office is largely a fixed expense related to the value of the services performed, not a pure variable cost related to the amount of orders processed. This is further exacerbated by the fact that a majority of order placements are being moved on to those requiring the purchased service or product (users), as a logical evolution of ongoing ordering activity being separated from the contract negotiators' tasks.

HOW TRUE COSTING MAKES COMMONLY USED BREAKEVEN CURVES OBSOLETE

Figure 8-1 depicts the usual breakeven curve that appears in most academic textbooks on cost analysis. It assumes that fixed costs remain at the same level throughout, while variable costs are a straight line from the very first sale that becomes an account receivable. This type of analysis makes no attempt to delineate semi-fixed and semi-variable costs, which generally account for the majority of cost elements. These costs are usually referred to as mixed costs, or step costs or variable fixed costs.

To better understand this, see Figure 8-2, which demonstrates how many fixed costs vary at specific volume limits. In other words, many so-called fixed costs are fixed within limits, and then they step up (or down) to the next level of fixed costs.

Figure 8-1   Textbook Depiction of Breakeven Cost Analysis

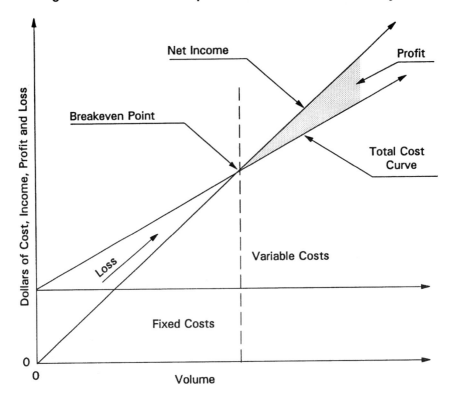

SEPARATING COSTS WHEN EVALUATING POTENTIAL COST IMPROVEMENTS

Profit/Volume Analysis is a technique of analyzing costs (and profits) at various levels of volume to determine the true:

- breakeven point
- relationship between profit and volume
- amount of fixed costs
- margin of safety
- cost improvement effect on profits (as well as effect of volume, and/or product or service price changes independent of cost improvements)

A grasp of these relationships is important in order to weigh the effects of various potential cost improvements, especially as these relate to limited investment resources, which force the manager to prioritize program initiations.

Figure 8-2   Step Costs as True Cost Analysis of Fixed Costs

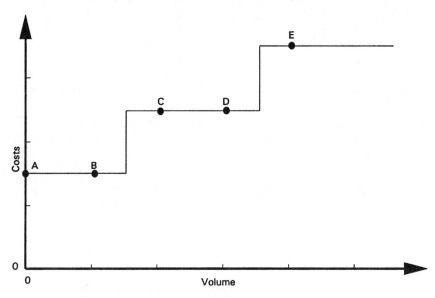

EXAMPLES - Supervision, Materials Handling, Building Costs,
Purchasing, Inspection, Maintenance, etc. As well as many
Staff Services such as Legal, Accounting, Data Processing,
Personnel, Training, etc.

THREE METHODS TO DETERMINE BASE
DATA FOR PROFIT/VOLUME ANALYSES

There are three accepted methods to determine the base data required
to perform a meaningful P/V analysis. The manager should decide on
the technique which is both results and cost effective.

ANALYZING EACH COST ELEMENT
SEPARATELY IS THE MOST EXPENSIVE
CLASSIFICATION TECHNIQUE

The most accurate and expensive approach is to analyze each element of cost in order to classify them as fixed, variable or mixed. This
requires capturing and separating cost factors as they occur in actual
practice. In Chapter Seven, where the leveraging approach was covered, the reader is advised to consider choosing, to analyze in detail,
but 1 out of 5 cost elements that would probably cover 75%–85% of the
total costs being considered. This could reduce the cost of data collection without harming the basic purpose of this exercise.

USING ACTIVITY SAMPLING IS A LESS EXPENSIVE APPROACH TO GAINING TRUE COST DATA

These same data may be collected by activity sampling, described in the next Chapter (Nine). The collection technique is far less expensive, but the results will be approximations of the total population of events drawn from reliably observed random samples. This technique may require an unacceptable span of time to garner data of any significance, even though the total time commitment for the analysis would probably be less than 15 minutes per day.

FITTING CURVES TO PLOTTED POINTS CAN DETERMINE TRUE COST FACTORS

A popular and fairly accurate way to determine the true cost types for each cost element, utilizes the point plotting and line fitting approach, which can be handled off-line by any personal computer, or with a terminal to an EDI network. This can also be done fairly accurately by a visual point plot followed by a manual approximation of a line of regression, such as that described in the following paragraphs. The manual method also will help the analyzer understand the expected results to be obtained by using available computer mathematics.

This technique requires collecting data such as that shown in Figure 8-3. Shown are sample data collected as they relate to the base data of "standard hours produced," the volume portion of the p/v analysis in some companies. Some service companies use dollars of sales as the volume consideration. Your financial manager can determine the most propitious base figure to define volume, by selecting same from: hours expended, budgeted costs, gross or net sales, weighted number of orders shipped, completed projects, pounds produced, etc. The main criterion is that the chosen base figure is representative of the volume of output, be it in dollars produced, end result, or hours of output.

Figure 8-4 is a graphic presentation of the figures collected in Figure 8-3. A regression line was eye-balled for both operating supplies and set-up labor. (As stated previously, a least squares line of regression could be calculated.) Both of these cost factors are usually considered indirect costs, which are then added to a base for costing, sometimes as a percentage add-on.

Note that the regression line for "operating supplies" intersects the "y" axis not at zero, but at $0.65m. This is the fixed portion

Figure 8-3 Sample of Data Collected
for Cost Identification

A large job machine shop has as two of its items "Operating Supplies" and "Set-Up Labor." A study of cost records revealed the following data:

(000's omitted in Columns A and B)

		A	B
Month	Std. Hrs. Produced	Cost of Operating Supplies	Cost of Set-Up Labor
J	26,000	$1,400	$2,300
F	27,000	1,650	2,230
M	28,000	1,800	2,700
A	24,000	1,250	1,770
M	21,000	1,150	1,125
J	21,000	1,450	1,300
J	20,000	1,300	1,220
A	23,000	1,160	1,710
S	29,000	1,430	2,770
O	30,000	1,800	2,730
N	30,500	1,610	2,780
D	25,000	1,600	1,720

of a mixed cost, which is used in the formula for a straight line as follows:

$$y = a + bx$$

where:

a= the fixed portion of the cost factor measured from zero to the regression line intersect of the "y" axis

b = the multiplier, which is the result of dividing the "y" cost increase by the equivalent increase in the "x" factor of standard hours produced. (This multiplier is also referred to as the tangent calculation of opposite over adjacent.)

x = the base cost factor, which in this case is standard hours produced per month.

Thus, the formula for the mixed cost of operating supplies is: Any point on the y axis = 650 + 300/3,000 times standard hours produced. This formula can be used to budget or predict the mixed cost factor called "operating supplies."

**Figure 8-4   Graphic Presentation of Individual Mixed
and Variable Cost Factors**

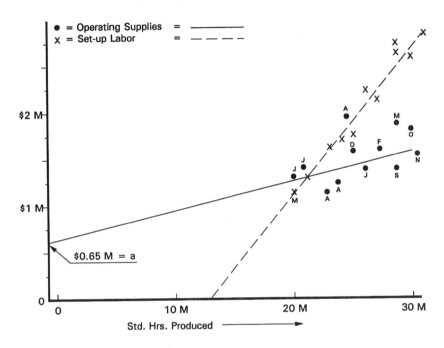

Std. Hrs. Produced ⟶

USING THE LEVERAGING PRINCIPLE IN TRUE COST ANALYSIS

As was discussed in Chapter Seven on leveraging, when seeking cost improvements you should determine those areas where a small effort can leverage up to a large effect on costs. For operating supplies, the fixed costs associated with this mixed cost, account for about 45% of the total cost in the average monthly operating range. Thus, it would be simpler to analyze this single cost factor—which is probably an add-on percentage figure in actual practice—than to review the many variable costs also charged as "operating supplies." This cost improvement selection process will also be covered later in this chapter when Activity Based Costing is discussed.

Set-up costs present another opportunity for the manager. It appears that this cost is a pure variable cost starting from minimum set-up hours required when only 1300 standard hours are produced. Most likely, below a certain number of hours produced during the month, set-up costs are absorbed as the indirect portion of direct labor hours. Since set-up hours are usually more expensive than the usual direct

Figure 8-5   An Example of a Minimum Fixed Cost Ratio in a Mixed Cost Element

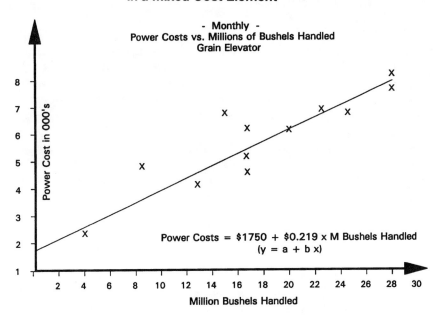

labor hours being supported, it may be appropriate to compare an increase of all set-up costs being absorbed by direct labor vs. the present arrangement. This may indicate a trade-off, when compared to a minimum loss of standard hours produced vs. a reduction in overall costs to produce these same standard hours.

Figure 8-5 depicts another example of a mixed cost analysis. This time the cost base is "bushels handled" in a grain elevator, compared to the mixed cost factor of power supplied to handle these millions of bushels, plus other required power uses.

Note here that the fixed portion of the mixed costs is overwhelmed by the variable portion by almost 5:1. In seeking cost improvements, it is obvious that a project to reduce the cost of administrative office and parking lot area lighting, should command a much lower priority during capital project approval time than a small variable power cost saving related to the physical handling of the grain. It would take a $5,000 fixed cost saving to equate to a variable cost saving of $1,000 per bushel handled. This is confirmed by a look at the calculated power cost formula:

POWER COSTS = $1750 + $0.219 × Millions of BUSHELS HANDLED

TOTAL PROFIT/VOLUME ANALYSIS REVEALS OTHER COST REDUCTION OPTIONS

As was stated earlier on in this chapter, analyzing each cost factor is a much more precise technique than determining a broad, overview relationship gained through a total company profit/volume analysis. Any detailed analysis entails more time and cost than any overview analysis, even where the formulas are directly programmed to convert the raw input data. Where a good correlation of plotted points is achieved in an overview analysis, this may allow the manager to choose a leveraged approach to the analysis of the detailed cost accounts, i.e., by choosing to analyze but 1 out of 4 cost accounts it may be possible to achieve the maximum initial cost reduction results that will drop to the bottom line.

CONSIDER THE LEARNING CURVE EFFECT

The learning curve effect can be factored into all of these profit/volume analyses to:

- determine incremental increases in costs for successive quantities of newly introduced products or services
- provide a more factual basis for estimating both start-up and learning costs to be incurred prior to the initiation of full-scale operations, as well as to consider where full-scale operations are never to be achieved
- provide buyers with an objective and analytical device for negotiation with potential suppliers, based both on past order and price experiences as well as on projected cost reductions to be gained on future orders placed with these vendors
- serve as a base analytical tool for make-or-buy decisions, by comparing past, present and projected in-company estimated costs with outside bids for the same work

The learning curve analysis is a significant step in cost reduction tactics because:

- in the early stages of the introduction of new services or products, efforts are concentrated on "making it work." Debugging and redesign efforts usually result in higher than anticipated costs when a full-scale sales and/or production effort is launched.
- when the emphasis shifts from stabilizing performance to cost reduction, the learning curve effect is no longer a factor, such that costs fall into the "straight line" of predictable results from planned cost reduction efforts.

Caution: Cost records must be established so that costs are segregated by individual products and/or services, and this data must be provided by batch or individual quantity as the start-up progresses. This is important since the learning curve effect is a graduated, sometimes accelerated costing analysis, usually not applicable to non-start up products or services.

Although not obligatory, the prudent manager should consider the learning curve effect when budgeting costs for start-up operations. This will assure greater cost estimating accuracy as well as provide for a better definition of cost improvement opportunities.

SIMULATING TOTAL COMPANY PROFIT IMPROVEMENT FROM POSITIVE COST REDUCTION ACTIONS

As stated earlier, the P/V analysis can also be used to examine total company cost improvement options before turning them into actions. This can best be described by the example that follows.

Figure 8-6 shows a simple profit and loss statement drawn from an average period prior to any contemplated cost reduction actions being taken. This information is plotted in Figure 8-7.

Figure 8-6 Example of Monthly Profit and Loss Statement

MONTHLY PROFIT & LOSS STATEMENT
(Before Any Cost Reductions)

Income—Sales

Product A—50,000 units @ $2.40 apiece = $120,000
Product B—40,000 units @ $2.50 apiece = *$100,000*
  Total Sales $220,000

Expenses	*Variable*	*Fixed*	*Total*	
Material	$ 44,000	$	$ 44,000	
Labor	50,000		50,000	
Indirect Labor		5,000	5,000	
Tools	7,500	7,500	15,000	
Supplies	5,000	5,000	10,000	
Depreciation		20,000	20,000	
Selling Expenses	4,000	30,000	34,000	
Administrative Expenses		35,000	35,000	
	$110,500	$102,500	$213,000	
Total Expenses				213,000
Profit				$ 7,000

Figure 8–7   Profit/Volume Chart - Monthly

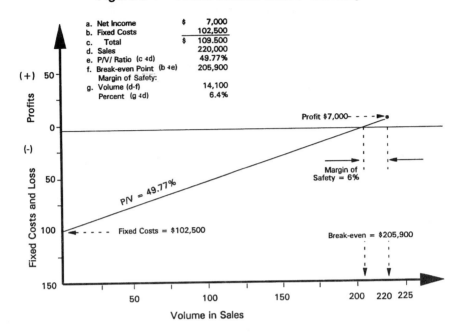

(Note—If the individual costs are not detailed by fixed vs. variable portions, the total of these two elements can be derived by the very same technique shown earlier on in this chapter, i.e., by simply plotting a regression line from sales vs. profit (and/or loss) figures from a representative past series of monthly data for individual cost factors.)

Now, consider the following calculations in Figure 8-7:

- The P/V ratio is gained by dividing the total fixed costs that are absorbed plus the profit (or loss) realized, both divided by the volume base, which in this case is net sales.

- The breakeven point is derived by dividing the total of all fixed costs by the P/V ratio. Compare this realistic approach to understanding mixed costs to the figure which might have been derived by the traditional breakeven analysis shown in Figure 8-1.

- The margin of safety can be expressed as a measure of volume, which in this example is sales, or it can be expressed as a percentage of total sales, i.e., sales above the breakeven $14,100 or as 6.4% = $14,100/$220,000 x 100.

Our purpose is to simulate the effects of attempting various fat cutting options as they impact the bottom line profits. Remember, our goal is to cut the fat, not the muscle. Therefore, let us assume that our

first comparisons will measure those actions which will be taken to reduce fixed costs, including fixed portions of mixed costs, by contem-
plating the following actions:

- Improved tool designs will allow for price reductions which were
  being quoted by outside contractors.
- New small tool requisition system will be installed.
- Maintenance crewing procedure will reduce two-shift crews by
  two persons per shift.
- First line supervisors suggested new monthly supply requisition
  expense budgeting procedure.
- Disposition has been recommended for eight little-used, multipurpose tools in machine shop.
- Beginning this month, routine buying will be conducted by
  users, as opposed to all requisitions having to be handled
  through the Purchasing Department.
- Tying the new order entry system to the EDI network reduces
  entry requirements by two personnel.

Figure 8-8 indicates the simulated results of these actions.

Figure 8-8   Simulating Fixed Cost Reductions

MONTHLY PROFIT & LOSS STATEMENT
(With reduced fixed costs)

Results of the actions:

Income—Sales $220,000

Expenses	*Variable*	*Fixed*	*Total*	
Material	$ 44,000	$	$ 44,000	
Labor	50,000		50,000	
Indirect Labor		4,000 (a)	4,000	
Tools	7,500	7,000 (b)	14,500	
Supplies	5,000	4,500 (c)	9,500	
Depreciation		20,000 (d)	20,000	
Selling Expenses	4,000	28,000 (e)	32,000	
Administrative Expenses		30,000 (f)	30,000	
	$110,500	$93,500	$204,000	

Total Expenses 204,000

Profit Before Taxes $ 16,000

Figure 8–9 Profit/Volume Chart - Monthly (With Reduced Fixed Costs)

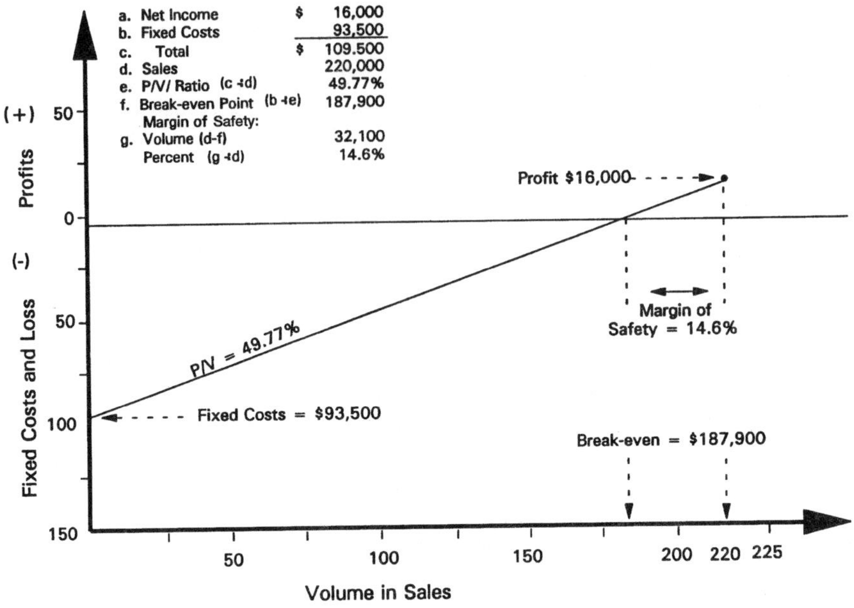
a. Net Income $ 16,000
b. Fixed Costs 93,500
c. Total $ 109.500
d. Sales 220,000
e. P/V/ Ratio (c ÷d) 49.77%
f. Break-even Point (b ÷e) 187,900
Margin of Safety:
g. Volume (d-f) 32,100
Percent (g ÷d) 14.6%
Profit $16,000
Margin of Safety = 14.6%
P/V = 49.77%
Fixed Costs = $93,500
Break-even = $187,900
(+)
Profits
(-)
Fixed Costs and Loss
50
0
50
100
150
50
100
150
200
220
225
Volume in Sales

Figure 8-10 Simulation of Reduced Variable Costs Only

MONTHLY PROFIT & LOSS STATEMENT (With Reduced Variable Costs)

Results of the Action:

Income—Sales				$220,000
Expenses	*Variable*	*Fixed*	*Total*	
Material	$ 43,000 (a)	$	$ 43,000	
Labor	48,500 (b)		48,500	
Indirect Labor		5,000	5,000	
Tools	7,500 (c)	7,500	14,500	
Supplies	4,500 (d)	5,000	9,500	
Depreciation		20,000	20,000	
Selling Expenses	4,000	30,000	34,000	
Administrative Expenses		35,000	35,000	
	$107,000	$102,500	$209,500	
Total				209,500
Profit Before Taxes				$ 10,500

Figure 8-9 is a profit/volume expression of these potential results. Note the effects of the reduction in fixed costs on:

- increased profits from $7,000 to $16,000,
- reduced breakeven point from $205,900 to $187,900
- increased margin of safety from 6% to 14.6% while the p/v ratio remains the same at 49.77%.

At the same time, recommendations for reducing variable costs have been proposed, while holding fixed costs at the level as they appear on Figure 8-6. Actions to reduce variable costs are as follows:

- Incorporate the value analysis direct materials' cost reductions proposed in the last quarter.
- Add the proposed single source, partnering proposals advanced by the purchasing department, which will reduce outside labor content and increase quality yields by sub-contractors.
- Introduce group workloads to empower direct labor to increase hours produced vs. hours of attendance.

Figure 8-10 depicts the simulation of these cost-cutting actions; while Figure 8-11 is a graphic p/v display of the results shown in the

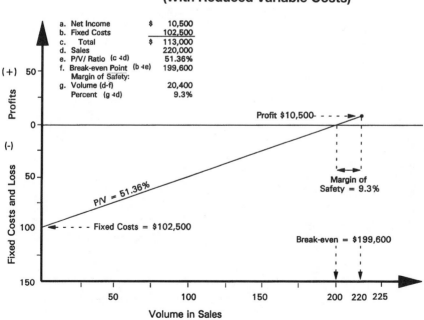

Figure 8–11 Profit/Volume Chart - Monthly (With Reduced Variable Costs)

Figure 8-12   Simulated Reductions In Both Fixed and Variable Costs

MONTHLY PROFIT & LOSS STATEMENT
(After Reductions in Fixed & Variable Costs)

Income—Sales $220,000

Expenses	Variable	Fixed	Total
Material	$ 43,000	$	$ 43,000
Labor	48,500		48,500
Indirect Labor		4,000	4,000
Tools	7,000	7,000	14,000
Supplies	4,500	4,500	9,000
Depreciation		20,000	20,000
Selling Expenses	4,000	28,000	32,000
Administrative Expenses		30,000	30,000
	$107,000	$ 93,500	$200,500

Total Expenses   200,500

Profit Before Taxes $ 19,500

Figure 8–13   Profit/Volume Chart - Monthly (After Reduction in Fixed Costs)

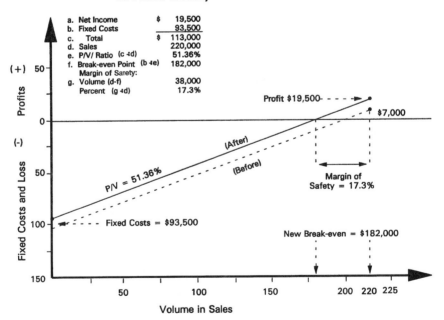

previous Figure 8-10. Comparisons with the base P/V analysis show the simulated increase in profit and margin of safety, as well as the decrease in the point of breakeven.

Figure 8-12 and the P/V graphic in Figure 8-13 are the most likely occurrence when a cost reduction program is underway, since they show a simultaneous reduction in both fixed and variable costs. This will obviously also include the fixed portion of variable costs as well as the step reductions in fixed costs. Comparisons with the base P/V situation are both obvious and positive.

As was stated in the opening chapters, cost reductions must be shown to drop to the bottom line on a continuing basis if we truly are cutting the fat not the muscle.

USING THE HIP ROOF CURVE TO SELECT COST REDUCTION OPTIONS

Simulations of the effects of cost reductions become even more informative when increases in volume are also simulated, sparked by price concessions based on cost reductions; and when various products and services are compared on a profit/volume basis, as to their contribution to overall profitability. See Figure 8-14.

Figure 8–14   Example of a P/V Hip Roof Curve

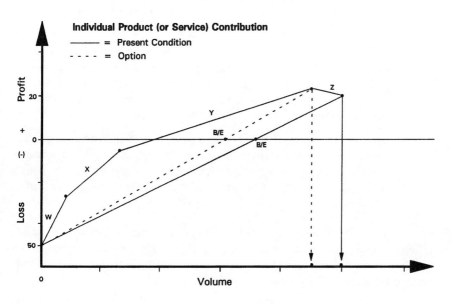

The profit/volume curve depicted in Figure 8-14 is called a hip roof curve. Products or services are plotted in descending order of their individual p/v ratio values. The total p/v curve can be plotted from reviewing a few past representative years' actual history of profit vs. volume. (One can also review a competitor's annual reports to picture their profit/volume history.)

Whichever technique is applied, from mathematical analysis to eyeballing regression lines, the hip roof curve of individual product or service p/v relationships will meet the total company p/v line at the profit or loss actual or projected value.

This type of p/v analysis presents the following cost reduction options:

- What is involved in order to stress cost reductions (or price increases) to make product "Z" profitable? Consider the formula for the p/v curve as:

RATE OF VARIABLE COST ABSORPTION = COSTS ABSORBED / VOLUME REQ'D TO ABSORB THESE COSTS (THE P/V RATIO)

when approaching other options:

- Product "Y" has, by far, the greatest volume of sales. How much of this is price related, such that a very small cost reduction, reflected in a very slight price reduction, can algebraically increase sales of this item as a leveraging affect? Or, in the face of inflationary pressures throughout the industry, how much can the volume of sales increase for "Y" when the price remains as before for this single item?

- If product "Z" is eliminated, or the item is priced to at least achieve breakeven, will the resulting profit decline be insignificant when your customers seek product "Z" from your competitors; while, at the same time, removing some "W," "X," and "Y" related product purchases from your company?

- What is to be gained if your company's total volume of "loss leaders" are driven to your competition? Will this force the competition to realize greater losses when they suddenly must absorb the increased sales of product "Z"? Or, have they figured out a way to provide product "Z" at a profit?

The hip roof curve p/v analysis need not be performed graphically. It was shown this way in order to highlight relevant managerial cost reduction questions and options. When cutting the fat (costs), you should be aware of the potential effect on muscle (profit).

USING ACTIVITY-BASED COSTING TO IDENTIFY COST REDUCTION OPPORTUNITIES

The tidal wave of cost accounting focus on true costing peaked in the early 1990's with the flood of applications of Activity Based Costing (ABC). Instead of cavalierly applying the percentage costs of overhead, indirect, and administrative costs to direct or other base costs, the accounting community pressed for true costing in the application of these add-on costs.

ABC is now being used to uncover hidden costs, as well as those that have been routinely absorbed in gross percentage add-ons without question as to their relevance or size. This has led to dramatic new analyses directed towards gaining true costing as well as cost improvement. In fact, the proponents of ABC have enthusiastically proclaimed that you will be able to trace virtually every dime of overhead right to its source.

As far as gaining true costing to cut the fat, ABC does make a significant contribution under the following conditions:

- where the add-on costs of indirect, overhead and administrative costs are significant relative to the base direct costs.

- as a rule of thumb, where add-on costs are approximately 40% or more of the total cost structure, ABC can lead to significant cost analyses resulting in pricing and bid modifications.

- unnecessary indirect costs are pinpointed as a prelude to either greatly reducing, or even eliminating them

- negotiating with vendors, especially in competitive price situations, can be fruitful where true costing of percentage add-ons is specifically questioned, requiring new price justifications

- most and least profitable customers can be re-defined, in order that this will lead to dedicated actions by the marketing and sales groups

- prices can now truly reflect adequate profit margins

- by applying the leveraging concept (see Chapter 7), storage and distribution true costing can lead to management decisions regarding holding warehouses vs. custom preparation of orders from fewer locations and at earlier stages of production.

- the ABC analysis will lead to a reevaluation of existing procurement and sales contracts

- support crews can be reorganized, regarding both number of personnel required and specific skills available, so that they can more effectively support the efforts of direct operations.

The greatest cost savings occur where departments and support work have never before been analyzed as to their true contribution to profitability. Savings can be achieved through studying both desired and available support vs. "merely available for use." In Chapter Ten, the charge-back system is described as this affects the use and charging of support services.

CASE STUDY: USING A SKILL / TIME ANALYSIS TO DETERMINE TRUE COST

A purchasing department in a Pennsylvania company consisted of a total of eight personnel acting as buyers, negotiators and expeditors. The cost of the department was traditionally spread over all products shipped, so that the dollar value of all products shipped, net accounts receivable, absorbed all the procurement department costs. In this way, the total costs of that department were always totally absorbed by the total of net dollars to be received.

A detailed skill/time analysis indicated that three of the nine buyers routinely negotiated lot purchases of mill and warehouse grade metal products, primarily firebox steel, rolled sheets and cast housings, as well as copper and cupernickel raw materials.

One individual, requiring minimal internal support, was responsible for office supplies and routine production buying contracts (for welding supplies as an example).

Four of the department's personnel were involved with implementation of the partnering approach with providers of unique electronic and gearbox assemblies. Their time was mostly spent in:

- performing on-site evaluations of potential suppliers leading to single sourcing based on pre-award surveys,

- quality training for vendor certification,

- merging scheduling of the main facility with delivery promises and capacities at vendor sites,

- performing evaluations for purposes of applying and paying performance incentives to suppliers, based on cost reductions instituted, quality improvements recommended and installed, and miscellaneous improvements in logistical standards by common carriers working with the company's own vehicle fleet.

This latter group of four buyers were engaged in procuring only 19% of the total material costs. But, their specific support costs included extensive travel, some with overseas residencies, a new, fully-equipped training facility, and 80% use of data input time by secretarial-type personnel. Thus, their total costs were calculated to equal 71% of the total purchasing expenditure.

A first attempt to proportionately spread costs was to apply usage figures of cost per line item. This proved to be totally misleading when analyzed. Routine purchases of hundreds of line items required substantially less procurement time and support expense than the negotiation and bidding procedures for assemblies to be provided by dedicated suppliers. An attempt to evaluate time and skills required by line item procured was also misleading, since only minimal time was required by some raw material purchases while maximum time went into cementing partnering relationships. Charging time spent by commodity code also proved to be a costly and very inaccurate procedure for proper application of costs.

Finally, a 50-year-old procedure, activity sampling, was installed. This procedure took less than 30 minutes per day to provide much more accurate chargeback experiences. (Activity sampling is described in the next chapter.)

You can see that accurate charging of procurement time and skills was a lot different from simply applying a percentage factor based on the value of product shipped. The end result was to make the company more competitive in bidding certain products, initiated a cost/benefit study for projects underway in the department, and led to cost reduction initiatives in areas never before studied in detail. Thus, true costing made a significant difference in this company's strategy for retaining old customers and gaining new ones through proper pricing based on more accurate indirect and administrative costing data.

CASE STUDY: DETERMINING THE TRUE COST OF MAINTENANCE SERVICES

A Texas food packer bid for every job based on locally-added labor and equipment productivity (cost vs. output) and profit needs. Quality losses and material costs were fully controlled by the prime customer, whose product was packed in their name by the co-packer. Therefore, proper pricing, based on true costing, was a paramount consideration as they daily competed in bidding wars.

The plant maintenance department accounted for 40% of the total cost of both direct and indirect hourly-paid labor. Since the plant was highly automated, from delivered stocks through to palletizing and warehousing of finished goods, a minimum of machine tenders (42% of the total labor cost) were required for changeovers, random inspections, and minimum materials handling. Yet, the machine tenders were directly charged to the lines they ran and the production which they produced, while maintenance labor costs were prorated by the total output of cost/case of good product produced.

A very simple study showed the main function of the maintenance group was to keep the aging equipment running . . . which was how its effectiveness was judged by plant management. The newest lines, four of the fourteen which were packing aseptic juice box products, needed very little of maintenance employee attention. The older lines, ten of the fourteen which were old glass and can lines, accounted for most of the maintenance skills to keep going.

It was the aseptic product lines that were the fastest growing sales areas. Starting from almost zero, production on these juice box lines grew at a rate of about 350% per year for four years, before tailing off in the last two years. Quoted prices by competitors were eroding their volume of aseptic business, based on the competition's lower price quotes to perform the exact same operations. To meet this competition, the company lowered prices, cut profit margins, and aggressively sought enough customers to stay in business.

By re-evaluating the support costs provided by maintenance, a whole new costing procedure turned the Company around. The product line hip-roof, profit/volume curve displayed a host of new pricing options, as well as laying the ground-work for needed cost reductions in the maintenance function. Just as importantly, it re-focused the attention of all levels of management to true costing for all other important support services.

CASE STUDY: HOW CHANGING THE COST BASE BECAME THE MAJOR FACTOR IN TRUE PRICING

An Illinois company was a major supplier of glass bottles to the soda, beer and food products industries. Their major competition was branching out into alternate packing modes. At the same time these competitors were true costing their remaining glass lines in order to make a profit comparable to their other new packaging products.

Since the Illinois company had no alternate packaging products, the new competitive pricing meant a life or death struggle to stay afloat. The Board of Directors mandated that present management either meet the competition's pricing structure, in order to keep their present glass volume, or invest heavily in alternate packaging processes through either acquisition or borrowing for new plant start-ups.

The President decreed a sense-of-urgency true costing study be initiated. This was to be a crash application of experienced judgment for all allocated costs, in order to (1) apply these true cost factors ASAP, and (2) highlight cost reduction options for all management to see.

One of the initial analysis results bears mentioning here in this chapter; others will appear in Chapter 10. The cost of direct operations was found to be based on the weight of glass being worked. Thus, a 32-ounce jar carried more of the direct operating costs than a 16-ounce one. After all, it was reasoned, it took longer to process the heavier jar, and the production output justified this, since heavier jars, by sheer amount of glass alone, accounted for a weightier price in the marketplace.

An example, that convinced Company executives that pursuing this path was folly, became the sample shown to all employees in their cost reduction training. There was a turning (finishing) operation which finished off the glass bottle tops (necks) after they were formed. These tops, for any weight of jar, took the same cap size and were identical to each other as a universal closure application. There was no way that the turning operation took twice as long to perform on a 32-ounce bottle than on the 16-ounce bottle . . . slightly longer was an acceptable number, of course, but never twice as long!

The analysis revealed:

- where over-pricing was out-of-line with reality,
- where cost reductions were urgently needed to maintain the glass bottle business, and
- where leveraged actions could show immediate savings that would drop to the bottom line.

HOW TO APPLY DIRECT COSTING TO REDUCE OVERALL COSTS

There are three steps to follow when applying direct costing factors to service or staff areas, in order to properly allocate these indirect or other overhead costs:

1. Select the support costs that are significant from those that are insignificant by the leveraging procedure described in the previous chapter. You will probably find that 25% of the

percentage add-on costs for indirect, administrative and overhead charges will account for about 75% of these total cost additions to the base.

2. Analyze the significant few cost factors selected in paragraph #1 by:

    - direct charging costs as they are incurred, and where they can be captured in a routine manner through the present cost input system, or

    - applying activity sampling to gain a significantly better true costing of the add-on factors, or

    - providing experienced estimates to get started. At a later date these "best guesstimates" will be verified and modified as specific true costing studies progress, or

    - applying a combination of all of the above.

3. Immediately begin using the developed true costing data for applications for better pricing, as well as to provide insight into cost reduction areas to emphasize and prioritize for required actions.

SUMMING UP: Cutting the Fat with True Costing Techniques

One of the major true costing benefits for cost reduction comes in the exposure of the fixed and variable portions of most total costs. This allows for both isolating areas of opportunity to cut the fat, as well as allowing managers to prioritize their analyses and ultimate improvement actions. You'll find the best evidence of this when examining "old icons" such as span of control, inventory add-on costs, and purchase order costing.

By simulating the effects of fixed, variable and mixed cost reductions, you can test the resultant effects on the profitability of the enterprise. The major technique that is employed is profit/volume analysis which establishes a true costing breakeven point, a margin of safety, and, most importantly, a curve that separates the fixed costs plus the fixed portions of mixed costs from the pure variable costs in the cost absorption process. Examples of these cost improvement approaches were sprinkled throughout this chapter.

An important part of profit/volume analyses is the learning curve and its impact on costing. By determining the experiential effect on incremental volume increases, buyers have a valuable tool for negotiating with potential suppliers, as well as a better method for analyzing buy vs. make decisions, especially when introducing new products.

The hip-roof profit/volume curve not only shows the relationships of products or services to one another as contributors to bottom line results, but also points out cost reduction opportunities by individual products or services for the purpose of selecting areas for improvement, and setting proper cost reduction strategy priorities.

The rise of activity based costing (ABC) has given new meaning to the cost analyses of overhead charges. The shift to detailing add-on costs for indirect, overhead and administrative functions has led to more specific breakdowns of these add-ons, i.e., much more specific than the usual percentage applications which have been the prevailing dogma during most of the Twentieth Century.

True costing techniques provide new opportunities to examine costs whether they be variable, fixed, mixed or add-ons. The end result is both to demand better analysis, and to re-define priorities for cost reduction analyses.

MANAGING YOUR TIME MORE EFFICIENTLY CAN SNOWBALL INTO A COMPANY-WIDE EFFORT

"I don't have the time to improve my management of time!" is an often repeated excuse for procrastination before initiating a personal waste-reducing effort. Yet, as discussed in Chapter Seven, if you see problems as opportunities for improvement, it is possible to direct both yourself and your employees to better use this valuable company asset. Just the use of leveraging will improve time use, by emphasizing applications in just 20% of the managed areas to achieve 50% of the possible improvements. This chapter will focus on the opportunities for cost reduction through improved time management.

Leveraging your time management effort is far more productive than mere exhortation, or applying a veiled threat, such as, "Do better!" It is a recognized management function to provide the most efficient tools and techniques to all who work with you. As a manager, you are, therefore, required to do the following:

- Study your own management of time objectively.
- Know the tools available to improve the use of this asset.
- Provide informal and formal time management training to your employees. This is similar to introducing your employees to any other method for improving operations either in the office or on the factory floor.

APPLY ASSET CONTROL TO TIME USE ON A DAILY BASIS

Time, like talent and effort, is a company asset to be preserved and improved. Better use of the time asset surely does not come from delaying time analysis, or from always accepting a lower priority for this asset improvement task than that supplied to address daily fires with fire fighting vigor. An unacceptable statement from any manager would be, "I don't have time to manage!" Likewise, the statement, "I don't have the time for time management improvement" should also be treated as unacceptable.

The key to improving your time management is accurately knowing how you and your employees currently spend this company asset. This requires the use of a simple leveraging tool called sampling. This tool should be used to gather facts in order to reach an acceptable "factual" conclusion about time use. This and other such management tools for gaining this important data are the focus of this chapter.

The resulting asset utilization conclusions will be far better to work with than the usual subjective perceptions drawn from temporarily documenting time use by keeping a voluminous personal diary. I can emphatically state, from my years of experience documented in my best-selling book, *Managing Time,* that keeping time diaries is a waste of time.

A cornerstone of the widely accepted, decades old management-by-objectives approach, modified and adopted by today's strategic planners, is related to cost reduction through improved time management as follows:

- dedication to asset preservation concepts through planning and control by all levels of management,
- a system of bench-mark controls to assure that asset planning techniques are successful, and
- proper allocation and application of time management principles in proportion to the value and priority of the total asset improvement effort.

HOW TO CUT THE FAT THROUGH THE APPLICATION OF TIME MANAGEMENT

Most time management programs that fail do so when they become paperwork games; i.e., where managers learn the acceptable buzz words, play them back as objectives, go through the motions of filling out analysis forms, make some minor noticeable changes, and then report on the success of same. "See; we're doing it; just as was requested." Sometimes, specific projects are chosen, and then passed off as next year's objectives. However, regardless of the management-by-objectives approach practiced in your work environment—from none to "playing the game" to total dedication to realistic improvements that will drop to the bottom line—there are advantages to choosing some degree of personal commitment to improved time management.

Oscar Wilde said, "Most (people) are consistent in managing their time, and consistency is the last refuge of the unimaginative." A much simpler commentary was passed along by Peter Drucker in *The Effective Manager:* "The effective manager knows where his time goes." This is the first step in improving your time management.

To demonstrate the premise that very little time need be spent to improve your time management—either by analyzing the present use of your time, or installing simple but ongoing improvements—consider the following technique. Twenty years ago, I introduced this simple routine to my clients' personnel:

1. Before you start any task during a day at work, take 30 seconds to ask a simple series of questions. If you start 10 tasks in a normal workday, this time use analysis technique would consume all of 5 minutes of your workday! If you still insist that you don't have time to improve your time management by spending these 5 minutes a day, then you have serious internal motivation problems.

2. During the 30 seconds allotted for this analysis, ask the following questions:

   • **Why is this task being done at all?** The highest form of operational improvement is elimination. This is far superior to seeking improvements for a task that could be eliminated altogether (thus eliminating the following questions).

   • **Who should be working on this?** Can the task be delegated? and, to whom? One of the major deficiencies of overworked managers is thereby confronted, evidenced by the lament, "I am the only one who can perform this task, since no one else is either capable or trained. Besides, I like doing it." When a manager is immersed in fire fighting, rarely is any time set aside for fire-prevention activities. Thus, the cause of the problem becomes the effect, and, like a cat chasing its tail, produces a never-ending and fruitless cycle of activity. With very little effort, the manager engaged in perpetual fire fighting can justify not training someone else, or allow for delegation, by stating, "I can't stop to train someone else, or delegate; I have too much to do."

• **When should this task be performed?** Is doing this task now, at this moment, the proper priority? How is this task related to today's job ranking of all tasks scheduled to be performed?, or is this just a job that has been waiting around the longest? Are priorities set by need or by arbitrary, set-in-cement-for-no-reason due dates? Some simple desk management techniques will be shown later in this chapter that allow for a "children's hour" and/or the establishment of the creative time interval in any busy executive's day.

• **What improvement can you apply to this task?** Can you reduce the amount of data required? or use access to the computer files through EDI vs. the manual hunt and search approach? or is the work repetitious of other tasks, but inserted for the "belt and suspenders" crowd? or, can we reduce the time for selling an idea by improving the presentation method, thus making it easier for the approver to say "Yes!" to a significant but small portion of a total scheme?

• **Where should this task be accomplished?** Would it be better to move approval levels to the ultimate user, instead of making their decisions for them, followed by requesting their concurrence with our already-reached conclusion?

✓ Develop the self-analysis process yourself. Assume the responsibility to custom-design your own set of analysis questions that fit your job as you perceive it to be, i.e., related to your pre-determined or agreed job objectives.

✓ Either act immediately to alter the current practice of riding the treadmill of work-without-analysis, or make necessary cryptic notes to further analyze and gain approval for selected changes.

✓ Schedule the time necessary to install the improvement by assigning a reasonable priority—one that matches potential gain to the investment of managerial effort.

If you can't find five or ten minutes a day to analyze for improvement, skip the rest of this chapter. Use this saved time to develop new excuses for procrastination! For the remainder of readers, consider the investment of five-minutes a day to produce, at the very least, one cost effective improvement per day.

CASE STUDY: HOW A SMALL COMPANY EXAMINED THE CAUSES OF THEIR QUALITY PROBLEM BEFORE DEALING WITH THE EFFECT

In the drive to improve quality performance, an Ohio company developed a system for stringently qualifying suppliers, training their personnel on-site, certifying performance, and developing corrective procedures to overcome any detected failings. The cost of producing the product rose dramatically, while customer satisfaction remained fairly constant, as gauged by delivery acceptances and continuing brand loyalty purchasing practices.

A simple test was conducted by the Quality Assurance Manager. He had long been suspicious of the specifications demanded by the company's design personnel as to both necessity and economic common sense. His quality assurance philosophy was, "Everything can be done better, but at what cost and to what end result?" On a cost/benefit basis, he felt that certain specifications exceeded the requirements of the ultimate customer in the price range of the end product.

To test this premise, he assembled a sample of his company's rejected products that were both internally manufactured as well as parts received from suppliers of sub assemblies. He carried these rejects to various customer locations, whose total business accounted for a total of 2/3 of annual sales volume. At these locations, he discussed the rejected products' quality characteristics with on-site quality assurance personnel. He found that 94% of the rejected products were totally acceptable to these customers!

HOW TO OVERCOME THE OVERKILL SYNDROME

Does your company spend more than necessary in time and funds to overcome a problem that may be a "paper tiger"? Specifications for quality depend on the requirements of both the ultimate purchaser and the ultimate user. This is not a call for producing junk, and then hoping that enough of it passes through to make a decent profit. Rather, it is a call for a rational approach to establishing criteria for quality acceptance, which should be based on both the needs of the ultimate purchaser and the target price range of the individual product or service. It is a significant time waster to spend much effort on phantom problems.

To improve time management requires both analysis and acceptance of more realistic responsibilities by the parties that are authorized to take action. One saving effect can come from the elimination of knee-jerk, impulsive reactions to phantom problems. Elimination of massive efforts to drive to a solution should be preceded by a logical analysis of the true problem to be resolved. This is the lesson to be learned from the Ohio company's efforts that were needlessly wasted in the above-described problem resolution.

Carry this one step further to a situation which may exist in your company. If a design group is held responsible only for establishing "safe specs," but not for the economic effect of tolerance and other specification mandates, where is the incentive to review and revise design criteria to ease operational costs? "That's not my job!" can be a costly mind-set for the group that formulates the rules of acceptance for purchasing, capital equipment investment, inspection procedures, packaging, storage, and transport.

A major time management concept simply states that you must examine the cause of a problem before dealing with its effect. Such a procedure brings efficient problem solving into the arena of time management for cost reduction effectiveness.

HOW TO GAIN REPRESENTATIVE DATA OF THE CAUSES OF TIME MISMANAGEMENT

As stated in the prior section, a true picture of the causes of a situation, i.e., problem origins, is necessary to improve both your own time management, and that of your associates. Yet, the literature is full of techniques that tell you what to do to eliminate time wasters only. For example, most of these time management applications will save you pennies while you assume you are attacking the dollar causes of your time mismanagement. Worse still, there is an abundance of popular yet unscientific methods that popularize keeping subjective time diaries.

HOW TO EXAMINE YOUR PRESENT ACTUAL TIME USE

To maximize your efforts to improve the management of your time, it is essential that you examine the present actual time use required to carry out the most important functions of most managers, namely, planning, organizing, delegating, communicating, reviewing, controlling, coordinating, listening, advising, deliberating, problem-solving, decision-making, and most important of all, improving. Unless we improve our management of time when performing these vital functions, we may be dealing with penny solutions while dollars of time value are ignored.

Yet, time management seminars and how-to books are extremely popular. This is because we all feel we can do better, love the description of time wasters, relate to the case studies which define improvement possibilities, and we feel good about the fact that others have the same problems as we have. But, ask the following questions:

- Have we learned time management techniques to improve our use of the manager's time?

- Have we been shown how to collect objective time use data that truly represents the causes of the present operational situation?

- Have we installed a time management improvement system that can both measure results from an objective base situation, and be economical enough to warrant ongoing analysis vs. the usual one-shot application approach that is so very popular?

HOW TO PERFORM AN OBJECTIVE ANALYSIS

You must begin with an objective analysis of how you are presently using your time. Ranking your time wasters or keeping a time diary for two weeks are two examples of subjectively analyzing your management of time. The approach to be shown in this section overcomes the major deficiencies associated with these two popular approaches:

- Time diaries rarely track the most important problem faced by most managers—interruption time. Time diaries may show, "2 hours spent preparing presentation from submitted statistics." Yet, as much as half that time was spent fielding interruptions by staff, telephone, personal calls, visitors, etc. Interruption time is rarely logged, or in any way accounted for, and may consume up to 50% of the individual event's elapsed time.

- Instead of listing types (categories) of time usage, most time analysis recording techniques list activities performed. Since the highest priority for time usage improvement should relate to improving the quantity of valuable management time, all observed activities should both define and summarize as they are reported. It is important to separate and report creative, routine, busywork, direct and indirect management activities, as well as documenting idle, unavoidable delays, personal and travel time.

- The data collected may not pass the usual test of sampling significance. How valuable is keeping a time diary only during the two weeks of your busy season? or, keeping a diary of your personal time usage, where only you make the subjective entries, and cumulate and review the summaries . . . especially where you have a pre-determined concept of what the problem is and how it can be resolved?

- The data collector (you?) may sense that the results achieved do not warrant the excessive time required to maintain the record-keeping. If the data collection seems to cost more than the ultimate improvements are worth, this usually provides a motivation to abort the process by declaring the project completed.

- Further impetus for abandoning a time management analysis-for-improvement approach comes from the unavailability of hard data that there has been any improvement, i.e., other than one may feel better after having made the attempt. The feel-good result has sustained many a manager who will not admit that the whole exercise did not produce any result other than "we worked on improving our time management." This is a commonly used statement that usually appears on year-end reviews of activities and is totally unrelated to any savings that drop to the bottom line.

Thus, you must start off with a time management data collection device that is:

- objective, such that it is not prejudiced by pre-conceived ideas of causes and cures,

- representative of overall time usage, not just the time the data is collected

- simple to understand and use,

- definitive as to time usage by managerial work categories,

- adaptable to summarization of raw data over a representative period of time,

- conducive to capturing both interruption and personal time use,

- meaningful because it separates managerial function time use from indirect type activities (dollars from pennies)

- significant to the manager when it allows for analysis leading to improvements,

- inexpensive and non-intrusive to operate, such that there is little opposition to continuing the process,
- capable of documenting savings as the data collection continues to demonstrate the positive effects achieved after improvements are installed.

HOW TO USE THE PROVEN ACTIVITY-SAMPLING APPROACH

It has long been known by pollsters, scientists and most educated laymen that random sampling is an acceptable device to measure total population statistics within the limits of data collection reliability. Simply by assuring the objectivity and randomness of the sample data, coupled with applying a validity test to determine the parameters of reasonable acceptance of these data, provides the observer with ratios (percentages) that can represent the entire population of events.

The simple time management data collection philosophy is that a manager can draw meaningful conclusions, relevant to present time use, by random sampling of the population of actual events. Some simple rules to follow begin with determining collection cells. The first rule is: Select any categories that have significance to you, both for documenting important aspects of your managerial activity, and as an aid to analyzing present time use leading to improvements. The following example will demonstrate this simple concept.

DISREGARD PRIOR CONCEPTS OF YOUR TIME USE

In the beginning you will tend to have many more categories than you will need for examining and improving your management of time. You will also have many misconceptions about your time use. For example, I used to think that I spent vast amounts of time training and instructing my staff. So I listed this as a major time user to be studied. Yet, over a period of one year's study (about 16 actual hours during that year), I found that I never cumulatively spent more than $3/4$ of 1% of my total time providing instruction or training my personnel! There will be other misconceptions which you will discover after selecting categories that prove to be insignificant, and, you may find some that you have actually overlooked.

Since I have been performing sampling of my time usage for almost 15 years now, let me provide you with categories that I have found to be most useful. However, let me again state that you may choose any

Figure 9–1   Activity Sampling Data Collection Form

Activity Category	Date _____ Daily Observations	Cum.	Cum. %	Date _____ Daily Observations	Cum.	Cum. %
1. DIRECT WORK a. Communicate b. Plan c. Control d. Improve						
2. INDIRECT WORK a. Get Supplies b. Arrange Travel c. Travel Time d. File Retrieval						
3. SPECIAL ACTIVITIES a. Telephone b. Meetings						
4. IDLE a. Choice b. U.D. c. Personal						
5. ABSENT						
Cumulative Totals			100%			100%

categories at initiation as well as when you are well into the collection of data. (See Figure 9-1).

Let me again state that the total time to gain a useful, reliable sample should take less than 5 minutes per day. Since the study is conducted on random days, as well as days when one is not on out-of-area travel, the total time consumed may approach 50–60 hours per year. This calculation is provided for those who are still resisting the initiation of an activity sampling study of their time use, by continuing to state, "I don't have time for time management!"

HOW TO CATEGORIZE WORK FOR FUTURE ANALYSIS

At first, chances are that you will lump INDIRECT with DIRECT WORK, omit IDLE and PERSONAL, and not see the value of the category, ABSENT. The explanations of categories may prove to be a valuable guide to get you started:

- **DIRECT WORK** consists of all of those tasks a manager is required to perform, and by which his remuneration and effectiveness as a manager are judged. This includes the following:

  - planning
  - controlling
  - improving
  - training
  - listening
  - communicating
  - organizing

This is the category that we hope to maximize in our utilization of managerial time. Therefore, it is frustrating to find that the amount of time spent here is usually far, far less than we predetermine. Consider yourself fortunate to spend more than 35% of total time working in this category's activities. This information will come forth from your initial analysis performed over a representative period of time, say three months.

- **INDIRECT WORK** are those activities that support DIRECT WORK. They are easily identified as necessary tasks that are worth cents of your time to perform. These tasks could be delegated to anyone paid far less than the manager, and could be standardized, combined with other like tasks, simplified, and, best of all, eliminated. Included are such activities as:

  - getting office supplies
  - arranging travel plans
  - completing your expense voucher
  - reproducing materials
  - delivering a verbal message
  - filing or retrieval from physical or computer files

These are some representative examples of types of tasks performed that require a pay scale far below that for the average manager; at least well below the remuneration for managerial tasks labeled, DIRECT WORK.

- **SPECIAL ACTIVITIES** are functions that could fall into any of the listed categories, but have been singled out for special study by the manager. My very first SPECIAL ACTIVITY was time on the telephone, which I felt was a major concern. Normally, telephone time would be part of the first two categories listed above. I thought I spent half my time with the black tumor in my ear. By selecting telephone time as a special activity, to be isolated from other tasks observed, I was surprised to learn that a representative sample showed that 12.8% of my time was consumed by time spent on the telephone. I now run at close to 6.5% of my time using the phone. This is due mainly to new procedures I instituted. These new procedures were based on my analysis of the numbers derived from the sampling study. If you are an employee in a small company, where everyone works in support of each other, the sampling will have much more success if all participate. A "special activity" for one individual may be "direct work" for another.

• **IDLE and PERSONAL** both have the same negative effect on the use of managerial time; hence, they are here grouped together. However, many managers choose to list them as separate categories, since much of this time may be due to circumstances beyond their control, called UD for unavoidable delay. This category consists of time spent on non-work activities, such as discussion of the Monday-night game on the tube. If you feel that this is a necessary activity for building morale, set up such a category. Obviously, idle gossip represents IDLE time usage. Getting coffee for yourself or your secretary is a PERSONAL task. Both PERSONAL and IDLE time will never be eliminated from your workday. However, it is worth your while to reduce the time spent on these categories to create more time for DIRECT WORK activities. I worked with an extremely inefficient executive who spent 42% of his office time performing PERSONAL and IDLE functions, and then proceeded to take DIRECT WORK home, to the chagrin of his family. Dozing or daydreaming are obviously IDLE. Waiting for information or people is either an unavoidable (UD) or avoidable delay (AD), but classified as IDLE in either case. Checking home to ascertain your child's temperature, or calling for a house painting estimate, are PERSONAL uses of your managerial time.

• **ABSENT** is a leveling category which is needed to balance out the selected observation times at 100%. Although you are in the office, somewhere, it would be imprudent to have the observer conduct a search to determine your whereabouts and activity being performed at the instant of observation; plus, it probably would not serve any gainful purpose for this activity sampling study.

To repeat: You may select any categories that will have meaning for you in determining time use now, and that, in the future, will be meaningful for selecting improvement areas and applications.

HOW TO SELECT RANDOM TIMES
FOR OBJECTIVE OBSERVATIONS

The next step is to select random times for observation. Two practical rules will help:

1. To assure objectivity, observations are best performed by someone other than yourself. However, self-analysis can be done so

that the observed and the observer are one. However, having your secretary or managerial aide observe for 5 minutes a day is a far better approach.

2. Observing at random times on random days will assure the collection of data that is useful for the purposes stated. Your computer can spit out random times, just as it does for selecting LOTTO numbers on a Quick-pick basis. Or, you can buy a book of random numbers, usually published by a computer hardware company. I suggest you use the white pages of your local telephone directory, which is an inexpensive and easily understood catalog of random numbers. (See next section.)

APPLYING SIMPLE RANDOM-SAMPLING RULES TO GAIN OBSERVATION TIME

The rules for using the white telephone book pages are as follows:

1. For each new day, turn to a random page in the directory.
2. Select a sample size and sample days. You will find that working in multiples of "10" will allow for easy conversion to statistics of time management that you can use for improvement. Thus, for the purposes of this example, 10 numbers per day are being sought for observation reference points.
3. For the 10 numbers chosen, consider just the last four digits of each individual telephone number. See Figure 9-2.
4. Discount all first digits that are larger than "1."
5. Disregard all times that are outside of normal work times, or when sampling would be impossible, such as observations in hazardous areas.
6. Select times for observation, using the 24-hour clock approach, i.e., where 1441 equals 2:41 PM.

If you are being sampled by your secretary, managerial aide, a peer, or your administrative assistant, they need only list the selected times in chronological order on a slip of paper for easy access. If you are sampling yourself, I have found that the use of individual random time entries on 3×5 cards allows the upcoming observation time to be easily noted and used.

RECORDING THE SAMPLE OBSERVATIONS

This next step requires a few practice runs for the uninitiated. Instantaneous, knowledgeable and objective observations are required. However, we are seeking a guide to time use, not a scientific study for

Figure 9-2   Selecting Random Observation Times
from the Telephone Directory

Sample Page from Telephone White Pages

Last 4 Digits	Time Selected
8231	2:31
2716	NA
9914	9:14
1441	2:41
6983	10:23
2914	9:14
0041	NA
1080	11:20
2936	9:36
4302	3:02
7611	NA
1232	NA (Lunch)
1601	4:01
3136	1:36

10 Numbers

reaching an earth-shaking conclusion. In actual practice, errors will be made in observing categories, i.e., between work and non-work, selected sampling times will be missed, and categories will be confused. In the long run of observation times, most minor errors will be digested by the system as you drive for a report of gross time use that is representative.

The observations taken at these random times should be instantaneous. The observer should not wait for a desirable observation (DIRECT WORK?) while the manager's telephone conversation with his/her latest paramour draws to a conclusion. Fixing the observation, or changing the random time does not allow for the desired result of collecting objective data for time management improvement.

Figure 9-3 is an example of what an activity sampling form might look like after two days of ten observations each. The entire process should take between 2 1/2 and 5 minutes per day for the observer. This includes selecting the random times and calculating the cumulative percentages by category. In addition, about one minute per day will be consumed by plotting the cumulative percentage figure by category. (See the following section on sample validity checking.)

Experience has shown that sampling performed on an average of three days per work week, over a three-month stretch of time, will provide realistic and representative data. The next section will provide a more scientific approach to determining sample size.

Figure 9–3 Activity Sampling Form After Two Days of Observations

Activity Category	Date _____ Daily Observations	Cum.	Cum. %	Date _____ Daily Observations	Cum.	Cum. %

1. DIRECT WORK
  a. Communicate
  b. Plan
  c. Control
  d. Improve
	III	3	30%	ЖHↃ I	9	45%

2. INDIRECT WORK
  a. Get Supplies
  b. Arrange Travel
  c. Travel Time
  d. File Retrieval
	II	2	20%		2	10%

3. SPECIAL ACTIVITIES
  a. Telephone
  b. Meetings
	I	1	10%	I	2	10%

4. IDLE
  a. Choice
  b. U.D.
  c. Personal
	III	3	30%	I	4	20%

5. ABSENT	I	1	10%	II	3	15%
Cumulative Totals	10	10	100%	10	20	100%

When I am sampled, I do not know the times selected by the observer. Having this knowledge might prejudice my activities during the observation times selected. It is for this reason that new observation times are selected for each day sampling is to occur.

Cumulative percentages are developed for each category, so that a running percentage is available at any point in the study. This is a vastly superior technique than that used by the proponents of time diaries. Those who have kept time diaries know that the most onerous part of data summarization is sorting out the cumulative time spent on various activities from a purely narrative diary. Worse yet, gross diary times never pick up all, or any of the interruptions that occur during a reported event. Thus, gross diary times may not be truly representative of actual managerial time spent, which is a shame, considering all the effort expended to collect diary data.

In Figure 9-3, on the first day, 3 out of 10, or 30%, of the total observations indicated that DIRECT WORK was being performed. On the second random day of observation, 6 out of 10 observations (60%) showed the same activity being performed. You could calculate that this average is:

$$\frac{30\% + 60\%}{2} = 45\%$$

Although your mathematics would be correct, this would be a very time consuming calculation for each category after each sampling day . . . as the sampling days grow from 3 to 50 during the course of the study. Thus, a cumulative sample calculated each day is a far more practical approach. For example, the calculations after the second day's observation for the category DIRECT WORK show:

$$\frac{\text{cumulative observations}}{\text{total observations}} \quad \text{or} \quad \frac{9}{20} = 45\%$$

The remaining question is, "When do I have enough observations to have figures that represent actual time use?"

WHEN TO CONSIDER THE CUMULATIVE RESULT REPRESENTATIVE

Any statistician would quickly respond that, within defined limits, say plus or minus 5% error acceptability, use the formula for calculating standard deviations from the mean. Let me assure you that there is a very acceptable short-cut to arriving at approximately the same point of sample reliability.

Figure 9-4 is a graphic illustration of plotting the cumulative figure each day of the sample by category. Note that for DIRECT WORK, the first plot was for 30%, and the second cumulative figure was 45%, which was the cumulative figure after the second day of observation on Figure 9-3. The numbers "28," "36," "29," and "34," which follow for the next 4 days, are all cumulative figures.

In the beginning, there will be wild swings in the cumulative totals, which is to be expected from small cumulative samples. Consider a baseball player who is shown to be hitting .450 (9 for 20) after just two weeks of the season, perhaps dropping to .250 (15 for 60) in the fourth week. A few hits here or there can have a dramatic effect on his batting average early in the season. That same player will probably

Figure 9–4   Plotting Cumulatives for Each Sampling Category

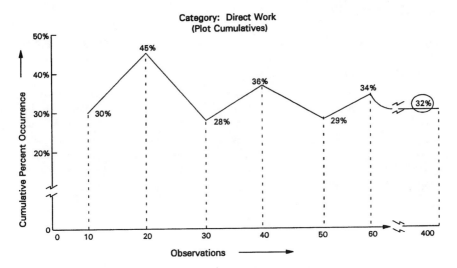

Category: Direct Work
(Plot Cumulatives)

end the season near his typical average, even if he goes 4 for 4 (or 0 for 4) on the final day.

As the cumulative sample grows larger (the denominator), the cumulative observations by each category (the numerator) is less affected by radical change. Therefore, at some point, the plotted cumulative curve for each category will level out and barely fluctuate as new sample days are added.

The mathematics of the standard deviation formula will calculate the point where the fluctuation is less than 5% plus or minus from the mean. The plotted curve can give you similar information as is shown in Figure 9-4. After 400 observations, of about 10 observations for 40 days out of 60 working dates in three months (or between 150 and 200 minutes during this entire 3-month span), the curve is virtually flat no matter what individual days are added. Thus, a relative factor of reliability in the observed data has been achieved. This completes the required sample study.

A logical short-cut is to plot the cumulative percentages for only the major categories, since, if the major parts of the whole (all selected categories) solidify around a representative percentage, the rest of the categories will also be stabilizing as part of the whole. However, you will probably find that it is easier to plot all of your 5 or 6 categories' cumulative totals, than to worry about missing a possible important change in cumulative values occurring in those areas where you have skipped the plotting process.

HOW TO USE THE COLLECTED
SAMPLING DATA

After completing the sample study, you will note some general changes in time use that will have to be addressed. Some are very obvious, such as reducing PERSONAL and IDLE TIME by sheer discipline. Other changes require a review of the causes. Surely, a manager would be interested in reducing INDIRECT WORK and adding this gain to DIRECT WORK time available. No manager should be satisfied with spending only 32% of his/her time on DIRECT WORK. (See Figure 9-4.)

Since SPECIAL ACTIVITIES may include DIRECT WORK activities, this figure should be added to the total percentage. Remember that SPECIAL ACTIVITIES are those you had singled out to be studied separately. (For example, I always included telephone time in my search for time management improvement. Since some of my telephone time is personal, I separated this from business-oriented SPECIAL ACTIVITIES.)

Many managers, after defining telephone time as a significant time user, have instituted changes in the handling of both incoming and outgoing calls. For example, they are taking advantage of many computer, fax and telephone features, including automatic call-back, voice messaging, wireless response, interoffice faxing, using your managerial aide, electronic mail, changing reception call handling, call forwarding, EDI, speed dialing, interactive messaging, and, of course, sheer personal discipline.

Managers are always surprised when they see the classification of time after the sample is completed. Very few of us believe that we spend so much time on IDLE or PERSONAL activities, and so little on DIRECT WORK, as compared to INDIRECT WORK. It is my experience that when the INDIRECT WORK category shows up as so large as to overwhelm DIRECT WORK, I am confronting a manager who has difficulty delegating work, by assuming "Only I can do this job!" The "only I" syndrome commits many a skilled and experienced managerial and technical person to having very limited time to perform the required management tasks of improving, delegating, controlling, planning, organizing, training, listening, etc. The hue and cry of these skilled workers performing as managers is, "I have no time to manage properly!" Activity sampling can provide the data to foster needed improvements in managing managerial time.

HOW TO MEASURE IMPROVEMENTS
IN ACCEPTABLE QUANTITATIVE TERMS

Was there a cost improvement made? After installing or deciding on time management improvements, you now have the tool to measure the results of this improvement effort, i.e., the very same activity sample.

Performing a sampling study, after actual improvements have been instituted, allows for a comparison of actual before and after data.

This comparison allows you to measure the results of adding new equipment, support services, discipline, personnel and/or providing additional skills training vs. the costs and inefficiencies of the just-measured past practices. The cure should always be less costly than the positive results derived from the cure. This is where you separate the time management approaches that make you feel good from those that produce cost effective results. Consider what the magnification of these results could mean if sampling and improvement were adopted on a company-wide basis!

HOW TO HANDLE INTERRUPTIONS

Management publications are loaded with narrative denouncing interruptions. The assumption garnered from reading this literature is that one can practically eliminate interruptions through applying better managerial discipline. I believe that this sort of result is reserved for kings and certain chief executives who are interrupted only when they want to be.

In actual practice, interruptions, even those based on a fairly structured exception basis, are and probably always will be a part of an executive's life. Therefore, it is far better to assume that interruptions will continue, but you should be aware that they can be reduced in quantity and improved in quality.

Examine your activity sample. How many of the categories are under your direct control? How many calls or visits to your office are made by others purely on a whim, or because of an actual need for your face-to-face personal input, opinion, or specific information that only you can provide? Thus, it is important to evaluate not only the results of your time usage, but also the causes.

WHY ARE YOU BEING INTERRUPTED?

Some interruptions are a direct result of your stated and practiced management style. If you are an "open door" manager, or strive to be, you desire every one of your troops, as well as every visitor, to have free access to drop in at their convenience to see you. But, at any time? on any matter?

- Can you determine if some of these visits are for the purpose of using you as a crutch?

- Could the decision be made by the visitor without your approval, but he or she would feel more comfortable if you do it for them?
- See if you encourage this situation, by functioning as if you are the only one allowed to make decisions that cannot be overridden.
- Is your concurrence even necessary?
- Is the decision level too high for every single situation?
- Would leveraging (See Chapter Seven) allow for a delineation of decision levels, such that penny-effect decisions related to low level results, could be decided without your direct input? Would this not allow you to spend more time on dollar projects?
- Are some interruptions informative? If so, did the face-to-face communication warrant the time urgency of an oral statement made by you?
- Could a brief note suffice? Or a faxed or voice mail memo that would allow you to receive the communication so as to be read at your leisure?
- Does your office layout encourage passersby to drop in with idle talk? Do you encourage this interruption by leaving your door open with your chair facing the entrance?
- Do you express an urgency to receive certain information that is not warranted? "Tell me as soon as credit is cleared for the Jones order!" is an urgent call for an interruption.
- Can you make a distinction between "need to know now" and "would like to know at your convenience"?

GROUPING INTERRUPTIONS FOR BEST RESULTS

Interruptions should be grouped so that various people can see you at the same time on the same subject. This will eliminate the need to handle all interruptions as individual events.

In Figure 9-5, you will note an interruption diary I kept when I was a very junior executive. Note that two hours and 45 minutes were consumed by interruptions. Assume that at least $1/2$ of this time could be considered in the DIRECT WORK category. This still leaves a load of valuable time that could have been planned and used for more productive managerial purposes.

Can you encourage others, at the very least your employees, to group their questions and discussions during their meetings with you? It is probable that you group work in action folders when you prepare to meet with your manager. Your secretary learns to collate your requests, using such tools as signature files, comment folders, and time

Figure 9-5   Sample of a Personal Interruption Diary

A PERSONAL DIARY

Date: _____

Interruption	Time	Description	Comment or Possible Improvement
1	09:04-09:18	John gave out cigar for new son	Shorten time spent
2	10:00-10:08	Charlie needed help	Did he really?
3	11:41-11:43	John called me to confirm meeting next week	Secretary could have taken the information
4	12:00-12:11	Charlie still needs help	Did I give good enough information the first time?
5	13:16-13:19	Mary wants next Wednesday off	How about a note?
6	13:28-13:36	Mary needs concurrence signature	Could have been grouped with point 5 above
7	13:55-14:11	Charlie needs help again	Consider replacing Charlie
8	14:39-15:18	George has wife problems	39 minutes!?!?
9	16:12-16:41	Attend weekly meeting chaired by yourself	Why is it held weekly?
10	17:01-17:36	The boss needed "hand holding"	Can I be honest with him?
TOTAL	165 minutes		

commitment diaries, when preparing for meetings with you. As such she has grouped the work by types of action required by the manager, and the papers in each folder are probably also prioritized by both urgency and time dating.

Why not set an example by grouping and prioritizing your oral requests, made both in person or on the telephone, when contacting your employees? This approach allows for the activation of the principles of the Pygmalion Effect, as characterized by Dr. Sterling Livingstone of the Sterling Institute. He stated that employees tend to emulate their bosses' work characteristics, both the good and the bad. If you avoid unnecessary interruptions by your own employees, and also reduce their length by priority grouping subject matter during telephone calls and visits, they will soon begin to use this very same practice.

Are you interrupted because your previous instructions were not understood? Many evidences of poor communication show up in interruption analyses. Keep these three basic rules in mind when providing instructions or when making requests of others:

- It's not what you say that counts; it's what they hear.
- It's not what you write that is followed; it's what they read.
- It's not what you mean that is significant; it's what they understand.

When you are not specifically understood, some employees will come back to you for clarification; thus, your poor communication is a time waster, and the cause of the interruption. More often, those who do not understand your communication, provided either orally or in writing, will avoid beginning the task requested, postpone necessary actions awaiting clarification, or perform partial work, or none at all. Thus, your poor communication becomes both a cause for an interruption and an employee time waster. Remember, poor communication is primarily the sender's responsibility.

Are you the victim of those who arrive unprepared at either your office or at your meetings? Does this cause you to be involved in using group time to again discuss previously covered details, leading to an examination of the facts leading to the previously announced conclusions? Such redundancy is an accepted time waster by executives who revel in detail, even redundant detail, to justify their decision that was pre-determined. This situation is best described by the age-old statement, "Don't bother me with facts; my mind's made up."

Do you need to take the time to train your employees on proper preparation for one-on-one meetings with you, as well as the requirements of adequate preparation for group meetings? You can do this by informally expressing your need to have employees come prepared with factual project status, experienced opinions, and both problems and potential suggested solutions, not just prepared to "dump the monkeys onto your back." Show, by example, the types of questions you expect to have answered. Define a completed stage or task. Explicitly define the milestones in project management and problem solving, which logically lead to better decision-making. (See Chapter Six.)

Learn to control personal interruptions by honestly saying, "Yes" when asked, "Are you busy?" Can you learn to say "No" to those who by-pass the chain of command in order to speak to you?

Can you distinguish between business and social courtesy requirements? If you are gardening in your back yard, and your neighbor stops to chat, it would definitely be a discourtesy to state, "Go away! Can't you see that I'm busy planting tulip bulbs?" Conversely, when you are confronted by the company busybody while at work in your office, and you are asked, "Did you hear about Harriet and Joe being caught in the parking lot?", you could respond, "No. I haven't. But, I must continue working on this proposal right now; so, let me get back to you as soon as I can." There is a different code of social behavior required in the office from that which is practiced when you are at home.

Again, you will never completely eliminate interruptions. They will continue to be a part of everyday life at both your office and at home. You can, however, reduce their quantity and increase their quality.

SUMMING UP: Spreading the Improved Time Management Concept

Leveraging the time you spend on improving your time management, by determining the areas where the return on your efforts will provide the maximum results, can set a significant example for all of your employees and peers. After all, time is a company asset which you will be seen to be conserving. A further motivation should come from those objective observers in your company who believe that cutting the fat should include, if not start with, improvement of the manager's use of personal time.

Time management improvement doesn't require that much time. For an expenditure of but 5 minutes a day, the manager may come up with 2 to 3 fresh approaches to everyday tasks. Surely, you can spend this minute amount of time to scratch the surface of the layers of fat that surround your daily workload with the practice of inertia . . . "keep going as before, until you see the light at the end of the tunnel . . .", if there is a light. The obvious counter is, "Work smarter not harder!"

To initiate such an approach requires that a manager gain a factual picture of present time use. Activity sampling is a methodology that is both more objective than time diarying for data collection, and consumes as little as 5 minutes a day for collection, summarization and reliability analysis.

Activity sampling has been employed in England and the U.S. since the 1930s as an accepted methodology for gaining reliable information that allows for meaningful improvements. Just as important, actual results achieved can be measured by this self-same technique. The first step is to divide your time use into meaningful categories, i.e., meaningful to you when the collected data calls out for positive action. For this reason, the manager is given the prerogative to choose any categories that he/she feels can accurately capture present time use as the causes that cry out for positive changes.

A key element to assure collecting useful data is the use of random sampling. For this reason, observations must be made at random times and on random days. A third-party observer should also be seriously considered, in order to assure objectivity in collecting random observations of current practice.

When reliability of the sample data has been ascertained, you will usually be surprised to learn of the small amount of time spent (less than anticipated) on direct managerial duties, and the large amount of time (more than realized) spent on indirect support work, as well as that which is consumed by idle and personal time use. Obvious improvements come from the reduction of time spent on non-managerial tasks, while simultaneously applying this saved time to maximize time to perform those direct managerial activities of planning, controlling, improving, coordinating, selling, training, communicating and other valuable management functions.

Using the leveraging philosophy, you will seek to gain large savings from either small effort, or through accurately choosing and improving those few areas of concern where maximum savings can be realized. The key here is that this is no longer a wishful supposition, because the sampling activity will proceed after the improvement has been initiated, in order to quantify the effect of the change.

Consider the massive affect on the business entity if just 10% more managerial time could be made available by the same talent that is now in place. You can cut the fat through positive action by a community of personnel devoted to achieve the same results as the slashers who are bent on cutting the fat, without regard to possible muscle damage.

CHAPTER   10

CONTINUOUS IMPROVEMENT (KAIZEN) THROUGH CONTINUOUS ANALYSES

One-shot cost reduction activities can be momentarily fruitful, but keeping lean, after excess fat has been removed, should be the desirable long-term objective. Like dieting, keeping it off may prove to be a more difficult task than initially taking it off.

APPLYING COST REDUCTION DISCIPLINE ON A CONTINUING BASIS

One answer is to apply the same discipline on a continuous basis that was applied during the initial thrust at reducing excess costs. This assumes the same sense of urgency will exist long after the fire has been reduced to embers. Any medical doctor will tell you that when the patient has great pain and is disabled, as well as fearing for his life—all prescribed medicines are taken regularly, exercise is performed on a strictly observed schedule, and abstention from smoking and alcohol consumption is practically absolute. But, a few weeks down the road, when the dire symptoms have eased or disappeared, the former patient probably has relapsed to the usual undisciplined health care approach. After all, they say, "I feel better now that I followed your instructions last month."

The key to cutting the fat and keeping it off is to install a monitoring system (the "test" in management terminology) that not only reports the continuation of those practices that worked, but also sets targets for continuous improvement, and measures progress against these new moving targets.

The Japanese call this approach to continuous improvement, "kaizen." The U.S. contribution has been in the area of developing improvement ratios, while raising the periodic reporting and control of the entire process to a visual involvement by the topmost managerial levels, in order to emphasize a personal commitment to continuous improvement.

The main objective is to apply continuous improvement in every area of operation on and off-site to include suppliers, contractors, transport services, and other elements of the supply chain. In addition, a complete plan for continuous improvement involves customers, temporaries, support agency personnel as well as anyone remotely related to receiving or delivering the company's services or products.

CASE STUDY: HOW TO USE REVENUE PER EMPLOYEE AS A BASE

A Wisconsin firm, dealing in coatings and finishes for original equipment manufacturers' products, uses the ratio of revenues per employee as a base, not just for maintaining the status quo, but also as a basis for their budgeted ratios that reflect an expectation of continuous improvement. They found that this approach forced all levels of their management team to constantly seek productivity improvements, especially in flat market periods where volume could not, by itself, allow various supervisors to meet their stated targets. The evaluation of the ratios for the utilization of their most expensive asset, labor, was being conducted on an ongoing basis. This constituted their testing.

TEST, MEASURE, TRAIN . . . THEN DO IT ALL AGAIN

Continuous improvement demands a continuing review of those practices that have worked, plus an ongoing investigation of what is new and applicable to your specific local operations. This requires a detailed review of practices that have worked by all affected parties. Thus, if a modified process of dealing with your transport carriers has resulted in diminished freight charges for the same or even increased volume, both the buyer and the supplier must find out the details of this success.

This is the test phase of control in the continuous improvement procedure.

The next, or simultaneous step is to further review specific cost improvement applications to add to the present system. But, the testing forces the ongoing analyses to continue. Some examples of tests follow:

CASE STUDY: HOW FIRST LEVEL SUPERVISORS CONTROLLED TIME USE

Figure 10-1 illustrates the results of a two-month study, which produced a follow-on application of a new scheduling technique in a job shop. This company produces short, sample processing runs of dye chemicals for major clothing manufacturers. The work is all custom-defined so that no two runs are alike, but the standards of time and material cost leave little room for error or employee/worker procrastination. Getting it right the first time was an important criteria, but getting it done profitably was of equally high priority. The objective was to improve the percentage of processing time during the average workday. The figure for category #1 historically was about 24%! As the reader can see in Figure 10-1, the initial attempts at work scheduling drove this percentage to 37%, which was a more than 50% increase in processing time. Continuous improvement demands that the testing continue, so that the quest for improvements continues.

CASE STUDY: ELIMINATING TIME CHARGED TO IRREGULAR ACTIVITIES

A Pennsylvania manufacturer of heat control units spent most of its engineering time estimating future work, based on its past history of performance, while producing like products. Every job was won or lost on the basis of price, past delivery and quality performance and reputation. Yet, as successful as they were in their field, only one of every three bids resulted in a successful award. A study showed that their quality was not the problem, in fact their product performance record made them a leader in their field. But, customers, such as school principals, public service department heads, municipal superintendents, and the like worked from mandated capital equipment budgets. Thus, there was no doubt that price was the major factor in awards won or lost.

Figure 10-2 shows the results of a study to define the major variable cost, direct labor. Through a benchmarking test, it was found that the 50% level of direct labor activity on actual production work was below that attained by four out of five competitors. The 30% attributable to production unmeasured activities, entitled "job difficulty" in

Figure 10-1   Example of Continuous Testing
of Process Time Utilization

TIME/USE CONTROL BY SUPERVISORS:

One of the most important elements of cost, controlled by a supervisor, is time. The three basic categories of production or service time usage are:

1. Process time
2. Man time
3. Idle time

The concern pays for all three. Analysis of these categories relates to the following:

1. Process

   37%

   a. Machine capabilities
   b. Materials used
   c. Holding and locating devices
   d. Release and aside devices
   e. Condition of equipment
   f. Machine settings
   g. Environmental conditions
   h. Materials handling
   i. Etc.

2. Man time
   (not internal time)

   27%

   a. Training and skill
   b. Maintained pace
   c. Job difficulty
   d. Interest, attention, and physical capabilities
   e. Etc.

3. Idle time

   36%

   a. Environmental conditions of heat, dust, noise, etc.
   b. Process delays
   c. Personal time
   d. Supervision and instructional
   e. Distractions
   f. Complete idleness
   g. Travel time
   h. Etc.

most manufacturing concerns, became the target for analyses, since "idle" and "indirect time" use were well within acceptable limits. (Note the definitions of production unmeasured time, which the company called PUSH for production unmeasured service hours.)

In Figure 10-3, a leveraging analysis revealed that three of the ten departments accounted for 56% of the total time charged to this category. The constant testing of results attained produced actions that showed a 17% reduction in production unmeasured hours in but one month. When the work design crew began testing results by individual

Figure 10–2   Example of Use of Direct Labor Cost

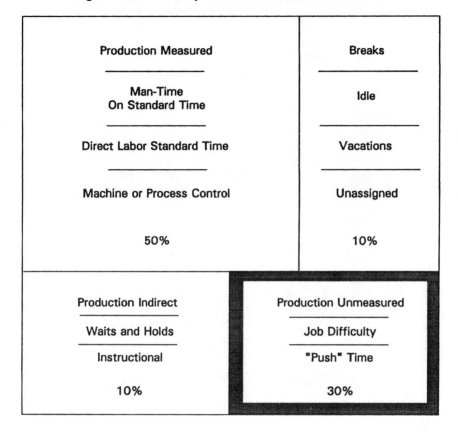

Production Measured	Breaks
Man-Time On Standard Time	Idle
Direct Labor Standard Time	Vacations
Machine or Process Control	Unassigned
50%	10%

Production Indirect	Production Unmeasured
Waits and Holds	Job Difficulty
Instructional	"Push" Time
10%	30%

DEFINITION OF PRODUCTION UNMEASURED (PUSH) CATEGORIES

1. **No Job Standard** - This type of push occurs where no standard has been determined on standard type work.

2. **Anticipated Special Push** - This push occurs on special work where no standard exists, or an estimated standard is adjusted.

3. **Unanticipated Push** - This push results when irregular tasks occur or unforeseen difficulties arise on a normal operation.

4. **Job Training** - Those hours incurred and charged to push when training a new employee.

operation in these three departments, 23% of the total jobs accounted for 75% of the total time allocated to this category.

In Figure 10-4, continuous testing, that led to improvements, ultimately reduced the job difficulty figure from the initial 30% to a very acceptable 6.8%!

**Figure 10-3   Leveraging Analysis of Departmental
Production Unmeasured Hours**

November 30–December 4
PRODUCTION UNMEASURED HOURS SUMMARY

					Hours By Code			
Department #	Total Hours	% Total	% Accum.	Not Coded	1	2	3	4
6	361.7	23.3	23.3	56.2	44.1	—	164.4	97.0
10	350.3	22.6	45.9	36.7	253.8	58.8	1.0	—
1	168.2	10.9	56.8	29.3	88.6	24.4	25.9	—
5	139.0	9.0	65.8	.5	67.2	12.5	58.8	—
8	137.7	8.9	74.7	137.7	—	—	—	—
2	117.2	7.6	82.3	40.0	41.5	31.3	4.4	—
3	111.5	7.2	89.5	40.5	71.0	—	—	—
4	107.2	6.9	96.4	9.7	59.4	1.3	36.8	—
7	39.2	2.5	98.9	21.9	2.2	—	15.1	—
9	17.1	1.1	100.0	1.2	12.7	—	3.2	—
	1,549.1			373.7	640.5	128.3	309.6	97.0
	100%			24.1%	41.3%	8.3%	20.0%	5.3%

Codes:
1. No Standard
2. Anticipated Special
3. Unanticipated
4. Job Training

The test phase of continuous improvement is really a well-defined and quite specific analysis of pertinent cost areas. It will pay you to use the leveraging techniques described in Chapter 9 to illustrate both results and leveraged options for further improvement.

USING ACTIVITY BASED MANAGEMENT (ABM) AS A TESTING TOOL

Proponents of the theory and practice of re-engineering seek to re-design operations and organization by relating tasks currently performed to those functions required and needed to be performed to meet the business objective. For example, does an advertising agency have to own its own print shop? Can your local city management have waste

Figure 10-4   Leveraging Analysis of Individual Operations' Production Unmeasured Hours

Accumulated Descending Production Unmeasured Hours Reported by Operation

Rank No.	Opr. #	Accum. % of All Opr. Reporting	Production Unmeasured Hours Reported	% of All Production Unmeasured Hours	Accum. Hours	Accum. %
1.	321	1.1%	129.2	8.3%	129.2	8.3%
2.	919	2.3%	129.1	8.3%	258.3	16.6%
3.	4401	3.4%	103.9	6.7%	362.2	23.3%
4.	330	4.5%	99.1	6.4%	461.3	29.7%
5.	917	5.7%	70.5	4.6%	531.8	34.3%
6.	322	6.8%	70.0	4.5%	601.8	38.8%
7.	532	8.0%	67.5	4.4%	669.3	43.2%
8.	270	9.1%	65.1	4.2%	734.4	47.4%
9.	724	10.2%	54.0	3.5%	788.4	50.9%
10.	941	11.4%	47.2	3.0%	835.6	53.9%
11.	416	12.5%	45.0	2.9%	860.6	56.8%
12.	534	13.6%	43.5	2.8%	924.1	59.6%
13.	615	14.8%	40.0	2.6%	964.1	62.2%
14.	401	15.9%	38.8	2.5%	1,002.9	64.7%
15.	320	17.0%	37.5	2.4%	1,040.4	67.1%
16.	728	18.2%	31.4	2.0%	1,071.8	69.1%
17.	904	19.3%	27.0	1.7%	1,098.8	70.8%
18.	915	20.5%	25.1	1.6%	1,123.9	72.4%
19.	910	21.6%	21.4	1.4%	1,145.3	73.8%
20.	719	22.7%	19.6	1.3%	1,164.9	75.1%
21.	310	23.9%	19.4	1.3%	1,184.3	76.4%
88	950	100.0%	.2 Hrs.	.1%	1,549.1 Hrs.	100.0%

COMMENT:

10% of the operations, reporting production unmeasured, account for 50% of the hours reported.

23% of the operations, reporting production unmeasured, account for 75% of hours reported.

removal contracted out instead of having it done as an in-house function? If an airline is in the business of moving passengers and freight, why must it operate its own on-site maintenance with all the attendant labor and spare parts costs and problems?

HOW CONTINUOUS IMPROVEMENT USES ACCURATE COSTING TO ASSURE ACTIVITY BASED MANAGEMENT

A very important test tool used to augment the re-engineering philosophy is Activity Based Costing (ABC), briefly covered in Chapter 9. When re-allocations of indirect, overhead and administrative charges are based on actual measured activity, the results of re-engineering studies can truly be appreciated. However, continuous improvement demands that these measurements and related reports continue to drive the ABC analysis.

Obviously, all improvements to direct work procedures, materials and services used, as well as purchasing activities, should broaden the base and the incentive for ongoing improvement. Thus, the testing of burden costs is a significant part of continuous improvement.

Activity Based Management (ABM) allows managers to escape the traditional mind-set of historical performance measurements. By applying ABC principles to those functions which were heretofore percentage add-ons, the measurement and improvement of these burden functions become a natural by-product. Each indirect, overhead and administrative function has always been handled by traditional accounting procedures—procedures which calculated burden rates based on arbitrary bases such as direct labor and materials. Analysis of these costs, by functions performed by these overhead organizations, has uncovered a whole new set of measurement and accounting tools to analyze costs.

Naturally, true costing also leads to improvements in areas long overlooked, and perhaps never analyzed for improvement. The simple theory behind ABC is that managers should emphasize analysis of cost drivers, not just the total costs themselves. In this way, costs are attached to functions performed by these burden departments. This allows for two immediate analytical questions to surface:

1. Is the burden function worth its cost as a service that positively supports the base function of the operating entity? If burden is charged in an appliance wholesale distribution company by base hours of pickers, packers and materials handlers, a percentage allocation of total procurement costs by these labor hours expended may mask some ongoing costs for

insupportable functions. For example, what is the relative value of sales entertainment and travel expense, which will increase in the budget when more direct warehousing hours are expended? This is especially pertinent where this increase is solely driven by order size increases, which may be totally independent of ongoing sales efforts.

2. By leveraging costs of those activities performed by the burden function, analysis of the benefits derived from these costs can commence. Such a descending array of costs leads to significant cost reductions due to increasing the cost/benefit ratio.

HOW A PURCHASING GROUP
CAN FOSTER COST REDUCTIONS

A typical purchasing department performs three major functions, namely:

- Managing basic operations, such as issuing purchase orders (where this function has yet to be delegated to a user group), aid in the scheduling of contractors and other suppliers, initiation of scrap sales, promotion of salvage and modification of obsolete and defective items, expedition of delayed shipments, correction of billing errors, approval of accounts payable invoices from receiver data, assessment of vendor and industry lead time changes, insertion of buying data into the MRP system, etc.

- Acting as prime supplier contact for selection, contractual negotiation, quality certification, rating of overall performance, bid preparation and coordination of responses, pre-award surveys and audit, assessment of damages, evaluation of contractual clauses, extrication from losing contracts through buyouts or legal remedies, etc.

- Getting involved in new systems and product/service development, working with product/service design functions, procuring custom (one-of-a-kind) materials and services for the research and development function, aiding the sales and marketing group through sampling procurement in the open market, developing and updating materials requirement lead times, integrating procurement files into the Electronic Data Interchange (EDI) network, aiding in the operation of make-or-buy decisions, and performing value analyses.

In addition, administrative functions are performed that include the usual data entry, reporting of progress, attendance at production, design, sales and quality assurance meetings, providing procurement staff personnel service support, as well as the myriad of other services each firm requires of any operating department.

Since most of the above-described procurement services are not sensitive to the volume of work produced, or even the volume of sales delivered, the usual cost absorption approach is to treat the whole purchasing function as a pure fixed cost. Consider that it makes no difference if the procurement is for 5 or 50; no more work is required of the data entry clerk, the payment approver of shipping dock receivers, or the various managers in the department.

With Activity Based Costing, the purchasing function is not reviewed solely in terms of salaries, fringes, travel, data processing equipment, supplies and the like; but, rather, what does it buy and how is this function performed. By attaching cost factors to such functions as invoice approval, analysts can lock in their cost improvement efforts on high cost functions that may add little or no value to the product or service ultimately supplied. A further advantage relates to the identification of costs that can be eliminated by capital investment in both technology and operational improvements.

CASE STUDY: CREATING SAVINGS BY TRUE COSTING OF THE PURCHASING FUNCTION

A Missouri casting company found the following cost breakdown of purchasing operational time very useful for finding areas to cut the fat:

- selecting outsourcing partners 28%
- entering and communicating engineering change orders 18%
- attending staff meetings (called by others) 15%
- expediting late or urgent deliveries 14%
- training and certifying suppliers 11%
- contractual negotiations, including resolution of problems arising from existing contracts (delivery, quality) 9%
- examining and entering lead time changes 2%
- scrap, rework, salvage and re-supply activities 1%
- special reports required by management 1%

The above activities accounted for $2/3$ of procurement personnel time; an additional $1/3$ of procurement personnel time was spent on long-range projects and administrative functions. The percentages for the nine activities were determined by work sampling (described in the previous chapter) over a period of three representative months at a cost of about 11 minutes per day.

IDENTIFYING CORE ACTIVITIES

The first step was to identify activities which added little value to the overall function. Instead of randomly looking for these cost reduction targets, the consultants worked their way down from the largest time users to the smallest. This recognized the leveraging principal that large gains can come from small savings in significant areas of cost.

The next step was to ask "What can be eliminated?" This approach recognizes the well-known cost reduction philosophy that states, "the highest form of improvement is elimination!". There is probably nothing more frustrating than spending effort and other resources to improve an operation that could be eliminated. In this case, any activity that did not add value to the service rendered was targeted for elimination. The major targets were redundant paperwork, excessive expediting, and performing a job twice instead of completing it on the first try. In addition, those services that added little value for the benefits received were either combined with others, reduced through routinization, or modified to a fraction of their previously required time use.

Savings also came from the introduction of new technologies, such as from the introduction of bar-coded invoices, purchase orders and receivers. The managers learned that cost reduction efforts had to focus on areas of greatest opportunity to achieve the stated purchasing goal of running a supply management operation, not merely perform as a transaction processing group.

LOOKING TO CUT THE FAT

With this as the overriding philosophy, the purchasing group sought ways, through applying Activity Based Management, to cut the fat from non-value added functions in order to strengthen the muscle of value added ones. They pinpointed such needed value added areas as:

- performing value analyses,
- applying standardization and commonality studies,
- developing logistical transport routing and supply matrices,
- performing supplier audits,
- conducting pre-award surveys,
- reducing overall cycle times for engineering change orders,
- arranging consignment and vendor stocking contracts
- reducing time of materials possession to aid cash flow
- relating new product development to single sourcing and total quality control applications.

Thus, cost savings come not only from elimination or improvement of present activities through activity based management studies, but additional savings can also come from adding available technology and techniques for which little time was heretofore available. External savings may also be derived from working with your single source suppliers to whom you introduce activity based costing in order to have the generated cost savings reflected in price reductions to the supplied company.

No matter how these savings are achieved, an underlying principle is that the test results must act as a spark to continuous improvement, not an end in the cycle of test, train, and improve.

USE AVAILABLE COST REDUCTION CHECKLISTS TO PROVIDE A QUICK START TO THE TEST PROCESS

The concept of testing what exists against specific criteria for improvement is one of the oldest approaches to cost reduction, if not the original one. From the time of Frederick Winslow Taylor's experiments with manual coal shoveling in the 1920's, checklists for improvement have been developed by industrial engineers, methods and systems analysts, efficiency experts, and work simplification consultants. The purpose of using these checklists has been to provide some semblance of order to the testing process itself.

Random questioning of activities can never be as productive as an organized investigative approach that starts with a review of the overall business strategy to reach agreed goals. This organized approach then continues on through the organizational hierarchy to the questioning of those base-level activities as to their relevance to this stated objective. Coupled with the achievement of consensus approval for cost reduction actions, is the need for controls to assure that the selected cost reductions not only drop to the bottom line, but also can continuously be achieved if not continuously bettered.

However, since these checklists serve the purpose of allowing one to achieve a review of what is in a relatively short period of time, they are alluded to as a simplistic tool in the test phase of cutting the fat.

EXAMPLES OF COST REDUCTION CHECKLISTS

Figures 10-5 through 10-9 show various types of cost reduction checklists available. This small group of examples merely scratches the surface of the total number of available forms and questionnaires. These few were chosen to represent what's out there.

Figure 10-5 Example of a Simplistic Cost Reduction Checklist

ALTERNATIVE METHODS	ACTION REQUIRED	ADVANTAGES	DISADVANTAGES	FURTHER INVESTIGATIONS
COMPETITION	1. Create competitive spirit, provide awards & recognition 2. Provide comparative records and reports 3. Set up standards for competition 4. Record or chart improvement	1. Stimulates group thinking and team spirit 2. Makes available a continual progress record 3. Capitalizes on normal drive *to excel* (to produce more and better) rather than to defeat rivals	1. Competition may become negative or get out of hand 2. Requires exceptional leadership 3. Can become time-consuming 4. Quality may be sacrificed for quantity if not well motivated	1. Tensions arising from competing groups 2. Can emphasis be kept on *desire to excel* 3. Rugged individualism is declining as a motive force
TRAINING	1. Choose the subjects 2. Develop the course 3. Select instructors 4. Form groups 5. Provide facilities and schedules 6. Set a budget	1. Positive organized approach with singleness of purpose 2. Has permanent value 3. Create good atmosphere 4. Gives all an equal opportunity to learn 5. Is creative and developmental	1. High cost 2. Time-consuming in comparison to results attained 3. May meet resistance 4. Results last no longer than 2 yrs.—need constant refresher course 5. Hard to distinguish "fads" from subjects of permanent value	Inside or outside training Mandatory or voluntary Timing and learning Ability of group
TASK FORCE (or Management Groups)	1. Select a group and define the area or project 2. Set up schedule and time 3. Provide guidance regarding limits, rules, authority, business etiquette 4. Follow through	1. Multi-disciplined approach with cross section of management focused on the same problem 2. Small, flexible & self-starting 3. *Can get fast results* 4. Gives the team recognition	1. Can reach an impasse by getting non-solvable difference of opinion 2. May bypass normal lines of control 3. May lead to buck passing and/or uncontrolled meetings 4. Solution may be sound but impossible—hence hard to reject	Selection of individuals: 1. Self-starters 2. Cooperative 3. Keep on beam

195

Figure 10-6 Simplistic Checklist of Problem Indicators and Potential Solutions

Problem Indicator   **Cost Reduction Technique**

I. ORGANIZATION

A. Inability to pinpoint responsibility.

B. Poor policy formulation.

C. Difficulty determining "What to do, when."

A. Organizational analysis and orientation.

B. Executive training (appreciation and orientation).

C. Systems and procedure analysis.

II. PRODUCT DESIGN

A. Good product, no sales.

B. Good product, can't make it economically.

C. Cost higher than estimated.

D. New product research lagging.

E. Customer complaint—service problem.

F. Packaging cost out of line.

A. Market analysis, including analysis of pricing policy.

B. Manufacturing capabilities study and methods analysis.

C. Cost analysis and control.

D. Budget priority and scheduling analysis.

E. Reliability control.

F. Packaging engineering.

III. PLANT LOCATIONS LAYOUTS

A. Cost and disposition of labor unknown.

B. Evaluating location in terms of procurement and distribution cost variables.

C. Determining where to place equipment and how to provide areas of work.

D. Machinery replacement untimely and costly.

A. Labor area surveys.

B. Linear programming.

C. Work flow analysis in plant layout.

D. Dynamic machinery replacement analysis.

IV. PERSONNEL

A. Wage inequities.

B. Poor selection of personnel.

C. New (and old) supervisors do not realize they are managers and part of management.

D. Lack of incentive to do better.

E. Poor dossiers on personnel and no use of historical information.

F. Constant grievances relating to petty occurrences.

A. Job evaluation and job pricing.

B. Aptitude testing.

C. Supervisory training programs.

D. Incentive plans (not necessarily financial) including merit rating.

E. Creative use of personnel records and records improvement.

F. Employee attitude training.

Figure 10-6   Continued

Problem Indicator	**Cost Reduction Technique**

V. PRODUCTION PLANNING AND CONTROL

Problem Indicator	Cost Reduction Technique
A. Orders lost in the plant.	A. PPC procedure analysis.
B. Lots of paper work for little product	B. PPC procedure analysis.
C. Priorities not honored. Personnel do not know what follows what. Material "waits" and searches. People or equipment time not available. Excessive machine downtime for lack of work.	C. Better scheduling through MRP analysis, linear programming and lead time charting.
D. Over and undertooling for the job.	D. Economic methods analysis—tool control.
E. Inequitable performance standards which lead to soldiering and complaints.	E. Time study performance analysis and control.
F. Inefficient, costly and unsafe methods.	F. Motion study, training and standardization.
G. Return on investment and inventory extremely low, plus stockouts, deteriorating floor and crane wastage, obsolescence, etc.	G. Inventory control techniques including ABC analysis, reorder point and safety stock determination, economic order and manufacture quantity determination, records analysis, standardization of parts, parts numbering for usage.
H. Excessive machine downtime for maintenance.	H. Idle machine analysis. Preventive maintenance techniques.
I. Poor utilization of material handling equipment.	I. Work flow analysis. Plant layout changes.
J. Poor control due to lack of sufficient, timely action.	J. Reports and control surveys.

VI. PURCHASING

Problem Indicator	Cost Reduction Technique
A. Poor contract placement with unreliable vendors.	A. Pre-award surveys.
B. Vendors uncooperative due to poor past relations and misunderstandings.	B. Understandable incoming quality inspection plans, using statistical sampling plans and logical follow-up with vendors.
C. Costly component procurement.	C. Value analysis.
D. Purchased items not in condition of use.	D. Point and condition of use analysis, inventory studies, materials handling capabilities.
E. High demurrage cost.	E. Demurrage analysis.

VII. QUALITY

Problem Indicator	Cost Reduction Technique
A. Scrap and rework losses.	A. through F.
B. Customer quality service cost.	Quality control, quality engineering studies, machine and process
C. Rebates and complaints.	

Figure 10-6   Continued

VII. QUALITY (Continued)

D. Excessive inspection.
E. Downtime due to poor quality.
F. Excess setup cost due to poor quality.

capability analysis, statistical quality control techniques.

VIII. SALES

A. Opportunistic vs. planned sales.

B. Inequitable sales compensations.
C. Poor forecasts of customer demands.
D. Unit profit becoming total item losses.

A. Market research and sales approach controls.
B. Geographical potential surveys.
C. Statistically controlled demand analysis.
D. Break-even analysis, economic profitability analysis, including marginal analysis.

Be advised that every approach may contain the germ of a single idea that may have been overlooked during more sophisticated analyses. From personal experience, I have found that at least one useful idea comes to me each time I re-review the myriad of checklists that I have collected over the years. To improve on this approach, I have developed a computer directory of these checklists, allowing me to access appropriate sub-headings.

INITIATE COST REDUCTION TECHNIQUE TRAINING TO GAIN CONTINUOUS RESULTS

There is a common perception that if you motivate and empower personnel, they will, with their present skills, create improvements that will lead to cost improvements. Perhaps. But, consider that a group trained in the uses of the varied cost reduction techniques would have a much greater chance at ultimate success. Compare this to the much-heralded "quickie" improvements that result from one-shot motivational approaches. For this reason, cost reduction technique training should be an integral part of the concept of continuous improvement.

Figure 10-9 lists a group of negative statements by those not convinced that improvements are in their best interest. However, the list demonstrates the need to prepare potential cost reduction contributors with selling skills. The primary one is that people buy, not because you are selling, but because they see a benefit to their own perceived needs. These needs could range from the basic drive to ensure job security to the emotional need to be a part of their group's drive for recognition.

Figure 10–7   A Graphic Example of a Cost Reduction Checklist - Macro Look

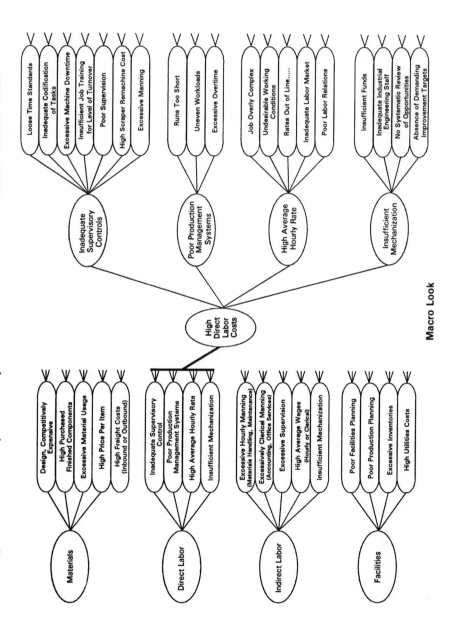

Macro Look

Figure 10-8   A Graphic Example of a Quality Cost Reduction Checklist - Micro Look

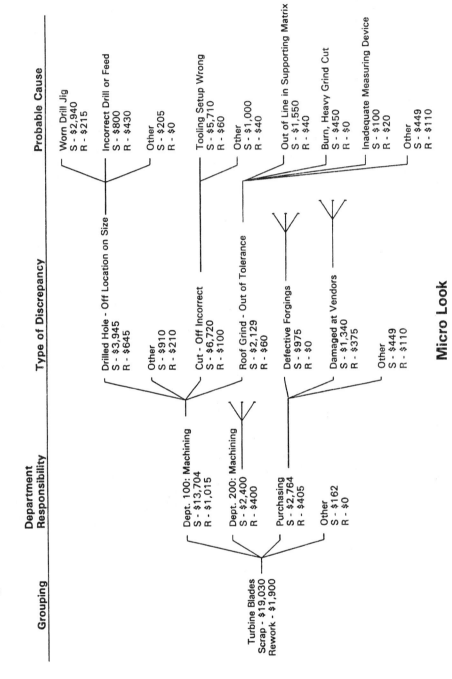

Micro Look

Figure 10-9   A Checklist of Responses You Should Be Prepared to Handle

60 Excuses for a Closed Mind:

1. We tried that before.
2. Our place is different.
3. It costs too much.
4. That's beyond our responsibility.
5. We're all too busy to do that.
6. That's not my job.
7. It's too radical a change.
8. We don't have the time.
9. Not enough help.
10. That will make other equipment obsolete.
11. Let's make a market research test of it first.
12. Our plant is too small for it.
13. Not practical for operating people.
14. "They" will never buy it.
15. The union will scream
16. We've never done it before.
17. It's against company policy.
18. Runs up our overhead.
19. We don't have the authority.
20. That's too ivory tower.
21. Let's get back to reality.
22. That's not our problem.
23. Why change it, it's still working o.k.
24. I don't like the idea.
25. You're right—but.
26. You're two years ahead of your time.
27. We're not ready for that.
28. We don't have the money.
29. Can't teach an old dog new tricks.
30. It isn't in the budget.
31. Good thought, but impractical.
32. Let's hold it in abeyance.
33. Let's give it more thought.
34. Top management would never go for it.
35. Let's put it in writing.
36. We'll be the laughing stock.
37. Not that again.
38. We'd lose money in the long run.
39. Where'd you dig that one up?
40. That's what we can expect from the staff.
41. We did all right without it.
42. It's never been tried before.
43. Let's shelve it for the time being.
44. Let's form a committee!
45. Has anyone else ever tried it?
46. Customers won't like it.
47. I don't see the connection.
48. It won't work in our plant.
49. What you are really saying is . . .
50. Maybe that will work in your department but not in mine.
51. The Executive Committee will never go for it.
52. Don't you think we should look into it further before we act.
53. What do they do in our competitor's plant?
54. Let's all sleep on it.
55. It can't be done.
56. It's too much trouble to change.
47. It won't pay for itself.
58. I know a fellow who tried it.
59. It's impossible.
60. We've always done it this way.

Whatever the goals of management, the objectives of any program that requires the cooperation and positive actions of others demands that:

- the participants clearly see "what's in it for them," and
- they are trained, either formally or informally, in the skills, techniques and disciplines of the program that is being promoted to them.

In this way, continuous improvement becomes more than a temporary fad that is justified by temporary improvements. Ask any promoters of zero defects, job enlargement, quality circles, task force technology, short interval scheduling, suggestions systems, and the like about initial successes vs. long term improvements.

Figure 10-10 depicts the KOBERT WHEEL, named for me by an Air Force General at the Air Material Command at Wright-Patterson AFB. As part of a research foundation study by Ohio State University, I was asked to provide a maintenance scheduling training program for 1100 world-wide personnel engaged in maintaining the B-52 fleet. Out

Figure 10–10   The Kobert Wheel for Self Analysis to Determine Job Performance Deficiencies in Understanding Responsibilities and Authority re Cost Reduction

Cost Improvement Training Can Be
Measured by Determining Pre and Post Conceptions

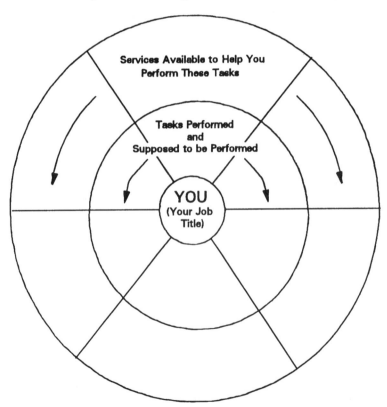

The Kobert Wheel

of sheer naivete, I asked the General, "What do the present incumbents think their task is relative to maintenance scheduling?" He responded, "Why don't you ask them!" Hence, the Kobert Wheel was born.

At the center of the Wheel, the survey participants placed their job title. (92% had this correct.) In the spokes of the Wheel, the future trainees were required to name those tasks they were now performing, as well as those they thought were required to be performed as a part of their present job. The results were a definite eye-opener to the General, since less than $\frac{1}{2}$ of the respondents indicated that maintenance scheduling was a function that they were either performing or were expected to perform! And, this was the topic that was chosen to be delivered to them. Imagine describing, through training, the newest maintenance scheduling techniques to a group that felt this was not applicable to their present jobs! Obviously, management had a pre-training task to define the specific requirements of the maintenance management positions to at least $\frac{1}{2}$ the potential trainees.

In the spaces defined by the tire of the Kobert Wheel, the respondents were asked to list those services available to them in the organization, which could assist them in carrying out their functions, as listed in the spokes of the Wheel. The results obtained were a real shocker. The answers were outrageous, in terms of the expenditures that the Air Material Command had made to support the front line supervisors.

Little knowledge of the established support departments, and their available services, were shown in the survey. A clear lack of knowledge of help available to the maintenance supervisors showed that training was required to illustrate the services that could be utilized upon request. These services included receiving cost data arrayed in some usable format, personnel delineated by skill and available capacities, available and scheduled equipment vs. deadline requirements for the maintained aircraft, priority work isolated by particular departments, and information relative to the pool of skills that might be tapped on a temporary basis.

It became obvious to all concerned that there was much work to be done to prepare for the mandated maintenance scheduling training program. This is the first step in assuring that training will be received and realistically applied. Since training is a key part of a continuous improvement program, you should make sure that the criteria for success are understood and agreed to before attempting to perform "shotgun" training, i.e., fire a blast, hoping that some of the pellets will strike home. By pre-determining the potential trainees' conceptions of (1) what their job is, plus what is expected of them, and (2) the personnel and staff available to aid them perform these specific tasks, planned training programs can be structured, aimed as a "single rifle shot" that will hit many more trainees with specific result-oriented training.

FOUR STEPS TO ASSURE
TRAINING FOR RESULTS

The usual rationale for sending an employee to a training program, either conducted on-site or at a public seminar, is to provide skill upgrading by seeing what's out there that the trainee may then employ back on the job. The sponsor of the delegate is hoping that the generalized knowledge in a specific discipline area can then be converted to a positive application upon the attendee's return.

This is at times an impossible task, where the trainee attends a feel-good seminar. At these, he/she is entertained with stories of problems encountered by the speaker, but no specific actions or techniques are presented that the delegate can apply upon returning to the real world of the job.

Part of this problem relates to the sponsor's naive hope that the attendee will be able to convert generalized knowledge received into specific local applications. Worse yet, is the expectation that the returning delegate's trip report will result in a whole group of motivated employees declaring that the described techniques can be locally applied for immediate positive results.

The following four-step approach is presented as an alternative, aimed at achieving a much higher percentage of positive change from the training expenditure in the continuous improvement cycle. It is intended for on-site training purposes only, the type of training that has proven to be the most effective when introducing and maintaining a cost reduction program designed for continuous improvement.

STEP 1: PLAN PRE-TRAINING TIME
ON-SITE FOR THE TRAINER

About 5 weeks prior to a planned on-site training program, the seminar presenter(s) is invited to spend meaningful time with each potential attendee at their individual workplace. The instructor is invited to gather opinions, facts, and general concerns from these future program delegates . . . relative to the CR program to be presented. For a group of between 10 and 15, this should take about 2 days of 45 minutes to an hour with each person.

If the instructor is so authorized, the concerns of the interviewees should be addressed at this first meeting. However, if the company would rather not have an "outsider" answer these important questions, they can be answered subsequently by the involved manager, or at the seminar. It would also be of help if the company establishes the ground rules for the instructor's interview, by either issuing a paper prior to the scheduled interview appointments, or by addressing the purpose of the upcoming interviews at a general meeting. The venue and format depend on the openness that exists between the potential trainee and other elements of management.

STEP #2: INCORPORATE THE INFORMATION GATHERED FROM TRAINEES INTO THE PRESENTED MATERIAL

The instructor will incorporate the main points raised by the potential trainees into the program. These subjects will be woven into the presented program by stimulating delegate discussion, using specific examples drawn from the interviews, and through "floating" potential solutions to the trainees. The advantage of performing Step #1 will now surface. Since the group will have met and become cursorily acquainted with the seminar leader at the initial interviews, many barriers to an open discussion of company problems and opportunities will be dissolved.

Since the training program will be attended by enrollees that have met the instructor, the attendees should have a lessened resistance to presenting logical solutions relative to the specific problems presented by the instructor. In fact, many of the proposals could be adopted at the seminar meeting, since they were presented as real life situations to a friendly audience.

STEP 3: PLAN A PHYSICAL FOLLOW-UP TO DETERMINE PROGRESS

About one month after the seminar, the instructor will return to interview each delegate that attended the seminar. The discussions will revolve around:

1. what cost reduction installations have been made, or have been planned, in the intervening time. These can be either by the individual or as part of a working group,
2. a discussion of the problems encountered, and
3. suggestions for overcoming obstacles.

The very knowledge that the training dates are but a prelude to expected participation in improvements generally acts to motivate the majority of the trainees.

A final oral report is provided to the sponsoring managers during the latter part of this visit.

STEP 4: REQUIRE A REPORT SHOWING POSITIVE TRAINING RESULTS

Training results, measured in improvement plans and installations are reported and monitored.

Training for results has an objective: positive actions by the trainees who feel the program met their concerns and was specific enough to indicate logical and supportable solutions. The payoff is not in the receipt of a certificate, a fistful of highly-rated evaluations, or just a general "feel good" emotion. Results are measured in plans, cooperation towards a common, accepted goal, followed by installation of projects which are proposed and supported by all involved. This should be the objective of the training phase in the continuous improvement cycle.

HOW TO MAKE COST REDUCTION A PRIME OBJECTIVE OF THE TRAINING FUNCTION

There are various, existing approaches to conducting training that should be noted before attempting to install the training for results approach, similar to that described in the preceding section. Some of the most commonly used strategies are:

THE SHOTGUN APPROACH

In this situation, a budget is established for training. This budget is related to past years' expenditures, expected income volume, and forecasted organizational changes. From all the training provided at conventions, on-site seminars or continuing education programs at universities, something good will occur. The theory behind this approach is that when you fire a shotgun, some pellets will strike someone, somewhere at some time. Improvements are reported when they do occur, and claims for recognition and justification are immediately pressed by the training group.

THE RIFLE APPROACH

In this style of training, it is imperative that the training group find a subject area(s) where training is obviously lacking, or where training has been mandated by a top manager. This limited area for training is then flooded with programs and stocked with attendees. A well-aimed shot is made with all the department's fire-power at one, or a limited group of priority objectives. If this shot misses, or barely grazes the target, try another rifle shot . . . assuming you have enough reserve ammunition.

COMBINATION OF THE RIFLE AND SHOTGUN APPROACH

Fire a rifle at some targets and a shotgun at others. The hope is that the combination will result in a specific gain attributable to the training function.

COUNT THE NOSTRILS AND DIVIDE BY TWO

This is also called "training by the numbers." If 100 nostrils are sent to training programs, this will equate to training 50 hot bodies. Compare this to the 80 nostrils (40 breathers) that were trained last year. It is obvious that the training program is 25% more effective this year than last! If no one believes this, tell them, "Count the nostrils."

ALL TRAINING IS VALUABLE

This theory starts with the concept that some training is better than no training at all. It graduates to the premise that everyone can benefit from some training all the time. This is a widely-held philosophy among professional societies' and regulatory agencies' training directors, who mandate a specific attendance at annual seminars for certification. These human resource developers justify themselves and their staff by the numbers of attendees at their selected programs. It is related to the count-the-nostrils approach, but varies by the method of selection of topics presented.

For the results oriented manager seeking positive improvements, the above approaches leave some questions begging for answers. For one, what is the zero base? If the present practice of training were discontinued, what would be the loss? Conversely, what savings can be indirectly attributed to the existing training programs? Is the training itself a method of rewarding or recognizing individual accomplishments? Do the graduates feel better afterwards? If the results cannot be tracked, should the effort be reduced? improved? increased?

When a manager sets down his objectives, it will be found that training will be one of them, perhaps not number one. However, resorting to training in order to overcome existing problems, allows the manager to say, "See . . . I'm doing something!" However, is this action the prime item on the shopping list of desired objectives? (It might very well be, if you are the Training Director, and have a training budget to spend.)

After concluding your list of prime cost reduction objectives and strategies, you will assuredly find training on the list. Now, the question is one of priorities. Do you require specific training in a narrow area of discipline? If so, why is someone being sent to a three-day seminar in Los Angeles? For the same cost, you probably could train 10 people on-site in the specifics of your defined problem.

HOW TO PREPARE A POTENTIAL TRAINEE
FOR THE COST REDUCTION SEMINAR

How should a potential trainee be prepared for a training program? Should the trainee be told of your objectives? How is the trainee greeted upon his/her return, especially those who come back with a fistful of ideas and notes? Do you ask for a trip report which is then filed away as a justification for the expense? Do you demand an oral report, followed by agreed appropriate actions? Do you ask for specific improvement proposals, utilizing a format that demands justification for any future expenditures? Can a sample request for improvement be submitted, which when adopted pays for the entire cost of the training venture?

All of the above relate to the steps that make training part of the program to cut the fat. The steps that follow are to assure that training is not just a knee-jerk residual of past inertia, or a personnel reward, or an expenditure one must just live with:

- Choose and get agreement on the objective of the problem resolution action which includes training. Prioritize this potential solution with other solutions proposed for problems awaiting resolution.

- Establish some criteria for success that are measurable. Even a simple statement of expected improvement will suffice; but, remember, the more imprecise the objective, the more difficult it will be to establish a criteria for success, as well as to justify the training expense vs. other priority needs. In the reengineering concept, agreed and necessary functions drive organization, staffing and expenditures, obviously including training expenditures.

- Establish limits of expenditure to meet these criteria for success. If you have unlimited funds, this step can be skipped.

- Schedule and justify training expenditures as part of an overall program to cut the fat, such that each expenditure fits the overall pattern so established (and approved).

- Allow for an expenditure of effort and time to monitor the results of the training expense. Provide a forum for suggested improvements. Demand a sample investment for an agreed improvement. If you cannot achieve a sample improvement, demand a plan for a simple installation. The returning trainee must be made to understand that he/she is part of a training for results effort—not simply a program of expenditure-without-return concept.

To prove the point that training for results has been lacking in the past, take a poll of those who have recently attended a convention or public seminar. First, ask for positive plans or actions that have resulted. The company will be lucky if the convention notes or the seminar workbook are still available. As part of the great American cover-up, the managers who wined and dined in Mexico City will all agree that they are now better managers, caught up with what is current, and prepared to execute positive actions based on this new-found knowledge. The training director will concur with this conclusion, and the divisional

VP, who authorized this expenditure, will point to the approved budget as justification for the approved expenditure for training.

Since the value of training is related to the results of this expenditure, you should re-read the preceding section which defined the steps in training for results. Figures 10-11 and 10-12 are included as samples of specific training programs that define their objectives and specifically state the techniques covered. Compare these to the outlines of programs that promise generic solutions for your very specific problems.

SUMMING UP: Assuring Continuous Improvement Using the Continuous Testing and Training Approach

Most one-shot cost reduction programs fail because they do not allow for a continuous cycle of "test, train, and then do it again". Thus, it is essential for creating a continuous improvement program that monitoring and testing activities be planned as part of the initial set-up. To do less will guarantee that the results will not be long-lasting, and will not act as a steppingstone to more cost reduction applications. The first slice in cutting the fat must lay the groundwork for both achieving the continuation of promised savings, as well as to act as the catalyst for further cost improvement.

To assure this, testing (monitoring) of activities should be formalized, so that realistic and approved targets can be set. In addition, the cost reduction program should be all-encompassing, to include suppliers, customers and, of course, all levels of the internal organization on down to first-level supervisors.

Activity Based Costing has bred Activity Based Management, encompassing a whole range of tools that continuously question functions as to their worth in the enterprise. Totally insupportable costs are the first targets; costs which are barely worth their investment/result ratio are the next functions to be analyzed. All functions are not merely reviewed in terms of the functions they are presently performing and have traditionally performed. Instead, all functions are tested in terms of the value they offer to the enterprise.

Many of these ongoing costs can be eliminated through the application of new technology, by being combined with existing functions, and through investment in savings-specific,

**Figure 10–11   Example of Specific Objective and Outline
(Vendor Certification Program)**

**Summary of 25 Key Benefits of
Attending This Course**

At This Seminar You Learn:

1. How a Vendor Certification Program identifies and solves manufacturing problems at their root
2. Why it is the quickest way to gain control of your operation
3. The eight essential steps in implementing a successful program within six months
4. Why and when JIT and Vendor Certification are synergistic
5. What Japanese manufacturers do that we don't, and should
6. An understanding of how Vendor Certification will change the culture, impact, and quality work life of your whole company
7. The positive impact of a zero defect program on your inventory turns
8. How to measure the true cost of quality
9. When paying more may be cheaper in the long run
10. How to select the suppliers you want without making enemies
11. Why you need a partnership relationship between supplier and manufacturer, and how to achieve it
12. Why company teamwork is the key to a successful Vendor Certification Program
13. How to eliminate those kinds of engineering changes that are more trouble than they're worth
14. A practical method to predict your post-implementation results, and when they'll begin to peak
15. The five inspection tools and techniques critical to your quality improvement process
16. The most effective techniques to improve and control your supplier base

Seminar Outline

*What Supplier Certification Is and
Why You Need It*

A. How vendor certification solves today's quality issues
B. Understanding the relationships to JIT and TQC
C. Why certification helps your company respond faster to changing conditions

*How You Can Integrate JIT and
Supplier Involvement*

A. Acquiring the right mind-set for JIT— Effects on the quality of work life
B. Requirements for achieving zero inventory
C. What planning systems are necessary to begin using value, using value engineering/analysis as a tool
D. Effects and challenges for engineering, procurements, and production
E. Formulating new and effective resolutions for logistics

*How to Achieve Total Quality Control
with Your Suppliers*

A. How to make the right product right the first time
B. Where, when, and how to use TQC techniques
C. How to arrive at zero defects
D. What cost/quality trade-offs you should and should not make with vendors
E. Defining and implementing the concept of TQC

How to Develop a "Win-Win" Relationship with Your Suppliers

A. Why price increases can generate savings when waste is eliminated

17. Potential pitfalls to avoid when selecting your suppliers
18. What to do when a "bad egg" slips through your vendor screening tests
19. Who in your company should be part of the evaluation team
20. How to conduct a supplier survey using our own, tested questionnaire and assessment techniques
21. Why a partnership relationship is critical to the success of your Vendor Certification Program
22. How to educate your team so they believe in the philosophy behind Vendor Certification
23. How to develop a report card on suppliers that monitors their performance every step of the way
24. What you need to include in every Purchasing Agreement
25. How JIT and Vendor Certification together produce total quality control

B. How and why of supplier selection—one vendor or many?
C. Techniques for evaluating suppliers
D. How to make a quality survey of vendors that enhances formation of a solid partnership
E. Who are the key players involved?
F. Typical time frames and steps for implementation of vendor certification

How to Implement the Supplier Certification Program

A. Methods that produce the most cooperation and why
B. Introducing the program with a supplier symposium—How to set it up and what to talk about
C. Why the role of vendor education and training is important
D. Which methodology best rates supplier's adherence to the program's objectives
E. What should be included in purchasing and quality agreements
F. Measuring progress and status—teamwork approach vs. performance benchmarks

capital investments. Another function test relates to buying time and other managerial assets to perform those functions that should be performed, but for which there has been no past funding or time dedication. Elimination and combination thus can present improvement opportunities.

Quick-and-dirty checklists provide a glimpse of how the testing function can be immediately applied. This improvement sampling approach gets the inertia for the continuous improvement cycle going. They become the base for application of more sophisticated analyses. But, beginning with the checklist approach, one can build towards future applications which support the popular South Pole Theory, which is: "When you are at the South Pole, any step—in any direction—is a step up (to the North)."

Another important step in continuous improvement is the necessity to support specific on-site training. Reliance on good old common sense by all motivated employees empow-

Figure 10–12   Example of a Specific Program Outline

**Program: Cut the Fat,
Not the Muscle**

*Investing in future profitability requires
more than just cost slashing*

- Squeezing cash from assets. . .not
essential services
- Be tough on disciplinary spending. . .
but, cost analysis is not a discretionary activity
- Spending maoney to make money
- Adequate cost analysis may mask
available cost reduction options

*Practical steps for moving a cost
reduction activity to a profit
improvement strategy*

- Determining which products or services should be eliminated, modified
or absorbed
- Analyzing worthiness of expense additions or reductions
- Factoring market share into required
actions for choosing applicable techniques
- Quantifying cost reduction opportunities by stimulating results that drop
to the bottom line

*How to view expenditures
as investments*

- Stimulating investment withdrawal
from marginal winners and outright
losers
- Evaluating the potential of future returns on investment
- Utilizing cost reduction strategies in
return-on-investment analyses

*Leveraging cost reductions
for increased profits*

- Using cost inequalities to help define
an overall cost reduction strategy
- Determining criticality of change by
quantifying expected results

- Utilizing the Pareto principle in the
analysis of homogeneous cost factors or categories
- Promoting small savings in significant cost areas vs. large savings in
insignificant areas of opportunity

*Separating blockbuster (revolutionary)
development from logical evolution
of existing products and services*

- Staffing a development team that focuses on cost reduction in the earliest phases of the project
- Providing the development team with
decision-making authority in the cost
reduction arena

*Partnering with your suppliers to foster
cost reductions that improve
joint profitability*

- Co-operation as a viable alternative
to the application of traditional price
negotiation techniques
- Involving your suppliers in new process, product or service development
- Applying cost structuring in pre-
award planning
- Applying J-I-T single sourcing practices to reduce cycle times through
investment in supplier certification

*Better time management as
a cost reduction technique*

- Matching time spent with work objectives and accomplishment values
- Determining the delegatable aspects
of your job
- How to improve your desk management
- Working with your secretary as a
managerial aide
- Improving both formal and informal
meetings by using the meeting call
approach
- The best uses of tickler files, to-do
lists and voice mail

How to utilize the distinctions provided by fixed, mixed and variable cost analysis

- Building a cost/profit/volume curve
- Working with the variable portions of mixed costs to isolated prime targets for cost reductions
- Conducting service or product profit analyses to isolated specific areas of leveraging opportunity
- CR phasing actions that reduce the break-even point

Gauging the impact of increased or decreased volume of sales on administrative cost ratios

- Fulfilling basic (ground zero) administrative service requirements at the lowest cost
- Measuring the output of units of service vs. the input of administrative cost elements
- Automating responses, summarizations, decision-making and communication by applying management-by-exception principles to data processing
- Eliminating excessive approvals by establishing levels of acceptance based on cost effects of decisions

The training for results concept

- Converting the training budget to a cost reduction commitment
- Quantifying areas where the leveraging of training costs can be used to provide the greatest CR opportunities
- Monitoring the training investment

Reducing materials cost

- Analyzing inventory possession cycle times in order to reduce cash commitments
- Instituting vendor and consignment stocking practices to reduce materials' carrying costs

- Performing bottleneck analysis to reduce ongoing work-in-process possession cost
- Applying turns ratios by components, cost centers and by storage facilities
- Evaluating costly safety stock requirements by stockout critical criteria
- Reducing stock verification costs by eliminating manual data entry into the computer system

Reducing costs of demand and preventive maintenance

- Using the maintenance skills matrix to allow for the application of pool scheduling techniques
- Maintaining maintenance inventories by criticality replenishment time
- Applying local area maintenance (LAM) approach to scheduling demand maintenance
- Criteria for use of outside maintenance skills and inventories

Why this Seminar is different from others in the field

Some old icons that mandated cost reduction schemes have fallen. Eliminating 'warm bodies' has always been the first approach to any cost reduction effort. After all, direct costs drive all other cost factors. In addition, the magnitude of personnel costs has served to place them as the number one attack option in order to leverage all other cost reduction actions.

In the heat of battle, management wants action not analysis. So, 'good soldiers' move quickly to reduce the personnel roster as the first, and sometimes the last effort before some other program becomes primary.

At the close of the 20th century, direct labor costs have shrunk to 10–15% of total direct costs in many industries. *(continued)*

Table 10–12 *(continued)*

Thus, even a 10% direct personnel reduction will only cut between 1 and 1.5% of total costs. Because of this change in cost cutting leverage, the simple cost cutting activities of previous managements are no longer filled with the same opportunities as before. Yet, reducing the direct workforce is still the first concern of most cost reduction efforts today . . . perhaps because such a strategy is both easy to perform and is highly visible.

A simple example of the new approaches can be demonstrated by the opportunities which now exist in a manufacturing or processing firm. A wise approach would now be to segregate those costs which are production related from those which are associated with absorbing past capital expenditures. In other words, a strategy to sell off excess capacity may prove to be more fruitful than expending management and sales efforts to utilize this excess capacity. This will also allow for matching direct personnel reductions to desired, not just existing, capacity.

No one will question cutting fat, but future profitability is at stake where you cut into muscle, bone and nerves of the corporate entity.

The conventional approach to cost reduction includes:

1. Do the same things as before, but at a reduced cost.
2. Perform the above by cutting capital and expense budgets across-the-board by a fixed percentage.
3. Then, as a possible next step, rethink how the compnay can and should be doing business.

Step 3 should be performed prior to, or at the very least during stages 1 and 2.

A painful search for alternatives should be an on-going program, but, at the very least should be performed during the mandatory and immediate cry for cost reductions. The major difference in strategy will be between:

- 'Save money!' and
- 'Improve profits!'

Both avenues of opportunity will conclude in some desired result at some point in time; but, the longer-range effect of the latter strategy of improving profits can also involve short-term cost-cutting measures. The application of the 'improve profits' strategy will result in a program that cuts the fat while it saves and even builds the muscle.

Who Should Attend This Course

There are two elements of management that should attend.

- In the large enterprise, middle and top management are under constant pressure to develop creative cost reduction programs. This is true in both large industrial manufacturing and processing firms, as well as in large service companies. Titles such as the following have been targeted:

  Financial Controllers
  Product Managers
  Directors of Operations
  Product or Service Designers
  Cost Reduction Committee Members
  Purchasing Directors
  Office Managers
  Marketing and Pricing Strategists
  New Business Developers
  Strategic Planners
  Information Systems Managers
  Plant Managers
  Capital Budgeting Planners
  Systems and Procedures Analysts
  Auditors.

- In a smaller enterprise, consisting of less than 100 personnel on staff, the single entrepreneur who has founded and developed the business is a prime target. Without the need for extensive reviews and ap-provals, he can move quickly to adopt the many 'cookbook-style' steps to installing a cost reduction program that cuts fat, but also strengthens muscle, bone and the nervous system of the enterprise.

ered to improve operations will get the company just so far. There are obvious limitations to the skills which employees will bring to the testing and analysis of operations as they presently exist. No doubt their most important skill is knowledge of particular operations. But, management must provide the larger view of overall functional objectives, investment limitations, and specific cost-reduction skill training.

Where to look is as important as what you are looking at. As described in Chapter 9, at the very least employees should be provided with true cost data, leveraged reports, and the tools for testing objectives vs. actual results obtained.

Training for results requires four steps, which include participation by the potential trainees in both the subject matter yet to be presented, and the actual installation of agreed improvements. In this way, training becomes an important part of the continuous improvement cycle. It allows for trainee participation in the selection of the training materials, as well as providing for an active role in the installation of improvements . . . this, by the parties most affected by the plan to cut the fat. In this way, the training function has an important role in assuring the success of a continuous improvement program.

There is no doubt that a continuous improvement program has a multitude of benefits over investing merely in a one-shot cost-cutting program. Today's managers must realize this, and take appropriate cost effective steps to assure ongoing cost improvements.

INCREASE PRODUCTIVITY BY POOLING TALENT AFTER THE APPLICATION OF TRUE COSTING

Arousing the will to work ranks a close second to maintaining this attitude. The problem is that too many productivity improvement programs are short-lived. Business history books are filled with concepts that worked dramatically for brief periods of time—then flickered and died out. Examples of this phenomena abound, and some were mentioned in Chapter 10.

Western Electric's Hawthorne Studies of the workplace environment's effect on productivity, Montgomery Ward's short flirtation with short-interval-scheduling, Volvo's experiments with job enrichment and enlargement, Maytag's employee suggestion motivation system, Texas Instrument's job restructuring program, General Motors' crewing and group technology applications at their Lordstown, Ohio plant, Corning Glass' productivity measurement appraisal at their Medford Works, General Foods' productivity payment scheme at their Topeka operations . . . all were successful at proving that employees work more productively as a team. But, the consequences of these programs lasted for but a brief interval of time . . . and the list of temporary fixes goes on. All of the foregoing cost improvements were media events at the time of their installation. Few aspects of these plans remain in existence today, most likely due to the lack of:

- a realistic means of monitoring the effects of solutions to existing problems

- the establishment of pre-planned action options to handle the unexpected, and

- continuing interest (drive or simple motivation) by successive managements.

As described in Chapter 4, hands-on management control is a key to the success of any organizational plan. This, of course, includes those cost reduction efforts that cut the fat but not the muscle. More about control vs. mere review will be covered in a later section of this chapter.

USING A TEAM APPROACH TO MAGNIFY INDIVIDUAL EFFORT

The history of the teamwork approach, during the dawn of the era of scientific management in the U.S., is spotty. The first attempts by Frederick Winslow Taylor, Henri Fayol and the Gilbreths were introduced and publicized from 1890 through the late 1930's. Their work revolved around workplace methods improvement and the measurement of standard pace for repetitive work. Hence, their concepts depended on crew motivation through balanced and measured work assignments.

Managers were responsible for aiding work crews through their activities as schedulers, expeditors, reporters and rewarders (or disciplinarians). Thus, crew activities did not depend on workers communicating with one another, employee empowerment authorized by top management, quality circles, or even employee committees seeking operational improvements. It was assumed that individual motivation, provided by both financial and non-financial incentives, would produce measurable, overall and long-lasting productivity improvements.

This view, of increasing overall performance by appealing to individual needs, was carried forth in the promotion of group incentives, highlighted by the introduction of both the Rucker and Scanlon Pay Plans during the middle Twentieth Century. Financial incentives, as rewards for group performance over base norms, were well publicized by the Lincoln Electric application and by Mitchell Fein's revolutionary IMPROSHARE payment for results approach.

Beginning in the late 1950's, the United States became the first nation in recorded history to employ more people in white collar than blue collar jobs. Thus, the World's first staff and service economy was born. Today, direct labor accounts for as little as 10% of all costs in the modern manufacturing and processing concern.

These facts posed new problems and opportunities for managers concerned with cost reduction, since cutting the fat now meant analyzing and improving staff and service operations which were rarely routine, repetitive, or easily described. This latter distinction relates to the fact that difficulty in describing any group of tasks makes it even harder to both measure and improve them.

LOOK FOR TRUE COST-REDUCTION OPPORTUNITIES

As the costs of overhead tasks were rising rapidly, factories were converting from mass production runs to customized, short-runs—flexible and lean manufacturing. But, the cost accounting systems remained stuck in the inertia patterns which allowed direct costs to be the driver and base for all add-on percentage costs. This worked out well when materials and direct costs contributed the lion's share to product cost, but overhead allocations are misleading when the ratio of direct material and labor costs decline in the total cost picture. What was adequate for financial reporting purposes became a millstone around the neck of those companies that had to bid against foreign competition, or local producers with more realistic cost accounting practices.

With the introduction of automated and very flexible, custom producers, the costs of overhead-type activities has skyrocketed to about 50% of total costs in the 1990s. Thus, producing small lots on short-notice customer demand, coupled with increasing product options have been accomplished with a greater reliance on reducing set-up and teardown change-over costs than previously. Managers have been quick to understand the opportunities associated with these trends as they relate to cost cutting options as well as to the necessity of accounting for true product costs.

Thus, cutting the fat without damaging the vital organs of the business, requires a knowledge of where to realistically search for cost reduction opportunities. In Chapter 7, leveraging was presented as a viable cost improvement selection technique. In this chapter, the use of true cost applications is re-introduced. The difference relates to any specific firm's cost and time frame considerations. When the barn is burning, a discussion of egg production would be unacceptable when considering the need for an urgent and immediate fire extinguishing drill. When the life of the enterprise is at stake, immediate cost-cutting cannot wait for a study of activities and their contribution to productivity and overall cost.

The leveraging approach can be used with any present accounting system; whereas, true costing (such as through Activity Based Costing, as described in Chapter 9) requires a much longer-term review, culminating in a modification of both the development and application of all cost factors.

However, there is an additional reward for those who can apply true costing. Markets for services and products can be more realistically selected by reviewing the profit contribution of products and services under a true activity costing system. This is done by comparing these newly generated costs to market prices after eliminating non-value-adding activities. Simulation models are a tremendous aid in this regard. Also to be considered is that many non-value-adding costs masquerade as overhead costs.

Analyzing true cost applications will identify areas for cost improvement that have previously remained hidden by the process of proportional overhead allocations in traditional costing systems.

HOW THE FAILURE OF THE ONE MAN/ONE JOB PHILOSOPHY LED TO THE BRINK OF ECONOMIC FOLLY

During the Twentieth Century evolution of the industrialized society, vast swings in the economic pendulum caused tremendous hardships for the work force, primarily for unskilled workers. For this reason, job security became a prime rallying point in the international labor movement. The cry went out for, "One man for one job!" leading to some horrific abuses and very bad press, which was especially hurtful for those involved in promulgating the higher vision of the progressive labor movement.

For example, the media had a field day with abuses such as:

- the fireman who was supposed to shovel coal for the steam boiler while accompanying the railroad engineer driving a diesel locomotive.

- the visual inspector who supposedly checked fluid levels and any introduction of foreign objects on the automated brewery filling lines. (The task was so fatiguing that the inspector had to be relieved every 15 minutes.)

- truckers who could deliver packages to a site, but were not allowed to unload or move them upon arrival.

- operators who were precluded from inspecting work, moving parts in or out of their workstation, or substituting for other workers to cover absenteeism.

- first-line supervisors who were precluded from aiding their employees by performing any worker-type task.

- the requirement for push-button operators and starters for automatic elevators.

These practices were mostly exceptions in the U.S. In England, prior to the onset of the Conservative Governments of the 1970–1980 era, a single worker complaint, regarding work that was requested in addition to a specific and agreed work assignment, would close an entire plant. In this way, unions practiced solidarity to resolve problems that resulted from their one person/one job philosophy, based on their drive for job security and higher employment. Productivity was considered a management problem; job retention and security was the worker's and their union's main concern.

Exclusivity of work by individual and group was the cornerstone of the communist systems in operation in Eastern Europe during the era before the Berlin Wall was dismantled. Thus, full employment was promoted, while products and services were produced for a society that paid dearly for the results of these make-work projects.

I shall never forget, in 1960's East Berlin, observing a 12-person work crew shovelling snow onto a cart that was pulled by a fellow human being. A single snow plow or blower could have replaced this crew, and supplied thousands of additional jobs in the manufacture and distribution of snow blowers. This experience brought to mind the patented speech of Walter Reuther in the 1950's, when he was the United Auto Workers (UAW) President. He attacked the Big-3 auto makers for pressing for automation in their antiquated plants by crying out, "Who will buy your products when produced by robots . . . surely not the robots?"

On a consultancy assignment in a Balkan country, since dissolved and impoverished by internal war, I needed information on an inventory level that was erroneously reported on the manual records. I was told that the designated "item counter" would arrive after the lunch break, since no one else was allowed to count these power steering drive parts for me. Furthermore, I, as a foreigner, was specifically prohibited from performing any worker's task.

I thought about this when the East German economy was absorbed by the Bonn Government. The inefficiency of the East German operations, including the in-place one man/one job philosophy, caused a major upheaval in the newly united Germany, including economic distortion, unemployment, factory closings and social unrest directed at foreign workers as scapegoats for their local problems. The non-competitiveness of inefficient operations caused massive unemployment and a strain on the national compensation system, resulting in an explosive fueling of the flames of bigotry and ultra-nationalism.

It is well accepted today that reducing the workforce need not reduce the functions required to produce goods and services. A flexible workforce, both in the office and in the factory, has been accepted as both a road to competitiveness and job security.

POOLING TALENT FOR INCREASED PRODUCTIVITY AND COST SAVINGS

Alfred P. Sloan, who built General Motors into one of the World's largest concerns in the period of the 1920's to the 1950's, mandated that no manager be promoted unless a trained replacement could fill the position being vacated by that promotion. Thus, it became a paramount goal of all managers to train a likely successor as quickly as possible. If your career depended on training a deputy, the motivation for molding a successor became far more urgent than, "I'll get around to it if I have time . . . after I take care of these daily pressing problems."

Middle management survivors of flagrant downsizing slashes often find themselves suddenly being given tasks which they are totally unprepared to perform. Little griping about the situation ensues, because these survivors are happy to still be employed. Yet, resentful employees give little in return in the way of trust, loyalty and enthusiasm.

They justify this negative attitude to themselves because; (1) benefits, salaries and perks are trimmed (except for the top managers), and (2) opportunities for promotions are less likely as levels of management are eliminated. At the same time, these middle managers suddenly have more responsibility for tasks that are dumped on them, with more people to manage than before, culminating in an increased work agenda. The new workload includes managing new and varied work skills, as well as projects for which they have neither experience nor specific training.

Any professional sports coach will tell you that the players in the game need very little extra training and motivation, compared to that required by those players sitting on the bench. If a company is to successfully cut the fat, it must take steps to ensure that muscle is maintained—if not strengthened—by expending the time and costs involved in cross-training middle managers.

Today, cross-training and group motivation of both workers and managers has led to:

- a quicker review of recommended actions for productivity improvement, since fewer individuals are needed to voice an approval.
- smaller work crews that can perform multiple skilled operations, so that specialists no longer wait on each other in order to perform single skill tasks. (See Example in maintenance crew operations described below.)
- cooperative efforts by employees, working in close proximity to one another, so that, "May I help you?" can be heard at all levels of the workforce hierarchy.

- group bonuses and other communal rewards create the environment of cooperation and meaningful empowerment for the ultimate individual good.

- improved indoctrination of supervisors, including training in how to train, listen, assist, motivate and cooperate as the prime criteria for success in climbing the management ladder.

Some applications of the above philosophy in action will help you to specifically visualize the potential, positive results to be derived from both pooling talent and cross training the existing workforce.

CASE STUDY: HOW TO IMPROVE THE MANAGEMENT OF MULTIPLE-SKILL GROUPS

An analysis of a 38-person buying department revealed that the size of the crew was rationalized by the purchasing manager as the correct number of personnel related to the special skills required for overseas sourcing. Subsequently, a list was made of the costs of foreign procurement that were related to the special purchasing skills embedded in the procurement department. By relating costs to the skills required, top management was able to compare the added cost of cross training to the benefits that could ultimately be derived from reducing the present staff to meet the projected workload.

The specific list of overseas buying costs demonstrates the variety of skills that had to be considered for the activities of overseas procurement:

✓ Surcharging terms relative to money rate volatility, especially for long lead time items requiring upfront materials purchasing commitments.

✓ Qualifying and certification agreements, especially those required by the international quality standard, ISO 9000.

✓ Search time and cost for identifying potential suppliers, including travel, translation, communication and the like.

✓ Tooling and set-up costs for start-up or pilot activities, including scrap allowances, initial design modifications, worker training, recycling, etc.

✓ Labor agreements including overtime and holiday pay, especially where future expediting is forecasted.

✓ Enforcement of penalty clauses as they relate to quality, the local environment and lengthy shipping leadtimes.

✓ Design change and obsolescence charges.

✓ Special packaging and packing specifications depending on carrier, customs and receiver requirements.

✓ Insurance at all stages of supply.

✓ Costs, location and size of inventory carried as a hedge vs. that which would support locally sourced parts and components.

✓ Agent commissions, taxes, documentation paperwork, customs duties, broker fees and port charges.

✓ Logistic charges for loading, scheduling, carrying, and unloading, including local transport costs.

These required skills were then rated by the manpower analysis group as to difficulty in acquiring them through formal and informal training, as well as the cost of acquiring these special skills with experience. But, the first step was to ask, "What functions are we performing vs. what functions must we perform?"

CROSS-TRAINING THE EXISTING STAFF

Since procurement had to fit into the total hierarchy of company activities, the supply function had to be tied to the overall competitiveness strategy. This alignment of sub-strategies to the overall objectives and schedule of implementation was considered crucial. The specifics of a global computer system, integration of supply with design, the establishment and enforcement of quality criteria . . . all were a part of the dock-to-dock procurement consideration. This required, among other programs, a re-alignment of customers and production to the procurement function, standardization of audits, provision of technical guidelines and on-site aid, etc.

For all of the above tasks, it was decided that, before increasing human resources, the present staff would be trained and exposed to experiences that would broaden their scope of capability. By year's end, the re-trained and retained procurement staff was accounting for a measured 31% increase in overseas procurement workload, including the acquisition of new suppliers from previously non-investigated sources.

The cross-training and functional analyses were vital tools for achieving this success. Additional credit was given to the empowerment of the purchasing staff, as well as the resolution of a specific list of productivity inhibitors. This important empowerment topic will be covered in the next example.

CASE STUDY: HOW TALENT POOLING CUT THE COSTS OF PREVENTIVE MAINTENANCE

A New Jersey processing and storage facility was staffed for both demand and preventive maintenance activities. Yet, the work-to-wait ratio of this skilled and expensive crew was about 50-50. This meant that $1/2$ of the hours available to the group was spent on non-maintenance activities or idle . . . this gathered from data gained from activity sampling (as described in Chapter 10). Even after all maintenance supplies were delivered to the site of the repair, thus reducing maintenance personnel travel time, this 50-50 ratio persisted.

Top management introduced an empowerment program to this site. All employees were trained as to what procedures and materials they could modify and/or eliminate without requiring supervisory approval (or even notification in some cases). They were also empowered to request company services outside of their department, under the same freedom of authority by which they could request aid from within their department. Probably the only restriction, outside of cost considerations, related to the very stringent safety and quality controls.

After a burst of initial enthusiasm resulted in some cosmetic improvements, a group of maintenance personnel decided that the major productivity problem was maintenance crew scheduling. This function was performed by a scheduling group that aligned the tasks required in some priority order, searched for skills that could be applied, ordered materials for the crews, and spent a great deal of time keeping fastidious notes for data entry to support cost control and status reporting requirements.

The maintenance group, after scheduling training was performed by a consultant, decided that a significant base requirement was for a skills inventory. This would aid in improving present scheduling practices, as well as provide factual data for cross-training needs. The group was empowered to work with the data programmers to develop this skills inventory matrix, as well as to work with middle management personnel to provide the subjective, as well as the objective, skills data needed.

The matrix (see simplified version in Figure 11–1) which was updated monthly, created the demand for cross-training. Based on the data in this matrix, the computerized scheduling system then aligned individual maintenance skills with crewing requirements for priority task completions.

The program was so successful that it was mentioned in the company's annual report as having saved $6 million during the first $1^{1}/2$

Figure 11-1　Sample of a Skills Inventory Matrix, Pre-Cross-Training

KEYS

1—Calibrate and/or inspect　　A—Can perform job in a minimum time with little or no supv.
2—Repair　　　　　　　　　　B—Can satisfactorily perform task with some supv. or instr.
3—Create or build　　　　　　C—Can do job after investment of more training or
4—Supv. &/or train　　　　　　　　experience

EQUIVALENT	CODE	Harris	Marny	Polest	Chi-Sam	Pohl	Smith	Boldern	Kinetti	Goldberg	Smythe	Sanchez
Temp. Controls	2	A	A	B	B	C	A	A	B	B	B	A
Temp. Recorders	3	B	A	B	B	C	—	—	—	—	A	A
Gas Analyzers	2	B	B	C	C	A	B	B	—	B	—	—
Gas Chromatographs	3	A	B	B	C	—	A	—	B	—	B	—
Integrators	3-4	B	B	C	—	A	A	C	B	—	C	—
Transducers	3	—	B	C	—	—	B	B	C	B	—	—
Speed Controls	3-4	—	—	—	—	—	B	—	—	B	A	A
Clock Systems	1	—	B	—	C	C	—	A	—	B	C	B
Pneum. Contr.	3-4	—	—	—	—	—	A	—	B	—	—	B
Actuators	2	—	—	C	C	A	B	—	—	—	B	C
Control Boxes	3	—	—	C	A	A	B	—	—	—	B	B
Tape Systems	2	—	—	C	C	B	B	—	—	—	B	C
Engine Safeguards	3	—	—	B	B	B	B	—	—	—	A	C
Alarm Systems	3	—	—	B	B	C	C	C	—	B	B	A
Circuitry	3-4	A	C	—	—	—	C	C	A	B	—	—
Vacuum Syst.	3	A	C	C	—	—	C	C	A	B	—	—
R. F. Designs	3-4	C	B	—	C	B	C	C	B	C	A	—
Computers	2-4	—	—	—	—	C	—	—	—	A	—	—
P. A. Systems	1	—	B	—	C	C	—	A	—	B	C	B

years of operation. Special credit was given to the maintenance group that was empowered to implement virtually every aspect of the program, with little or no further management approvals.

EXPANDING THE PROGRAM

From this very simple skills inventory, a computer scheduling plan was developed for both demand and preventive maintenance. The goal was clearly expressed to all who might even be remotely concerned:

"Preventive maintenance is required to reduce the quantity and cost of demand maintenance, while providing insurance against the risks of costly unexpected breakdowns which cause production stoppages."

In addition to cutting expensive downtime, quality targets were also set relative to the existing base scrap rate. Cooperation was both solicited and supported by other organizational groups who were informed of the need for their input into the new preventive maintenance program. In the beginning, this merely meant words on E-mail. After a time, targets were established by mutual agreement, and reports were received by diverse groups . . . reports that highlighted actual vs planned results, as well as responsibility for same.

The maintenance group was trained to:

- look for trends as they developed, especially in the area of linking adverse conditions
- analyze equipment maintenance and repair history
- spot changes from the norm in production or quality levels, so that maintenance could act to "fix things before they broke" . . . quashing the outmoded philosophy, "Don't fix it if it ain't broken."
- ask for the right data both for their own and production's needs
- spot "band-aid" approaches to serious problems that really required "major surgery," either immediately or down the line
- perform post-mortems that required analysis and review as to how to prevent serious situations from recurring as surprises, or as these problems might affect other similar systems in the company. (A well-understood example exists in the airline industry. When a carrier finds a surprise turbine blade defect in but one engine on one plane in its fleet of aircraft, all similar aircraft turbine blades on all engines may be required to be examined.)
- seek causes, not just solutions, for immediate repair problems.

Thus, a program to pool available skills and capacities resulted in the development of a skills inventory, publicizing of the objective statement, empowerment of the maintenance crew, and cross-training for needed worker flexibility. Essential to the success of the maintenance improvement effort was enthusiastic management support, which increased dramatically as the resultant traceable savings dropped right on down to the bottom line.

MANAGEMENT CONTROL
IS CRUCIAL TO CUTTING THE FAT

Anyone can plan and review. Most management reporting systems follow this pattern, with the addition of variance reporting and management-by-exception data. As was stated in Chapters 2 and 10, the concept of improvement, especially continuous improvement, requires management control, which is one vital step beyond mere review.

Control encompasses automatic adjustment of pre-set plans, where this potential corrective action has been envisioned in the planning stage. Hoping and praying that things will get better is a costly form of procrastination in today's fast-moving business atmosphere. Every plan must include potential options, to be exercised if events do not align with that which was expected and sought. Sophisticated planners even establish automatic responses to deviations from the expected. These responses range from immediate shut down to automatic selection of alternate processes, equipment, materials and manpower.

Ask yourself, when schedules are missed, budgets go awry, shipments fail to arrive, or the quality of work falls below expectations, do you:

- panic
- look for a scapegoat
- line up support for your excuse
- call a meeting where you dress down all who attend
- send a voice mail plea for expediting
- procrastinate, while hoping and praying that a solution will evolve
- act surprised and amazed that this could happen on your watch
- become defensive about any discussions of failure
- become extremely conservative when making or approving future schedules
- or, all of the above?

Establishing controls in the planning phase is the most propitious action for closing the management loop from planning right on around to effective re-planning. The test of this management control concept is simple. Make a list of all the emergency decisions reached on the spur-of-the-moment, many at panic emergency meetings of high level personnel, who are responding to urgent E-Mail requests to "drop whatever you are doing and come to the meeting!"

These calls will always exist, but hopefully on an exception basis, once a realistic control system is initiated in the planning phases of projects. The savings in management time alone may be impressive—granted that this would be difficult to quantify. Both considering and listing options in the planning phase will also lead to a better choice of options than when such decisions are reached at a panic-driven, unplanned meeting, where raised voices and incriminations may reign over rational thinking.

SUMMING UP: How to Assure the Long-Term Effects of Cost Cutting

As defined in the beginning of this chapter, many cost reduction and productivity improvement schemes have been introduced in a glowing fanfare of publicity and claimed savings. Very few of these still can be found. However, these temporary applications have provided the steppingstones for cost improvement as we are practicing it today. Unless we learn from these failures, we are bound to repeat them in the future.

Assuring a permanent installation of a new management cost-cutting technique requires that:

1. a realistic means of monitoring results exists or will be instituted (covered in Chapter 9 in the discussion of true costing and cost control)

2. an effort be made to maximize presently existing skills, so that you "do not throw out the baby with the bathwater." In this Chapter, talent pooling and cross-training are covered as well-received tools of both Directors of Human Resources and first level supervisors, and

3. continuing interest and support from successive managements.

Existing skills should be inventoried, both as a base data log to point out specific areas for needed upgrading and skill training, and as a source of knowledge to make teamwork more than just a feel-good slogan. This approach is especially important in administrative support, overhead and indirect tasks, where very few specific activities have been structured or analyzed.

When cutting the fat and attempting to save the muscle, middle management is a special area for concern. Through downsizing, its ranks have been decimated, but the remaining survivors are now asked to manage more employees and a wider range of skills. This added burden is readily accepted by those happy to be still employed. However, their motivation to excel and be creative with new cost reduction ideas is dampened by the real life facts that this new assignment will reap very little reward, promotion, or recognition as all budgets are slashed.

Management owes these survivors additional training in managing new skills, as well as better tools to supervise and motivate the expanded staff. Cross-training and skills inventorying should be considered prime, if not base, requisite additions for these managers. Cost reduction applications can be made permanent when all managers receive the tools and backing to participate after the fat has been cut.

Cross-training has some immediate and fruitful rewards, including: (1) quicker review and acceptance of recommended improvements because of a smaller chain of command, (2) the ability to gain new flexibility in the assignment of personnel, and (3) as a tool for recognizing and perhaps rewarding the super-achievers who are amongst us. Teamwork should not douse individual motivation, but should enhance and capture positive results as they relate to group performance. This is done by supplying needed data on individual employee skills to facilitate talent pooling.

A widely used and simple tool for capturing individual talent capabilities—assets that could be applied for the good of the group—is the skills inventory matrix. Crews can be assembled based on fact, not individual supervisory prejudices. Priorities and due dates can be tracked, and made the focal point for scheduling. The organization can be downsized by an analysis of the functions required vs. the capacities and capabilities of the existing staff.

Attacking overcapacity by specific area is a far more valuable approach to cutting out the fat than treating all human capabilities as equal in the percentage-cut-across-the-board technique. This latter approach to cost reduction allows for the underachievers and single-skilled personnel to be axed along with the superachievers with multiple skill capabilities. It may sound like a democratic approach to cost cutting, but the fat is severed along with valuable muscle, nerve and bone organs when all are deemed equal in the quest for future profitability.

CHAPTER 12

CUT THE FAT WITHOUT CUTTING CUSTOMER SERVICE

Whether you work for a private firm or in the public sector, your rationale for all cost reduction actions is to maintain, if not improve, ultimate customer satisfaction. Therefore, ultimate satisfaction of the customer must drive all management programs that seek to reduce costs while considering future prospects for continued service and/or profitability. This must be "a given."

SELLING THE COST-REDUCTION PROGRAM TO TOP MANAGEMENT

Cost reduction strategies must prove that they do not adversely affect customer satisfaction. This means the ultimate responsibility for success or failure of the program rests not on a single department or function, but on key top managers, and the executive board. Therefore, unless the cost reduction individual or committee does significant, proactive pre-planning, coupled with making a solid presentation to a top manager or management group, there is no assurance that top management will back the required decisions for action and funding.

A key element in selling a cost reduction program is in forecasting the potential results both as to profitability and customer service. Therefore, to win management confidence as a major contributor and developer of the total cost-reduction strategy, two critical steps must be taken. Both are based on the recognition that, without a strategic planning process in place, or at the very least a detailed understanding of the needs of your department's internal customers (design, production, procurement, quality assurance, etc.), the cut-the-fat approach may not succeed as a fully integrated total company strategy.

The proposal to top management must contain:

1. a fully developed and detailed analysis of internal requirements, and current inhibitors, as both relate to servicing the ultimate customer's needs, and

2. a written, strategic plan showing:

   - the schedule for implementation, including funding and commitments of support

   - the potential downside risks as well as anticipated upside gains

   - proposed reporting, reviewing and control procedures

   - provisions for both automatic and manual options to correct situations where actual results vary from forecasted targets

   - responsibility accounting for results that drop to the bottom line.

Remember, it is "what is bought" that is more important than "what you are selling." Think about what they want to buy, as opposed to what you want to sell, i.e., practice empathy for the buyer as the driver in assembling your presentation. The higher one goes in making a cost reduction presentation, the more it becomes obvious that the listeners to your recommendations must realize your proposal's effect on customer satisfaction. Obviously, cost reduction proposals, that stand a good chance of losing future business from presently satisfied customers, will be poorly received.

You may wish to consider a sample analysis based on interviews with (1) internal, potentially affected groups, as well as with (2) selected external customers. The purpose stated is quite simple: "What service/product do you expect from us to be able to compete more effectively in your markets?" In other words, "How can we help you perform better for your customers?"; or, "How can we help you better satisfy your customers?"

This type of questioning demonstrates your interest in their business, by demonstrating your regard for their ultimate customer. The following example demonstrates the potential good that can come from this approach.

CASE STUDY: HOW TO MAKE YOUR BUSINESS THEIR BUSINESS AS WELL

A procurement department in a Texas-based company, developed a program to cut $1/2$ their staff, while at the same time allowing for an increased ability to quickly and accurately respond to customer questions about their order status. Since 62% of the finished product, by value, was procured from diverse sources ranging from suppliers of unique electronic controls, to orders placed with manually produced glass-blowing facilities, answering status questions consumed a majority of the present staff's time and efforts.

First the customer's questions were placed with the sales people, who in turn questioned purchasing and production personnel to determine order status. The production people just read off the order schedule dates from their MRP generated data, much of which came from the procurement group's input on incoming shipment lead times. This data contained known and forecasted delays from a number of external sources; in the end, the supplied delivery times were a mixture of pure fact and much extrapolation based on experienced judgment.

Since there were so many variables in the meet-the-shipping-date equation, each customer question resulted in an investigation of all supplier inputs to satisfy that query. It was felt that a more immediate and much more accurate response could be provided after an investment in the system described below. However, the original justification for this installation was that half of the employee time would be saved, so that as much as 35% of the staff would either be made redundant or be reassigned to other duties.

WINNING THEM OVER

There were serious doubters in the management committee room that day; they had heard the story about future savings many times before as the justification for today's capital equipment expenditures. The doubters pointed to a slew of unfavorable post-mortems that were held to evaluate past capital spending vs. savings that dropped to the bottom line. These past expenditure failures were brought up repeatedly during the presentation, so that no decision was reached. The committee did ask for another look at the procurement plan in 4 weeks time.

This allowed the presenters to re-group, in order to prepare a proposal that would meet not only the needs of the doubters regarding future savings to be realized, but would also satisfy the hidden agenda of all concerned . . . "How will this affect customer satisfaction/service?" The sales group was authorized to conduct a limited sample telephone survey among representative customers as to what their needs were relative to the company's service and products. In response to the survey, 68% listed accurate information as to their order status as one of their top three needs, while an additional 19% listed this requirement in the top ten.

STRESSING CUSTOMER SATISFACTION

Armed with this data, the presenters from the purchasing department re-structured their presentation not only to promise cost savings, but also to demonstrate customer need satisfaction. Their specific proposal was for an integrated information system that included access by an auto-dial/auto-answer modem. This would allow for unattended communications with EDI (electronic data interchange) software. (It was important to note that files could be transferred to or from other micro, mini or mainframe computers already in the system.) In this way automated transactions could accommodate:

- purchase orders placed, canceled and modified
- incoming quality data
- part and assembly releases
- quote requests
- delay and advance shipping advisories
- E-mail
- shipping and receiving schedules
- supplier releases
- vendor and consignment stocking data
- all Manufacturing Resource Planning (MRP) and Just-In-Time (JIT) programs
- quantity and receiving forecast changes, both predicted and mandated
- lead time advisories for warehouse purchased parts and spares
- past delivery and quality performance comparisons
- charting of trends with statistical limits thereon
- management-by-exception notifications including expediting priority info by SEODO procedure
- location of physical stocks both en route and on site.

With all data entered immediately from various sources, a program, to distill this information into a forecast for end product delivery, was appended to the in-place MRP system. By doing so, customers were given access codes to segments of the total system, so that, at any time, customers could call and immediately receive through their own modems, precise and current order delivery information.

It was the potential satisfaction of a known customer need that put the proposed program across. The proposed savings through forecasted cost reductions were politely listened to, since "they (the committee) had heard so many plaintive stories from every pleader for funding approval." But, tying the cost reduction proposal to the most important demand on the company's services, that of their ultimate customers, carried the day.

USING LOGISTICS MANAGEMENT TO STUDY INVENTORY COST REDUCTION OPPORTUNITIES

The supply pipeline is the internal organization's segment of the total supply chain that progresses onwards to the ultimate customer. This pipeline includes warehousing and materials movement which are vital parts of today's logistics management responsibility. By integrating these supply functions into one organization's domain, cost reduction opportunities arise, especially where there exists a working interface with representatives of the ultimate customer . . . marketing, sales and design.

From either a forecast or actual orders in house, the logistics function gears itself for analysis of the buying mix through to the shipping schedule. As purchased goods roll into production schedules, transport and stocking locations gear up for the finished goods servicing of the ultimate customer.

Savings come from the extremely close relationship that is developed between daily and even hourly raw material, assembly, and end-product needs with the flow and possession of the material asset. In fact, the customer requirements are the independent demand that creates all other dependent materials' demands. By the flexibility inherent in a Materials Requirement Planning (MRP) system, small but vital changes in either supply or demand, trigger computer iterations that affect every materials schedule from suppliers on through to customers.

To receive materials that are not required for a week, due to a delay forced by another purchased or manufactured component, is no longer an acceptable practice. All material schedules for stocking, use, or movement are tied to each other by the master plan for lowest asset possession cost. (The process is known as netting.)

Problems arise where this system is not routinely audited. The primary concern should be customer satisfaction. Thus, the thrust of an

MRP audit begins with an evaluation of how well the existing system meets the customer's needs for delivery, information on status, and cost analysis. This has become increasingly significant where supplier performance in the area of cost reduction leads to a more permanent role as the single source supplier who can achieve increased profit advantages from proposed cost reductions in the supply chain.

CAPITALIZING ON THE EXTENDED-ENTERPRISE CONTRIBUTION TO COST SAVINGS

Today's relationship between contractors, suppliers and other vendors with the ultimate customer, are becoming clearer as well as closer. Cost savings up and down the supply chain are now both encouraged and rewarded. This network is called the value-added chain. This supply chain provides both the authority and responsibility for cost savings from base suppliers right on through to the customer, by introducing provisions for sharing any calculated savings so generated.

The suppliers of services and products are expected to assume the responsibility of studying and introducing improvements. They are empowered to make any changes that do not affect agreed specifications; and, more importantly, they are encouraged to formally propose those technical changes that require ultimate customer approval. Suppliers are then rewarded as if they were full-fledged members of the supply chain . . . which, in reality, they have become.

Just as the ultimate customer expects its suppliers to initiate and maintain an investment in research, process and product development and service enhancement, so, too, these primary service and product suppliers now require an ongoing effort from their own suppliers in the chain. This is done through review and participation in budgeted fund allotments that independently and aggressively plow back profits into improvement projects. In addition, requests are encouraged that lead to co-development of cost reductions with other members of the supply chain. The objective is to have a chain of supply committed to continuous improvement . . . not just to the usual process of continuous bidding, negotiating and contractual interpretation "haggling". In this way, the old adversarial system gives way to the teamwork approach.

This type of partnering is an outgrowth of the single sourcing policy that has become a hallmark of both Just-In-Time applications and the demand for total quality assurance techniques in manufacturing resource planning (MRP) systems. Procurement's responsibility has become that of seeking out, negotiating and qualifying suppliers, thus allocating the continuous day-to-day buying and expediting relationship to the actual user dealing directly with the supplier. This process has made suppliers full-fledged members of cost reduction team efforts at all levels of the supply chain.

Suppliers join in with the ultimate customers at design reviews, and contribute ideas and forecasted problems and opportunities to project planning for new product introductions. Many suppliers now have personnel permanently assigned to work, on-site, at customer locations. This has led to other savings, such that disparate suppliers have begun talking to each other about problems that have a common base and perhaps a common solution when working for a common customer.

Likewise, service alterations, mandated by revised schedule dates, provide new opportunities for applying cost reductions. Employee time and resources can be reallocated to take advantage of the new flexibility that advanced notice provides to these service suppliers. One of the most wasteful of human activities is thereby reduced, i.e., where personnel efforts and expenditures are used on a low priority task, while a higher priority requirement is forced to wait for open capacity and materials availability. The foregoing is usually a result of poor or no communication between suppliers.

The opportunity for major cost savings are the result of knowledge transfers on a routine, and perhaps daily basis, among all elements of the supply chain. This communication results in a style of management similar to the Japanese concept of "keiretzu," or "extended management of the enterprise." For American companies, the challenge is to perform this function legally, by encouraging competition and cost reductions through incentives, as well as through the use of managed competition.

Managed competition requires suppliers to pay an entrance fee by making a commitment to certified, continuous improvement, including quality registrar certification under ISO 9000 standards. This can ultimately lead to financial rewards (described in the previous chapter). The penalty for non-participation in the continuous improvement process is loss of this business to a competitor, who has been prepped and is waiting in the wings for a chance to demonstrate potential cost reduction contributions.

USING VALUE ANALYSIS AS A CUSTOMER-DRIVEN TOOL FOR COST IMPROVEMENT

Since the middle of the Twentieth Century, value analysis (and its cousin value engineering) have been exercised by the purchasing and engineering groups as their domain. The savings introduced and applied to supplier and manufacturing operations have been documented and rewarding to the innovators.

In today's supply chain philosophy, a greater role for value analysis has been uncovered. The ultimate customer, with a large stake in both cost and quality assurance, has joined in the value analysis effort both by providing incentives, and becoming an active participant in this activity by teaming up with their own suppliers. Management philosophers have claimed that this may be the best way to win in international trade competition, since U.S. global traders must match foreign government supply chain cartels in competing nations, without violating anti-competition laws in the U.S.

For the reader, whose company is new to the intricacies of value analysis, consider the following value analysis questions as they relate to the ultimate customer's needs to be price competitive:

- What is the core function of the end product or service, and how does the individual part, assembly, or supplied service meet this customer need? As a supplier, with encouragement from your customer, it may pay to invest in such an ongoing analysis of that which your company provides. Recommended cost improvements will be met with appreciation by your customers, many of whom will show their satisfaction by continued loyalty in their buying practices, or perhaps through financial reward.

- Can this core requirement be separated from secondary requirements and so analyzed for cost reductions?

  EXAMPLE: A Pennsylvania boiler manufacturer was supplied with a forged arm as a top support for the weight of the swinging front door. A secondary requirement for the top support was to act as a master hinge to aid the two tongue-in-groove pin hinges mounted on the side of the boiler. By separating the primary from the secondary functions, a much less expensive fabricated steel support was developed by the supplier. As a result, a long term supply contract was offered to them for 100 percent of the support business.

- Have the functional requirements changed over time, such that certain features are no longer required? The answer to this question can eliminate unwanted service or product features that add cost without value.

- Are specifications much different than when they were required for the original proposal that was sent out for bid? This is a very important area where customer input, on a continuing basis, can lead to cost improvements by motivated suppliers of services or products.

- Have new materials or processes been developed by the customer, which, over time, have altered the functional performance requirements for the part or service being supplied?

To maximize the cost savings from value analysis, it is imperative that the ultimate customer act as a true partner with his suppliers by providing vital quality and functional information along with revised specifications. In return, active participation gains should be rewarded with either financial gain to the innovator, or at the very least, motivation provided by increased procurement loyalty. The cost improvement rewards of true partnering in the supply chain start with open communication followed by motivated analyses.

STANDARDIZE OR CUSTOMIZE?

Ultimate customer input is essential in developing the strategic sourcing plan. The standardization process, coupled with commonality analysis, are very important cost reduction techniques in inventory management. However, their true success is dependent on technical guidelines usually provided by the design function. (Chapter Four of *Managing Inventory For Cost Reduction,* Prentice Hall, 1992, covers these two techniques in detail.)

Standardization is an ongoing analysis of similarly specified parts or services that may be reduced in number, and perhaps quantity bought or stocked. Thus, five screws can be replaced by one that does the job of all. On the other hand, commonality analysis is the study of disparate parts or services that are found to be linked by their common purpose.

EXAMPLE: I came across fourteen fastening devices in an electronics manufacturer's California plant. The redundancy of parts to perform this simple function was not obvious until a functional code was applied to the identification number, which classified their function as "fastening". This included the obvious and less than obvious examples such as: metal and wood screws, clamps, tack welding solder, bands, rivets, lock washers, bolts and nuts, tapping devices, glue, and even velcro strips.

When the unique classification was applied to devices that performed the fastening function, it was found that the design engineers had specified fourteen parts that could have been covered by only four in a standardized activity. This sample study was the tip of the iceberg. After a task force composed of design, production and procurement personnel was joined by a representative of the ultimate customers, 1600 classifications had been reduced to 387. This involved dramatic savings in both procured and stocked inventories, a solution which was not uncovered in the installation of their Just-In-Time system.

Commonality and standardization training are integral parts of most current engineering college curricula. Such training is also available through continuing education seminars conducted by universities, professional societies, trade associations, and by private training groups throughout the U.S. and Canada. The point of this example was to demonstrate the vital input that can be provided by the ultimate customer.

DEVELOPING COST REDUCTION CLUES FROM CUSTOMER COMMENTS

Most operational budgets are prepared by having managers repeat the categories of the previous years with new numbers related to forecasts of activities for the coming year. Yet, the budget can also provide a meaningful cost reduction tool for those managers who relate to customer input in regard to delivery, price and quality.

This vital information is usually supplied by a parallel system of information flowing to managers . . . data that can be as useful as merely receiving actual vs. budget figures. For example, customer satisfaction can be measured by reviewing information as to actual performance in delivering services or products. The data for performance criteria may be derived from the very source of satisfaction or dismay— your present customers.

The management reporting system should highlight, in a manage-by-exception format, both improvements and failures against these customer developed criteria. Sample categories of customer satisfaction could be:

- on-time deliveries vs. total deliveries to customer,
- line items delivered vs. line items backordered,
- returns as a percentage of shipment volume and price,
- invoice error rate
- financial budget variance vs. customer performance variance from targeted service levels.

This last comparison will highlight those departments that operate well within their approved budget, but whose customer performance level reveals a lack of consideration for basic customer needs. The primary goal should be to satisfy what is important to the customer, assuring that these needs are prime targets for both cost reduction and service improvement efforts. Future budgets should be so oriented towards customer needs, that impressive budgetary successes are applauded only if they are not achieved at the expense of the ultimate customer's needs.

It is quite possible for a department that greatly exceeds the planned budget to be demonstrating an incredible performance in satisfying customer needs. A simple cost/benefit analysis may justify these expenditures over the approved plan. This is better than castigating the budget planner, based solely on financial results that are viewed independently of the customer service factor.

Seeking continuous improvement should encompass both a financial review and an audit of the results of efforts, to maintain or improve customer satisfaction.

HOW TO MANAGE SALES STRATEGY IN TOUGH TIMES

During business downturns, indiscriminate across-the-board cost-cutting of the sales and marketing effort can backfire. Where the goal is to increase competitiveness and profits, it may be necessary to accept smaller margins in the short run, in order to keep your present customers. Loyal customers mean larger future profits when the business cycle reverses company fortunes. Thus, an across-the-board cut in budgeting for the sales and marketing staff during tough times may miss the mark, which is both short-term survival and regaining profitability in the long term. In fact, it may be a mistake to expect management to report consistently increasing profits in an economic downturn.

During an economic downturn, the usual practice is to exert pressure on the salesforce to sell more high margin, high priced goods and services . . . rather than those with lower margins. Likewise, pressure is exerted to chase after specific customers who buy these high margin items, in order to have them increase their purchases.

This strategy may be counter-productive where:

- profitability figures by either products, services or complete lines of either, are distorted by inaccurate cost data. (See discussion of Activity Based Contribution (ABC) in Chapter 9.) First, it is important to assure that the costs are driven by activity, not just by direct labor or material costs. Where only 15% of a manufacturer's or service provider's total costs are related to the cost of actually producing the service or product, the wrongful allocation of overhead costs will distort profit margins.
- a very wide diversified line of products or services may show overall profit margins accurately, but these margins may be significantly distorted by individual segments of the total line.
- the accounting system has not reflected the major changes that have occurred in actual practice, such as the installation of a

new Just-In-Time system, or the addition of a new incentive system or a major capital equipment brought on line.

Instead of jumping to initiate the activity of across-the-board cuts, consider using the salesforce's input for:

- establishing a priority study to determine where it would be most profitable to change the way the company is doing business, in order to combine the twin goals of decreasing costs and increasing productivity (and profitability). Who better to consult regarding customer requirements than the sales and/or marketing group, who can relate to core business activities that are minimum requirements for attaining customer satisfaction?

- highlighting areas of opportunity to improve customer service. Evaluate comments of your customers to determine patterns of problems that cry out for solutions. Do your customers adequately understand how to use your products or services? Would better customer orientation or training help? Should instructions provided by your salespeople be upgraded through improved training?

- promoting the input by marketing and sales into product and service design reviews at the earliest stages. (This approach is detailed in Chapter 13.)

- analyzing quality procedures to assure they are customer sensitive in the chosen price range. The sales and/or marketing groups can be part of the training and certification program for contractual suppliers of products and services.

- contributing to cost/benefit studies that are required to measure the effectiveness of planned improvements through increased capital expenditures. Can increased margins be expected (and actually measured) as an integral part of the sales input to these cost/benefit studies?

- recommending organizational changes that reduce the number of (and time taken for) overlapping and redundant approvals and concurrences. Does the company really need a belt-and-suspenders policy to protect the insecure managers among us? Must sales management approve:

  - production schedules?
  - procurement's certification and training of suppliers?
  - economic lot size determinations?
  - credit extension decisions?
  - writing off of account receivables?

Remember that sales strategies are major drivers of cost reduction activities. Thus, customer input, whether volunteered or requested, is a significant starting (or auditing) point for sales strategies that progress to directed cost improvements.

SUMMING UP: Using Sales Strategies in Long-Term Budgeting

It has been demonstrated that one of the chief reasons that the Japanese can bring a new product to market in record time is their rapid response to market changes. This is partly accomplished by their commitment to long-term budgeting for design and development based on a continuing long-term forecast of customer needs. Both the proposals and the money are placed in the long-term planning and budgeting bank. In this way, the funding to generate wealth-producing assets is made available no matter what the present condition of the overall economy.

For years, the American tradition has been to raise expenditures for product development based on marketing's recommendations in good times, while cutting back on this funding in tight times. Thus, marketing's input, as to customer product or service design needs, are usually modified by the economic environment much more than the long-term sales strategy.

Here are some valuable tips to improve long-term budgeting aimed at reducing the time and cost for product or service development:

1. Start by developing a long-term strategy that plans for the accumulation of long-term wealth, not just short-term profits. There is a common tendency to initiate the budgeting process by first establishing next year's profit goal, before identifying and quantifying the market. This approach amounts to living off tomorrow's profits without putting aside funds for the longer term. Two of the basic sources of long-term profitability (leading to what economists call "growth of industrial wealth") are:

   (a) markets and position in various target markets,

   (b) product and service innovation.

2. The accumulation of long-term wealth is best planned when considering short-term budgets as part of this profitability overview.

3. Build customer relationships for the long pull. This can be evidenced by funding customer training, providing on-site promotions, frequent distribution of communications, by newsletter and in person to explain new products and services under development, listening to valuable input as to their needs, matching their concerns with meaningful and timely action, and providing a myriad of other helpful promotion aids that demonstrate your commitment to your customer's concerns . . . primarily long-term profitability.

4. Do not cut the service budget in a downturn, since cutting service costs may be an expensive way to operate in the long term. When the cycle reverses, an inordinate amount of catch-up monies may have to be spent when lack of service begins to affect sales growth. Also, since quality is a perception as well as a documented reality to your customers, consider how service of your product adds or detracts from this vital customer image of your company. It may prove to be a good long-term investment to plan an increase in expenditures for service in both good and bad times.

5. Establish long-term incentives for top and middle managers, as opposed to providing rewards only for significant annual gains . . . sometimes at the expense of long-term profitability. It requires no special skill to arbitrarily cut back this year's expenditures for product or service promotion, new capital equipment and construction, skill and supervisory training, health care, and beautification, in order to generate good profits in the current year. Performance rewards, for five year rolling results achieved, should include such factors as market share growth, introduction of product or service innovations, and, of course, profitability.

Introducing long-term budgeting can provide the base for long-term profitability when cost reductions are planned for in the short-term budgetary process. In this way, long-term sales strategies can be the most effective base for funding long-term innovation and increased market penetration.

Marketing and sales projections should not only provide a calculation of volume and design criteria desired by the marketplace, but should also act as a long-term, cost effective base for growth planning and increased profitability. Since ultimate customer satisfaction is the key to accumulating corporate wealth, this factor must be continuously weighed in all cost-cutting decisions.

FINAL THOUGHTS ON CUTTING THE FAT, NOT THE MUSCLE

From the myriad of notes that I have put together over the years, based on over 35 years of asset management consultancy on six Continents, the following items are presented as an epilogue to the foregoing statements of in-place practices. They are important techniques based on accepted philosophies, but are mentioned here only as they relate to my selection of priorities for cutting the fat not the muscle, as described in the 12 previous chapters.

Therefore, the following are included as a miscellaneous, albeit important list of reader considerations for cutting the fat not the muscle.

USE A PRACTICAL DESIGN APPROACH TO GAIN COST REDUCTIONS FROM THE BEGINNING

Probably the single most important discipline in the world of manufacturing is the design function. This activity has a major impact on future profitability, especially as it relates to the ultimate customer's perception of the product and its features, cost (and price) vs. benefit derived by the purchaser. It is a commonly overlooked aspect of design, especially as it relates to service cost and reliability.

All design elements usually begin with a line drawn on a computer-aided design terminal by a design engineer. Yet, the impact of the design function on cost reduction is extremely far-reaching. Materials used, equipment and capital required, indirect expenses, personnel skills and capacities, quality testing, vendor requirements, plus a whole host of auxiliary services depend on the design function's output. To be cost effective, not just design effective, requires a design-for-manufacturing (DFM) awareness.

The traditional approach was to have design primarily reflect customer wants, as translated by the marketing function. This included parameters of price as well as functional specifications. Thus, the input of manufacturing to the design function was merely to continue adapting designed products to the processes available in order to aggressively aid the design-for-lowest-cost approach.

This approach was usually reinforced by the designers' attitude that his function was basically completed when the approved designs met the ultimate customer's needs. Except for minor engineering change orders that were dictated by subsequent customer, safety, regulatory or manufacturing needs, the product design rarely underwent a major overhaul solely for cost improvement. The most likely "change drivers" were quality, maintenance and safety considerations, which were more likely related to the skills and capacities of manufacturing and their suppliers. The foregoing describes the traditional relationship between the design, marketing and manufacturing functions.

At the same time, automation of an existing product manufacturing line—without redesigning the product—did not take full advantage of the promise of major cost reduction activities and principles, as advocated by detailed design reviews. However, by applying the principles of value analysis (what does it do? not just what is it?), coupled with the use of commonality (similarity) analysis of parts throughout an assembly grouping, some major savings were initiated. These disciplines mandated that product designers must not design a one-of-a-kind product, but must relate that product to all other products whose unique parts might be similarly used throughout the system. In this way, overall functional analysis drives the design function to expand its horizons to include the entire panorama of specifications. This is the basis of "design for manufacturing" as it is practiced today.

REVIEWING THE DESIGN WITH AN EYE TOWARD COST REDUCTION

The next step in fostering cost reduction in the design phase is design review. This is a formal process that allows for design contributions from a whole host of interested and vitally concerned personnel from various disciplines. It is a far cry from the free-form approach of the 1950's, called brainstorming, which had very few rules to control an open-ended critique of any situation. Today's design review approach is disciplined, goal-oriented and structured.

The essential design review rules are:

1. A concept review is held at a very advanced stage of product development, where the proposed design is roughly reviewed to ensure that quality and cost are within agreed parameters.

2. All design reviews, including the concept review, are initiated under a management policy that defines the desired outcome as it relates to agreed objectives, and which establishes the project schedule, assigns responsibilities for specific aspects of the review function, and budgets for all necessary resources required to perform these reviews.

3. An early design review is subsequently conducted during the first phases of the total review. At this stage, preliminary schematics and layouts are available, as well as early test results, proposed specification tolerances, materials selection, potential parts and service suppliers, and on-site skill and equipment capacity recommendations.

4. A review team, composed of personnel from a wide range of functional disciplines, is provided with essential data well before each step in the design review process. The key to the team's effectiveness will be related to the cooperative attitude developed between the designers and the reviewers. The thrust is to drive for mutual agreement on a schedule of actions and approvals.

5. The review is a critique, both positive and negative, which forms the basis for a formal procedure for acting on or rejecting the design team's recommendations. It is not uncommon to follow project management principles (PERT procedures as an example) in order to decide appropriate progress milestones, assess the probability of success, and pre-plan management options that will automatically kick in at failure points.

6. The design release review examines the final design vs. production requirements and design objectives. At this review point, drawings are authorized to be released to manufacturing for the conduct of pilot runs.

Applying formal design review principles, as described above, can be a major step in cutting the fat before it develops into "set in cement" product design. Introducing cost reduction in the design review stage can have dramatic results, compared to constant reviews of specifications that were decided upon independent of future procurement and manufacturing considerations.

GROUP TECHNOLOGY AS A COST-SAVING TOOL

In the late 1950's, the concept of group technology was developed at Cambridge University's Advanced Management Center in a project funded by the British Labor Government. The group technology concept was easy to adopt for new plant layouts, but extremely difficult to implement in older manufacturing operations. The objective of applying this concept was to group like production processes for both similar and dissimilar parts that required similar manufacturing processes.

The manufacturing cell thus would be able to produce parts and assemblies by exploiting the sameness of processing required that might be an inherent feature of dissimilar parts. The potential for manufacturing cost savings is obvious, since cost reductions can be achieved across many product lines when introduced and analyzed by process similarities, not just by product likeness.

The group technology process starts with identification of potential production and processing similarities for all designed products. This is initiated in the classification and coding procedures established in the design function. With a group technology system in place, designers need only enter the part design code to be supplied with a list of similar parts, i.e., similar in manufacturing processing, not necessarily similar in design. The design engineer may then only have to make a simple modification in design to accommodate the group technology theory for all similar processed parts.

Use of group technology procedures allows for the instant spread of savings that come from:

- value engineering (VE) of products, as well as value analysis (VA) of systems and procedures,
- single source partnering with selected and certified suppliers by the procurement group,
- the Taguchi Total Quality Control (TQC) methodology of multi-variable reliability testing, and
- standardization, interchangeability and commonality analyses.

There are obviously limited areas for application of group technology concepts. However, when seeking to attack the causes, not just the effects, of high costs you should consider the feasibility of applying group technology principles and practices to cut the not-so-obvious fat in the system.

HOW TO APPLY LOGISTICS MANAGEMENT PRINCIPLES IN COST IMPROVEMENT STRATEGIES

For the uninitiated, logistics management is concerned with the planning and control of inventories which are stored and transported, previously identified by such mundane titles as warehousing and traffic management. In the concept of analyzing a company's cost structure as it relates to the functions it needs to perform, logistics management is now being reviewed as this activity relates to the company's core business.

The main thrust, today, has been to investigate the methodology of contracting out (outsourcing) both distribution and warehousing activities. This follows the questions raised concerning the core business of the firm. Since well-run companies have adopted Just-In-Time as their inventorying philosophy, outsourcing analyses of logistics tasks have shot to the forefront of make-or-buy types of analyses. In other words, after answering the question, "What business are we in?", managers are asking, "Is there a less expensive way to have these services performed? In-house? Outsourced? or a combination of these approaches?"

The criteria for logistics management success are:

- customer satisfaction with delivery from fewer locations
- total cost reductions for the warehousing and delivery activities, and
- selected system flexibility to meet changing logistic requirements.

Specialized logistics contractors are an option to be considered for the above needs. These contractors are logistics specialists, and are certified as such under some of the provisions of the international quality standard ISO 9000 series specifications. They usually have unique and reliable advanced computer tracking systems, specialized tractor/trailer rigs, custom-designed aircraft and automated warehouses for picking and packing.

Thus, specialized logistics contracting is one of the highest growth business opportunities today. As such, the field has attracted some inexperienced, yet enthusiastic contractors, who will promise the world to get your business. It is also wise to consider the labor/management relations of your new logistics partner, since their work stoppages and make-work rules now become your restrictions as well. And, if they fail to satisfy your customer's needs, this will be your company's failure in the eyes of your most precious asset . . . your customer.

Probably the most important task the logistics manager can review that will assure promised cost reductions is data collection and processing. Can your customer access your system to expedite and locate individual orders? And, can this basic information pinpoint areas for improvement? Improved logistics management can help you cut the fat in many previously "unexplored" areas of the business.

HOW RE-DESIGNED COST SYSTEMS AID EFFORTS TO CUT THE FAT

In order for cost-conscious managements to maintain the proper focus and scorecard for the process of cutting the fat not the muscle, cost systems must definitively address at least three different targeted functions:

1. **Major costs:** Cost control of major operations is dependent on providing timely, detailed and accurate data to first level supervisors and other concerned managers. This information includes the usual costs of people, energy, space, contractors, materials, and overheads. The effectiveness of the data provided is partly measured by how well variances from normal are highlighted, as well as the ability to show costs in some manner representative of priority for action. (Chapter 7 discusses in detail a major cost highlighting process.)

2. **Product and/or service costs:** Accurate product and/or service cost measurement precedes the use of techniques for reducing the cost of marketing, design, selling, producing and delivering the product or service to the ultimate customer. The across-the-board type of slashing cost usually does not wait for such an analysis, which is one of the primary causes of fat cutting also mangling some essential muscle (described in detail in Chapter 1).

3. **Inventory costs:** Valuation of inventory at various stages of possession is essential to the control of the largest single current asset on the balance sheet of processing and manufacturing entities. The cost of goods sold should accurately reflect true costing (as defined in Chapter 8), in order to highlight targets that were overlooked in the Just-In-Time system. Cumulations by what functions are performed by any specific inventory (What does it do?) are an invaluable aid to the practice of value

analyses. Many enterprises begin this analysis in the design function by coding function into the identification label. Without such a classification system, product and service improvement may be a hit and miss activity.

Directing cost improvement activities to areas for the greatest potential return for the applied effort is a most effective asset conservation technique. Aimless, random selection of cost reduction targets can never be as effective as designing a cost reporting system that is geared to cost reduction action. Redesigning cost systems is a first and major step to consider when embarking on a meaningful approach to dropping savings to the bottom line.

There is a danger that companies will restructure their operations in a rightsizing move, without restructuring their cost accounting system. This can cause managers to receive less than meaningful data for the decisions they must make. Consider that decisions to be made to make or buy, expend more marketing funds to acquire new customers, make a capital expenditure now, and relocate facilities, all depend on the availability of adequate information as the base factor. Also, consider that continuous improvement coupled with re-engineering analyses create excessive demands on accuracy and availability of data to make dramatic cost/benefit decisions.

Most cost information is based on assumptions of how activities drive costs. When processes are modified, personnel reassigned and materials changed, cost accounting procedures must be adjusted, or managers may make poor decisions based on meaningless cost information. Activity Based Costing (ABC) attempts to correct these past assumptions to the newer realities of function driven weights. (See Chapter 10.)

However, the popular ABC approach, identifying and measuring the portions of current costs that are applicable to specific functions, fail when performed by committees of managers with axes to grind. It is strongly recommended that data on activity costing be objectively collected by activity sampling studies conducted by a third party group, such as industrial engineering. (See activity sampling details in Chapter 7.) Continuous activity sampling, tested frequently for reliability as it relates to the total population of events, seems to be the best approach to deriving a true costing base. For many office-type activities, this may involve as little as 5 minutes of analysis time per day to both keep current and to weigh cost improvement opportunities and savings.

Customer input can also be sampled with regard to:

- product acceptance in a given price range,
- profitability by product and by customer order trends,

- acceptance of a reduced product line,
- price vs. quality, and
- warranties vs. price at a given volume.

When a company acquires data from its customers that declares a product or service must continue to be provided, this places additional priority on reducing costs to be competitive and profitable. This customer information should drive the cost reduction priority system as well as the budgeting and reporting systems.

HOW TO USE STRATEGIC SOURCING TO DEFINE OVERALL SUPPLY STRATEGIES

Strategic sourcing is the application of supplier selection techniques, training and certification, as well as the use of a specifically designed audit of those selected to service or supply your company.

Three requirements must be fulfilled, which are the products of detailed pre-planning activities, including approvals:

1. Internal requirements by delivery and schedule, packaging specifications, data transfer, inventory possession details, inspection procedures both on and off-site, and payment and recovery terms must be produced and distributed in a written and readable form.

2. An objective list of cost reduction inhibitors should be gathered, discussed and reviewed for improvement.

3. The results of the above two actions should be captured in a written and approved strategic sourcing plan. Frequent audits of actual vs. planned activities and/or results should lead to a variety of cost savings applications, cooperatively recommended, approved and installed.

CUTTING THE COSTS OF OUTSIDE SERVICES

Key business services are provided by accountants, attorneys, management consultants, advertising agencies, investment bankers, and insurance brokers. A dichotomy of required actions usually exists. When contracting to acquire goods, savings can result from establishing long-term cooperative relationships with a few certified suppliers; whereas the value of service suppliers can be increased by working with more vendors.

All too often, managers have cozy, close executive relationships with their auditors, bankers and some consultants. Over time, the relationship becomes both convenient and comfortable. For this and other reasons, managers rarely consider switching bankers, accountants or lawyers. This means little or no effort is spent on checking a fee, add-on expenses, a requested increase, or prices charged by their competition.

Not only is this ongoing cost not compared with current market prices, but the advantages of checking out the competition are missed. Other professional associations may very well have an expanded list of experiences, including global expertise, as well as some new and innovative approaches to age-old problems in labor relations, tax exemptions, and inventory management for cost reduction, not just control.

If you are willing to switch service suppliers, and publicize this fact, the implicit threat to take your business elsewhere may prompt your current supplier to generate better remuneration terms, some creative approaches that were previously known but not offered, and prompt attention to some pressing needs. In other words, there are service savings to be garnered merely from the threat of competition. More specific actions to cut the cost of services are:

- Re-examine and tighten the auditing of service bills. This practice will pay dividends where the usual service bill is vague, cumulative over a period of time, and lacking justification, i.e., without detailed expense receipts, or hours expended by project and by classification of employee assigned to each project.

- Consider using monitoring services experienced in reviewing billing statements. This is especially productive when reviewing advertising bills with charges other than for the publication or broadcast of the message. This is referred to as a "vagueness-of-creativity" billing.

- Consider viable alternative services, such as arbitrators and mediation services, instead of relying solely on attorneys as adversary litigation counsellors. Litigation fees are one of the largest cost factors for legal services.

- Examine the advantages of using and/or developing in-house expertise. Can your firm be self-insured to reduce traditional property and casualty insurance premium payments?

- Fix prices, wherever possible, by overall performance, not just by service hours expended. In this way, open-ended agreements become results-oriented payment schemes. A project can be estimated by competent consultants, so that the cost of the installation of a new inventory management system can be weighed against the advantages to be gained. Securities underwriters can be employed on a firm commitment basis other than a best-efforts approach. Advertising payments can be linked to potential targets established in the test campaigns, and bonus rewards can be paid when targets are exceeded, or even met.

Many service providers will replace straight commission terms with:

✓ fixed fees for guaranteed services,

✓ commission plus fees,

✓ sliding scales for contingency fees, such as seen in liability suits, and

✓ suspension of payments for warranty work.

The bottom line is that many services can be performed on a more cost-effective basis. To do this, aggressive managers must weigh their reliance on cozy, traditional payments for these administrative and professional services vs. creating cost reductions through competitive analysis, payment for results, and a host of other creative schemes defined above.

TIPS ON MOTIVATING AND MAINTAINING SUPPLIER COST REDUCTIONS

New negotiating strategies are required for long-term purchasing contracts, especially where profit margins are shrinking and prices are becoming more volatile. The key is to make the contract a win-win situation for both your suppliers and your company.

It is in the supplier's interest to gain:

• the assurance of long-term volume guarantees based on cost reduction pass-throughs to your operation,

• specific price floors,

• a share in proposed cost reductions, and

• a clear definition of buyer and seller risks.

To counteract the historical nature of creeping price escalation, your firm should consider addressing this problem with both flexibility and some creative innovation in your purchasing policies. Some examples of these philosophies follow:

USING VARIABLE QUANTITY OPTIONS

This involves a clause allowing the buyer to have a quantity variance of say 25% from the contracted volume. This clause is activated when the market price dips below the contract price. This is called "index optioning," and works especially well where a spot market price allows you to make up the volume difference at a better price than in the contract. WARNING: clearly specifying which index is applicable can avoid costly future disputes.

VENDOR STOCKING

This is an agreement to have the vendor stock specific supply, guaranteed to be purchased by your company within a fixed period of time, probably one year or one season. Thus, the safety stock against unexpected contingencies is carried by your supplier, not your firm. Only after possession is taken is the invoice paid for the quantity received. Understand that Just-In-Time approaches attempt to decrease variable (not fixed) possession costs, which are near nil for vendor stocks.

CONSIGNMENT STOCKING

This is vendor stocking on your site, which is obviously not appropriate for very large or bulky items. The firm pays for these items as they are picked and used, and at the contracted price. This allows the supplier to do economic runs during their scheduled open capacity time, thus avoiding overtime pay, and other expediting costs, while locking up their customer's volume by contract. **IMPORTANT:** Warranty dated products should be considered very carefully, or not at all. Insurance should be carried by the owner, not the warehouser. Again, the premise of Just-In-Time savings relates to possession costs, which are primarily variable not fixed costs. For example, the warehouse, pickers, packers and materials handlers are in place whether the space is $1/2$ or $3/4$ full; but, variable possession costs relate to having to pay materials' invoices when presented.

LIMITING MARKET
PRICE FLUCTUATIONS

A clause may be negotiated whereby the buyer has the option to pay the lower of the index or the market price should specific prices fall below the contract price. If, however, prices rise in the marketplace at a greater rate than the index rate, you can exercise the option to use the index number, since it is lower. In either event, price savings can be gained, especially in volatile markets covered by long term contracts.

INCENTIVES TO SEEK COST REDUCTIONS

If suppliers are truly to be considered a part of the supply chain family, they should actively seek cost reductions to be reflected in price reductions. This could be based on agreed goals (targets), or be open ended, where a 50-50 split of savings is reflected in the price reduction. Again, this profit sharing is a supplier trade-off in order to gain the longer-term buying contract at specific guaranteed volumes. Where cost reduction targets are agreed, failure to achieve these minimum targets, results in set automatic price reductions. This is a perfect example of a carrot-and-stick motivation for garnering cost reductions down the supply chain.

The entire supply chain can be motivated to participate in your cost reduction efforts through the application of innovative and flexible buying contract terms.

HOW TO MAINTAIN EMPLOYEE MORALE DURING AND AFTER RIGHTSIZING

As stated in Chapters 1 and 3, almost all rightsizing events, whether one cuts into muscle or nerves as well as fat, will negatively affect employee morale. Morale must be managed through planning. Otherwise, unpredictable risks are taken by managements that are either fighting to regain profits or preventing corporate annihilation.

This planning relates to an overall policy of not just cutting costs, but also seeking to build a new, more cost effective organization. This involves:

1. a true calculation of both the tasks and the personnel that are to be eliminated. If the downsizing only reduces staff, but not unnecessary related functions, the remaining employees' workload may increase dramatically, perhaps to a point of impossibility and frustration.

2. a study of those remaining, specifically skilled employees who will be underutilized after the downsizing. Underutilization breeds a suspicion of imminent lay-off, which may result in make-work tactics being indirectly employed. "Waiting for the other shoe to drop" is a very costly attitude that may be adopted by the remaining managers and their employees. Carefully examine options and their potential effects on the remaining crew. Then, communicate your rightsizing plans as final, at least for a respectable time frame.

3. public announcements that tell remaining employees they will receive a clear statement of where the company is going. This new direction requires new individual responsibilities for many employees, which will involve less wasted effort and fewer layers of bureaucracy. Specific announcements to individual employees is a minimal effort task for the new company management.

4. asking for involvement by all employees in the re-design of both the functions and the organization to accomplish same. Involve employees in the definition of the core business. This action will also stop rumors that can revolve about secretly developed plans.

5. keeping employees informed about progress and problems. Rumors lower morale, overstate the company's problems, exaggerate remedial measures required, as well as fuel employee apprehensions and "worst-case" fears.

6. assuring that an effective outplacement procedure is in place, including placement to other company positions as a first choice scenario.

7. providing adequate severance pay and continuation of some benefits where earned by past performance, not just by position held. News of fairness to others travels almost as fast as rumored bad news. Steps 6 and 7 send a message to remaining employees that the company cares.

8. providing aid to the remaining employees that suits their psychological needs. This can be done by individual counseling, elimination of extravagant executive perks, introducing incentive plans so that employees can share in the new profitability, or allowing for more frequent and more open one-on-one meetings with and between managers.

9. upgrading all training programs and orientations to include a description of the new goals and how they will be attained, as well as a specific statement to answer the silent question, "what's in it for me?"

10. allowing employees to specifically and honestly state their view of:
    - planned cost reduction activities,
    - profit inhibitors,
    - performance expectations of and by their managers
    - expectations for reward
    - authority restrictions as empowerment prerogatives and limitations

It is important to precede any rightsizing efforts with planning for the expected morale problems. Managers should encourage future contributions of the remaining employees. This separates the desperate, one-shot downsizers, keep-us-in-business managers, from those concerned with building a long-term profitable enterprise from the new, diminished cost base.

Cut the fat not the muscle is a management philosophy that consists of a bagful of bold techniques pointing the firm in the direction of a profitable tomorrow. In contrast, percentage cost slashing—without planning for the effects of this drastic procedure—can defeat the prime purpose of cost reduction activities, which are long-term, ever increasing profitability.

The purpose of this last chapter was to add to the "kitbag" of techniques described in the preceding ones, i.e., techniques to attain this admirable goal of long-term continuous improvement. I strongly recommend that you acquaint yourself with the options available in the planning phase, so that a proper, specific, and site-specific approach is taken to cut the fat not the muscle, nerves or skeleton of your enterprise.

BASING RIGHTSIZING DECISIONS ON A FULL ANALYSIS OF WORK FLOW

The new terminology for re-engineering and retrenchment is "rightsizing." The rightsizing approach is especially important to apply where major staffing decisions are required to be made.

Rightsizing involves the analysis of work flow as it proceeds through a sequence of related tasks. The relevance of the work, its quantity and where it is performed become the deciding factors. As it is decided that the work can be reduced, eliminated, modified or outsourced, personnel and/or positions attached to these duties can be eliminated or re-assigned. Indiscriminate slashing of jobs does not require such an analysis.

During the analysis, it is important to make a distinction between permanent and temporary tasks. These value judgments should be made by an objective manager or team of qualified individuals. Temporary tasks should not receive a priority over permanent work, since staffing should be established for the performance of permanently needed, ongoing work. Temporary work can be staffed by overtime, temporary employees, or contracted services to cover the temporary overload of the human resource capacity.

The above can also be helpful when analyzing the tasks performed to support procedures which can be modified or eliminated. By analyzing a whole department's activities at the same time for all the procedures flowing through it, the analyst can pick up portions of tasks that may equate to a whole "hot body," or those related to an irreplaceable skill. In either event, matching the tasks required to the approved work procedures and flow, will allow for a meaningful and productive rightsizing.

These analyses should have been conducted in the normal course of business. This means that dramatic rightsizing is a reflection on the past inefficiencies of management's planning and staffing, relative to the utilization of the human asset. In most cases, however, the penalty of unemployment will mainly fall on the workers, not on the previously wasteful and inefficient managers.

INDEX

N

National industrial policy, 26–27
National Performance Review, 24
Netting, 231
Newtonian linear thinking, 106, 109
Non-linear thinking, 105–30 (*see also*
    Leveraging)
NPR, 24

O

Objectives, defining, 15–16, 28–29
Ohno, Taiichi, 64
"One man/one job" philosophy, 216–17
Opportunity curve in cost reduction, 115–22
    opportunity inequality curve, 117–18
Order, seeking through leveraging, 107–8
Outside sources, cutting costs of, 248–50
Outsourcing, 245
Overkill syndrome, how to overcome,
    163–64

P

Pareto, Vilfredo, 115
Pareto Principle, 66, 72, 79, 88
    Curve, 115–22, 130
    analyses, practical, examples of,
        118–22
    opportunity curve, 115–22
    opportunity inequality curve, 117–18
    sample generic, 116
    statement, 116
    10–50 curve, 117–18
    20–80 curve, 116
Partnering arrangements, 27–28
    as consensus tool, 65, 69
Personal commitment analysis, 127
Personnel cuts, across-the-board,
    problems of, 100–101
PERT procedures, 243
Peters, Tom, 113
Phantom problems, how to avoid, 163–64
Preventive maintenance systems, 23
    and talent pooling, 221–23
Prioritizing essential to time manage-
    ment, 128
Problems, failure to anticipate as reason
    for failure of cost reduction project,
    37–38
Procedures, changing, 91–92
Product costs, 246
Product design group, incorporating into
    cost reduction efforts, 97–98

Profit and loss statement, example, 143–48
Profit/volume analyses,131–32 (*see also*
    True costing techniques)
    hip roof curve, 149–50
    learning curve, 142–43
    leveraging principle, 140–41
    methods, three, to determine base
        data for, 137–40
    options, other, 142
    simulating company profit improve-
        ment, 143–49
Profitable solution, 57
Profitability, future, improving, 1–14
    analysis, importance of, 4
    borrowing to improve, 53–54
    cost reduction, 1
        caution, 2–4
        across-the-board cutting, 2
        diversified approach required, 13–14
        errors in analyzing,8–9
        profit improvement, relating to,
            11–13
    costs, allocating, 9–10
    declining, three warning signs of,
        51–55
        cash generation, insufficient, 54–55
        debt-to-assets and/or operating
            margins, rising, 53–54
        margins, slipping, 51–53
    discretionary spending, 4–6
        examples, 4–5
        identifying, 5–6
        spending money to make money, 6–8
    leveraging cost reductions, 105–130
        (*see also* Leveraging cost reduc-
            tions . . .)
    management control for planning
        success, 55–56
    sustained, and short-term cost reduc-
        tions, 100–102
    unassignable costs, eliminating, 10–11
        ABC, 11
    workforce, direct, 2–4,13–14
Purchase order costing, true costing
    and, 135
Purchasing, 122
Purchasing group, cost reductions by,
    191–94
Putnam, Howard D., 59

Q

Quality circles, fishbone diagrams and, 84
    (*see also* Fishbone diagrams)